THE UNITED STATES AND THE VATICAN POLICIES
1914-1918

THE UNITED STATES AND THE VATICAN POLICIES
1914-1918

DRAGAN R. ŽIVOJINOVIĆ

COLORADO ASSOCIATED UNIVERSITY PRESS
BOULDER, COLORADO

Copyright 1978 Colorado Associated University Press
Boulder, Colorado
International Standard Book Number: 87081-112-6
Library of Congress Card Catalog Number: 78-52438
Printed in the United States of America

For Mira

CONTENTS

ACKNOWLEDGMENTS

Many people and institutions helped me, in one way or another, in the writing of this book.

I am obliged to the following:

The British Council, London, for financial assistance; the Administrative Committee of the Charles Warren Center, Harvard University, for awarding me a grant to finish the manuscript; the Faculty of Philosophy, University of Belgrade, for granting me a generous leave of absence to work on it; Otakar Odložilik, late professor emeritus, University of Pennsylvania, Philadelphia, for interest and encouragement; Benjamin F. Brown, University of Kansas, for drawing my attention to the vast Sonnino collection; A.J.P. Taylor, for access to the Lloyd George Papers; Professors Oscar Handlin and Frank Freidel, Harvard College, Cambridge, Massachusetts, for interest and support;

The staffs of the Harvard University Library (Houghton and Widener Libraries), the Manuscript Division of the Library of Congress, the National Archives, the Catholic University of America (Washington, D.C.), the Yale University Library, the New York Public Library, the Public Record Office (London), the British Museum, and the Beaverbrook Library (London) for allowing me to use materials in their care;

Miss Rita Howe of Arlington, Massachusetts, for suggestions as to style; and

Professor Stephen Fischer-Galati, University of Colorado, editor of the *East European Quarterly* monograph series, for encouragement in preparing the manuscript for publication.

I alone, however, bear the responsibility for the contents of this book.

D. R. Ž.

CHAPTER 1
INTRODUCTION

A comprehensive study of the Vatican's activities in the sphere of international politics during World War I has yet to be written. Although it is not difficult to deal with certain problems and personages in the period, it is extremely difficult to study the Vatican as a whole. The evidence is fragmentary, there is an almost complete absence of published sources, and certain official historians, memoirists, and politicians have deliberately made contradictory and unsubstantiated statements in order to blur certain problems. It has thus proved difficult to give an objective analysis of the Vatican's policies and attitudes, and in certain instances historians have hardly touched on the problems that have to be dealt with. In short, the results heretofore have been unrewarding.

Nevertheless, historians are invariably drawn to problems such as these. Although the Holy See's inmost motives and decisions seem to be securely hidden behind the mist of time and the thick walls of the Vatican archives, now, for the first time, historians can begin to reinterpret its policies. The private papers of Baron Sidney Sonnino, Italy's foreign minister during World War I, have been discovered at his villa in Tuscany— a discovery of particular interest because Sonnino's papers contain the dispatches and reports sent to and from the Vatican in the period 1916-1919. Italian military intelligence broke the Vatican's code, screened its cables, and kept Sonnino abreast of almost every important action and decision it took. In addition, other documents have recently been discovered, notably in Great Britain. These new materials open up new vistas and possibilities for the study of diplomacy and international politics during World War I.

This study has been undertaken for several reasons. First, although there is a substantial historical output on Woodrow Wilson, there is no thorough and systematic analysis of his thought and reactions concerning the Vatican in particular and the Catholic church in general during the war. There is not even a study of American attitudes toward the Holy See during the war. The present study investigates some of the areas that historians have neglected. It is by no means a systematic analysis of the wartime relationship between the United States and the Holy See; after all, the relations between them were officially broken in 1868 and were never formally reestablished. As suggested, however, it will analyze numerous Vatican diplomatic initiatives—both open and secret—and especially the Vatican's reactions to the decisions of the U.S. government. The American response to papal moves and initiatives will be analyzed as well.

Second, these newly uncovered materials, combined with sources already available, help build a richer and more detailed profile of Vatican personalities—who, the reader will find, look different from the way they did several generations ago. Pope Benedict XV, Pietro Cardinal Gasparri, and many others—all are an almost inexhaustible source of interest for historians, and it is to be hoped that these personalities will finally secure a well-defined place in history. Likewise, it is hoped that this study will clarify the Vatican's wartime policies and attitudes. The pope's peace appeal of August 1, 1917 is well known, but his efforts to mediate between the belligerents, his views on the embargo, submarine warfare and the blockade, his temporal ambitions, and other vital questions all remain obscure.

Finally, this study will stress the importance of the Vatican's methods, that is, its diplomatic modus operandi, its policy makers, their strengths and weaknesses, their policies and preoccupations. If there is a wide variety of interpretations of the Vatican's wartime policies, it is primarily because of the Vatican's methods. The numerous public statements of Benedict XV, Cardinal Gasparri and others, press comments, secret interviews and consultations, covert instructions, and other sources—all can give rise to the most contradictory and unfounded conclusions. In the words of a perspicacious observer of the Italian scene, "the political activities of the Papacy are so many-sided, so shrewd, so astute, so indirect and tortuous that they tend to lead students of them, especially Americans . . . on a false scent." The search for the Vatican's methods should be very revealing, of both the Vatican's policies and policy makers. In fact, it may be said that the very nature of the task determined the form of its fulfillment.

During the war, the Curia teemed with strange personalities and characters—private chamberlains, advisers, and attachés to the embassies and legations—many of whom were suspected of questionable activities and of having a sinister influence on Vatican attitudes. Furthermore, the cardinals in the Curia, the congregations they headed, the representatives of the various church orders and the colleges had a substantial influence on the formulation of Vatican policies; the Jesuits and their head wielded considerable power and could affect, if they wished, every single decision on the part of the pope. The Vatican press, official and semiofficial (*L'Osservatore Romano, Corriere d'Italia*) or the Jesuit *La Civilta Cattolica* were under the direct control of the cardinal secretary of state, who himself wrote or inspired articles and editorials on subjects the Curia considered important.

These various personalities and organizations contributed, in varying degrees, to the ways in which the Vatican carried out its business, especially its foreign policy. It is sometimes difficult to ascertain who was responsible for what and how these pressure groups and individuals affected the decision-making process. Obviously, those who dealt with the Vatican, either officially or unofficially, had to confront the problem. Almost all were bewildered by the Curia's resourcefulness and imagination, its pretensions, its arguments and rationales—which were sometimes strong and incisive, sometimes weak and naïve, and often ignorant and prejudiced. Moreover, the Vatican did not hesitate, when necessary, to use thinly veiled threats.

The Vatican's place and role in international affairs—no matter how intriguing they may be—tend to escape easy definition. Clearly, as observed from different perspectives and angles, the Vatican is many things. First, by virtue of geography and history, it is an Italian institution. It is present in every aspect of Italian life, and it is dominated by Italian ecclesiastics, bishops, and cardinals. Since the turn of the twentieth century, the Vatican has never ceased to work for the preservation or promotion of Italy's interests; the popes after Pius IX were Italian patriots devoted to the defense of Latinity and Italianity. Second, the Vatican is also a European force. Its influence and presence are evident in almost every aspect of European life. More Catholics live in Europe than anywhere else, the Vatican derived much of its income from Europe; and it is Europe where the Vatican has cooperated most closely with the temporal authorities. The Vatican has also been most active in the Old World's involved religious and political affairs, in which its own manifold interests are directly at stake. From Europe, too, the Vatican extends its influence to Africa, Asia, and America. Finally, the Vatican is an international organization—the oldest worldwide, universal organization. Structured accordingly, it stretches its influence all over the globe, to wherever Catholics live and it has interests. All these factors have shaped the Vatican's outlook on the fundamental problems of Italian, European, and world affairs, although the personal inclinations and dispositions of individual pontiffs have frequently been at odds with them.

The Vatican's deliberate efforts to assure its temporal influence and authority during World War I raised complex questions about the proper relationship of the Vatican's spiritual powers to temporal affairs, its objectivity or partiality, its ignorance of a wide range of questions, and the bias and conservatism of Vatican policymakers. In some ways, Vatican authorities betrayed extraordinary fears and sensitivities. Yet despite all its shortcomings, the Holy See and its representatives carefully watched the domestic and foreign affairs of many countries, including the United States, thereby demonstrating its universal character and its worldwide interests and commitments. The Vatican also made it clear that it wished to be present when various international problems were settled, to participate in and influence the decisions that were to be made.

The clash between temporal power and spiritual authority during World War I—in Europe as well as in the United States—ended with the complete defeat of spiritual authority. This was perhaps unavoidable given the character of the war and the stakes involved. It was also a consequence of the Vatican's tendency, during the greater part of the war, to favor one set of belligerents. Although the Vatican pretended to be impartial and neutral, there is now evidence that its sympathies lay with the Central Powers, particularly with Austria-Hungary.

In its diplomatic activities, the Holy See officially offered its help to both sides on several occasions and continued to do so as long as its own interests coincided with the demands and pretensions of the belligerents. Despite its eagerness, however, the Vatican did not accomplish much in this regard. Its numerous initiatives to stop the war and start negotiations caused uneasiness and were ultimately rejected by both sides. Worse yet, both the Allies and the Central Powers suspected that the Vatican was the tool of the other side. The U.S. government was definitely convinced of this. In turn, the Vatican tried persistently to maintain a respectable position through pontifical pronouncements and even through pressure tactics. In order to bring about peace, the Vatican made several proposals: on a cease-fire on the battlefields (Christmas, Easter), on abolition of the naval blockade, on neutral trade and U-boat warfare, and on the definition of war aims. If nothing else, these initiatives confirmed the Vatican's awareness of the situation at any given time.

Because of its diplomatic activities and eagerness to take part in the work for peace, the Holy See became involved in the internal affairs of many countries, including the United States. Very early in the war, it realized that America's industrial and financial potential, if used exclusively for the benefit of the Allies, might ultimately make them victorious. This possibility was even more threatening because the majority of Americans favored the Allies, particularly England and France. The

Vatican, therefore, did everything it could to induce the U.S. government to stop exporting food, ammunition, and arms, as well as providing loans and credits to the Allies. If it could do this, the Vatican decision makers believed, the military operations would have to come to a halt: the Allies would be militarily, industrially, and financially exhausted. Not surprisingly, Vatican officials were rather indulgent about German submarine activities against Allied and neutral merchant shipping. They came to suggest that the British government should abandon the blockade if Germany abolished U-boat warfare on the high seas.

A very important vehicle, necessary to accomplish Vatican aims, was the Catholic hierarchy and clergy in the United States. It is instructive to study the attacks and accusations of the Catholic hierarchy and press against the administration's Mexican policy and their support for an embargo on the export of various goods and money. To these ever-burning problems, several others should be added. The problem of Ireland was especially sensitive both for the administration and the Democratic party. It became particularly explosive after the abortive Easter uprising in April 1916, the British execution of its leaders, and the administration's subsequent silence on the matter. Catholics also objected to the administration's Philippine policy and were successful, together with the Republicans, in defeating the Jones bill. The animosity of German-Catholics came as a result of their sympathies for their *Vaterland* and the administration's leniency toward the British and their usurpations of the high seas. The results of these developments were mutual distrust, accusations, and internal strife in both the Democratic party and the Catholic church.

As for U.S.-Vatican relations, the wartime period may be divided into two distinct phases: first, the years 1914-1917, when the United States was neutral, and second, 1917-1918, when it became actively involved in the war. During the first phase, the basic objectives of both the United States and the Vatican were analogous, if not identical. Each pretended to be neutral and even impartial. However, neither was able to carry out its aims. The Vatican failed because of its sympathies for and dependence on the Central Powers, because of its hostility toward Russia and alleged Russian designs in the Balkans and the Near East. The United States, on the other hand, was hampered by its constantly growing economic and financial cooperation with the Allies and by its obvious sympathy for Great Britain. Wilson and the pope, each in his own way, worked toward peace. Both the Vatican and the United States opposed the German U-boat warfare. The Vatican opposed it, if only halfheartedly, because of humanitarian reasons and because it feared that the United

States would be forced to side with the Allies. The U.S. government, despite domestic opposition, insisted on freedom of the seas, the right of Americans to travel and to transport their industrial products and raw materials without interference. Furthermore, both the Vatican and the United States initially opposed radical changes in existing political structures. The Vatican, as a conservative institution, naturally strove to preserve the status quo ante bellum, and even Wilson did not at first want to see the Habsburg Monarchy dissolved or the German Empire reorganized.

But in the second phase, after the United States entered the war in April 1917, U.S. and Vatican policies diverged considerably. Wilson soon envisaged a new world organization to secure future world peace and, with it, the ability to transform the nature of international relations. He soon insisted upon reorganization of Germany's government and tried to discredit the emperor, his bureaucracy, and the military establishment. However, the pontiff long held to his belief that the German imperial structure should not be radically changed nor its military power destroyed. The United States soon decided to support the demands of the nationalities of the Habsburg Monarchy for independence. But the Vatican opposed these demands and did everything to preserve the Habsburgs on the throne—even if Austria-Hungary had to be reorganized in order to do so. The Vatican's efforts to secure a seat at the future peace conference and its peace proposals elicited Wilson's disapproval and even contempt. Wilson regarded this as a spiritual sovereign's undue interference in temporal affairs. Besides, the Vatican's efforts were a strange mix of irreconcilable elements, ideas, and statements that had been lifted from the speeches of responsible statesmen from both sides. Wilson wanted no part of such a fragmented peace program. His ideals ran much farther than the pope's— as he soon came to believe that only he could offer leadership to the postwar world.

Too slowly, the Vatican came to realize and appreciate the political consequences of the United States' active involvement in world affairs. The Curia's decision-making process—with its faulty and biased information and special interests—did not adjust well to rapid and radical changes. This was inevitable. At the beginning of the war, the Vatican naturally was concerned primarily with the situation in Europe, where, indeed, much was at stake. It greatly resented the American intrusion into European affairs—for its first priority was to maintain the stability of the political, social, and economic order in Europe, a task it found complicated by the U.S. support to the Allies and by the spread of new ideologies. In fact, the Vatican was not ready—psychologically or otherwise—to adjust to the rapid entrance of Wilson and the United States onto the world stage. In 1914, at least, the United States (and the rest of the non-European world) was of secondary importance. By 1918, however, Wilson was at the center of the Vatican's attention. This change was highly significant: it was the Vatican's open recognition of the altered political circumstances at the end of the war.

Pope Pius X (1903-1914)

CHAPTER 2

THE VATICAN, THE EUROPEAN WAR,
AND AMERICAN NEUTRALITY

The outbreak of the European war did not come unexpectedly to the
Vatican: Austria-Hungary's intentions to punish Serbia for the assassination
of Archduke Ferdinand at Sarajevo in June 1914 were well known to
the Curia. Indeed, Pope Pius X and Merry del Val, cardinal secretary
of state, approved of the Austro-Hungarian note to Belgrade and
expressed their regrets that the empire had not taken this action earlier.
Pius X maintained that the Balkan nations were "barbarians," and Merry
del Val was especially distrustful of Serbia. They saw in Serbia, an
Orthodox state, a "corrosive illness," which, if allowed to develop, could
destroy the very soul of the Catholic empire. When approached, Pius X
refused to intervene in the interest of peace, since he came to believe
that Austria-Hungary was fighting a just war and that orthodox Serbia
must be repudiated. He thus completely disregarded the political
implications of papal support, underestimated the French and Russian
armies, and maintained that the German army was far superior to either.

When Pius X died, on August 20, 1914, the war was well under way.
The Vatican soon found itself overwhelmed by events, facing not only
the election of a new pope but also problems of international politics.[1]
Some—the "Roman question," the question of separation of church and
state, and the preoccupation with Austria Hungary were not completely
new. Others were indeed new, including the most difficult, the problem
of Catholic citizens' loyalty to their respective governments. In a very
subtle way, the confrontation among the European powers had started a
religious war. No church or religion had inspired or initiated this war,
but all the major religions—through their adherents—participated in the
actual hostilities, which pitted Catholic against Catholic as the French,
Italian, Austro-Hungarian, and German armies fought against one
another. Since the war was not only a contest between individual national
interests, but also among different cultures, civilizations, and spiritual
values in a larger sense, the Vatican found itself necessarily in the midst of
it. The adherents of the various religions became, consciously or not,
the tools of war. Statesmen and politicians closely identified them
with the ultimate destiny of their states, demanded that they pray to
God for the success of their arms. Through their churches the people

became warlike and nationalistic. As these factors seemed to weaken Catholic loyalty toward the church, the Vatican was forced to struggle against the governments, against growing nationalism among the flock, and against anything else that threatened to destroy its universal position.

Certain of the Vatican's tenets and goals further complicated the situation. The Vatican is an institution guided by its own "laws," for example, the drive for self-preservation and self-perpetuation and for the defense of all the rights and privileges it has acquired in the past (political, social, and economic). It also acts to increase the influence and power of the Catholic church around the world. Therefore, it was suspicious of and unsympathetic toward modern ideas and trends. Like wars, ideologies tend to weaken Catholic loyalties to the Holy See. Both the pope and the Vatican hierarchy were very much concerned at the prospect of a coalition between the socialists and Catholics in various European states, especially in Italy. The new pope, Benedict XV, voiced this fear in his first encyclical *Ad Beatissimi* on November 1, 1914, as well as later on, preaching against "the dissolution of societies, the weakening of morale, and the threats coming from socialism."[2]

As a conservative institution, that is, as an institution opposed to political upheavals and revolutions, the Vatican was bound to work for peace. It was natural. It made the Vatican more capable of defending its spiritual and political goals. Its interests, functions, and beliefs coincided harmoniously during the war, prompting the pope to act for peace. But here, too, the Vatican and the pope seemed inclined to take sides. Germany and Austria-Hungary, which included substantial portions of other nationalities within their boundaries, mostly Catholics (Czechs, Slovaks, Poles, Croats, and others), were to a great extent Catholic states. The Vatican, furthermore, realized that these powers were willing to give their support to its struggle against socialism and the entrance of the masses into active political life. On the other hand, it had little sympathy for the ideological and psychological warfare that Great Britain, France, and, later, the United States practiced against the Central Powers. Whether sincere or not, their slogans—to the effect that the Allies and America were fighting against Prussian militarism, for removal of dynastic absolutism, and for the realization of the principle of self-determination of peoples—could scarcely have received the Vatican's endorsement.[3]

Yet even among the Central Powers there were evident distinctions between zeal and trust exhibited by the Vatican toward Germany and Austria-Hungary, respectively. Germany, for obvious reasons, did not have the complete confidence of the Vatican and the pope.[4] Yet it was a state of law and order—and, as such, congenial to the Vatican. It also was a check against much-feared Imperial Russia, a fact that the Curia, as a careful observer of European power politics, considered very useful. Only during 1918, when Imperial Russia had disappeared from the political stage and when Austria-Hungary had become subservient to Germany did the Vatican change its stand and accuse Berlin of digging the Habsburg Empire's grave.

Austria-Hungary was the only great Catholic power left in Europe and in the world. The Vatican had shown a substantial weakness for the Habsburgs and supported them whenever it seemed necessary. As the war progressed and its effects became visible, the Vatican came to believe that the very existence of the Habsburg Monarchy was being threatened and that Catholicism was on the defensive. In political terms, the Curia considered Austria-Hungary and its dynasty as a bastion against the spread of Orthodoxy and Lutheranism. By supporting the Habsburgs, the Vatican insisted that it was defending Western civilization, Latinity, and Italianity, against barbarians from the East. Hatred of Russia and fear of Great Britain, hatred of Orthodoxy and fear of Protestantism, determined the Vatican's position toward the belligerent powers.

The Allies (Great Britain, France, Russia) were a strange mixture of policies, ideologies, and religions. They represented democracy and authoritarianism, liberalism and conservatism, and Protestantism, Catholicism, and Orthodoxy, respectively. Because of their political, social, and religious views and pretensions, they were regarded as anti-Vatican and anti-Catholic.

Imperial Russia was, certainly, the greatest threat to and an anathema for the Holy See. It was an Orthodox country, its religion was a part of the imperial structure and politics, and it was vastly ambitious and sometimes oppressive. It represented a great danger for Austria-Hungary and for Polish Catholics and Uniats in the Ukraine and Galicia. The Vatican also was disturbed by the prospect that Russia might spread its influence and domination over the Balkans and the Near East. In the Balkans, Russia posed a direct threat to Catholic elements there. In the Near East, it aspired to take over Constantinople and the Holy Places in Palestine. If the see of the Russian patriarchs were removed from Moscow to Constantinople, it was believed in the Vatican, union between the Eastern and Western churches would be prevented. Catholic influence in that area would be eliminated, and Orthodoxy would be favored in the Holy Places. For these reasons, the main object of Vatican policy for the greater part of the war was the removal of Russians from the Balkans and the Near East.

Since Great Britain and France seemed to approve of Russia's aspirations, they were bound to earn an extra measure of wrath from the Holy See. France, although solidly Catholic, had been at odds with the Holy See ever since the separation of the church and state early in the twentieth century. The latter considered the French faithless, atheistic, and vengeful against Germany. It also accused them of "producing more sinners than believers" in the twentieth century. It severely castigated French statesmen and politicians for their alliance with schismatic and aggressive Russia. It detested the rapprochement between France and Italy after 1902.

Great Britain was especially important to the Vatican. It was Protestant, its religious conduct was anti-Vatican, and it spread liberalism and the ideals of democratic reform. The Vatican considered England the major warmonger and accused it of supporting the warlike spirit of France. The Vatican was especially angry at the British government for its alleged role in bringing Italy into the war on the side of the Allies. The Vatican hierarchy accused England of forcing Italy to declare war against Austria-Hungary.

Over and above these considerations, there was a more mundane reason for the orientation of Vatican policies during the first years of the war. The Vatican found itself in a desperate financial situation after the death of Pius X, who was a poor manager of money and spent almost all of it on charitable work and relief, as well as building churches and monasteries. When the new pontiff took over early in September 1914, he was confronted with an empty treasury and was unable even to carry out routine operations; for the time being, he became dependent on contributions from the states and individuals. The situation became aggravated when the French government ordered the French bishops to stop sending money collected in France to the Vatican. German agents in the pope's immediate entourage realized the opportunity this offered. Monsignor Rudolf von Gerlach, the pope's private chamberlain, informed Mathias Erzberger, the leader of the Catholic Center party in the Reichstag, about the critical financial situation of the Holy See. Erzberger, with the full support and approval of the German government, collected a substantial amount of money among German Catholics and Protestants alike and forwarded it to the Vatican.[5] This relieved the pope's situation but made him, and the Curia, dependent upon Germany and on occasion ready to voice views that reflected Germany's desires and needs.

All these elements, factors, and prejudices account for the Vatican lean toward the Central Powers for more than three years of the war. They also explain, at least in part, the pope's reluctance to express his own opinions or pass judgments on the motives and actions of the belligerents. The pope found himself in an extraordinary dilemma, for example, when confronted with German destruction of a Catholic shrine such as Louvain in Belgium. His ambition to play an important peacemaking role and to mediate between the belligerents made it even more necessary for him to be silent about the causes of the war and the responsibility for the war. For the sake of political expediency, in fact, the Vatican and the pope limited their actions and proclamations to generalities or minor problems only.[6]

The conclave in the summer of 1914 elected Cardinal Giacomo Della Chiesa, archbishop of Bologna, as Pope Benedict XV. A follower of Pope Leo XIII and Cardinal Rampolla, the new pope was educated in the papal diplomatic service. He had a solid knowledge of politics and diplomacy, proved to be a competent administrator, and was a hard worker. He showed comprehension of a variety of problems, balanced judgment, and other necessary qualities. Confronted with the growing tensions and the spread of the war, he demonstrated an awareness of his responsibilities and a readiness to act.[7]

But the American, British, and French observers and diplomats were not much impressed with the new pope, and in some respects their assessments tended to agree. Gino Speranza, an American who spent most of the war in Rome as a correspondent and an intelligence-gatherer for the U.S. embassy there, found "the Pope younger, less astute looking than his photographs and portraits would lead us to believe, with a fineness of line and expression of face, indicative of determination and sensitiveness."[8] Duncan Gregory, the British diplomat long connected with the Vatican, had nothing nice to say about the new pope. He wrote that "the present Pope is a very decided mediocrity. He had the mentality of a little official, the inexperience of a parochial Italian . . . and a tortuous method of conducting affairs. He is not capable of rising to great heights . . . , is without any particular charm or personality and he is obstinate and bad-tempered to a marked degree."[9] The French ambassador in London, Paul Cambon, substantially confirmed Gregory's estimate of the pope. As he wrote to Lord Robert Cecil: "I personally know the present Pope from Madrid where we served together. He is an intelligent man, but with a mental outlook never rising above that of an ordinary first secretary. His attitude during the war ought to be ascribed to this weakness."[10] The Germans, for their part, appeared to be unhappy about the election of Benedict XV and initially ignored it. The German court, wrote a close observer, was "displeased about the choice of Cardinal Della Chiesa as he was known to share Cardinal Rampolla's views." After the pope's proclamation of September 8, 1914, however, the German Emperor changed his opinion and welcomed the pope's action.[11]

The conclave itself revealed the presence of a substantial German influence in the Curia. Cardinal Aidan Gasquet, an English Benedictine who acted as general manager and master of ceremonies in the conclave, found that the assembled cardinals did not sympathize with Belgium: in fact, Cardinal Mercier of Belgium was frankly told that his country was responsible for Germany's invasion because it had refused to allow Germany's troops to pass through. Gasquet noted that the ground was well prepared by Germany, Austria-Hungary, and Bavaria and that "the whole sentiment of ecclesiastical Rome was distinctly pro-German." He was also aware that pro-German sentiments and spies were present in the Vatican and in the pope's entourage. There was hardly any attempt to conceal this. Certain cardinals argued that the war was "entirely made by the English and French Freemasonry," which also endeavored to drag Italy into the war, the ultimate outcome of which would be to "overwhelm the Church."[12]

The pope's ablest and most trusted collaborator in the Curia was Pietro Cardinal Gasparri, the secretary of state. Gasparri was to act for many years in that capacity and came to enjoy the almost unique honor of serving two successive pontiffs. Gasparri was a man of enormous energy and determined will. As secretary of state, he excelled in forming the Vatican's policies, demonstrating great persistence and shrewdness. A French observer described Gasparri as an "improvised statesman, versatile character and, above all, not a too reliable friend."[13] Gasparri was politically close to the pope and never forgot that he was an Italian. Their views toward the belligerents were so similar, in fact, that it may be said that Gasparri was an interpreter of the pope's mind.[14]

Gasparri's views as to the responsibility for the outbreak of the war were clear. In his recently published memoirs, he levelled the full responsibility for the European conflict upon Serbia, its people, army, and king, that is, Princip had had the full cooperation of the Serbian army officers, who supplied him with a gun, and the tacit approval of King Peter I. Gasparri admitted, however, that the Serbian government, army, and nation would not have tried or approved of such an act unless they were sure of support from Russia, France, and England. Since Gasparri firmly believed that Serbia thus helped unleash a world war, it was no wonder that he, as well as the pope, considered its punishment by Austria-Hungary as justified.[15]

Besides the pope and Gasparri, Under Secretary of State Eugenio Pacelli wielded a good deal of influence in the Vatican bureaucracy. He was a young, rising star in the Curia and came to be considered the Vatican's best diplomat. Pacelli was unduly influenced by the idea that the Kaiser sincerely tended toward peace. Monsignor Bonaventura Cerretti was another papal diplomat, in fact the only papal diplomat well acquainted with North America and Australia. In 1908 he served in Mexico and as an auditor in Washington. In 1914 he was appointed apostolic delegate in Australia. Three years later, Cerretti returned to Rome and, for the rest of the war, directed Vatican policy toward the United States and earnestly worked for peace through compromise.[16]

Although the Vatican appeared to be au courant about Austria-Hungary's intentions to crush Serbia, American public opinion and the U.S. government were blissfully unaware of the pending crisis and its consequences. The assassination of Archduke Ferdinand drew substantial coverage in the press, it is true, but it was quickly forgotten.[17] In the last days of July 1914, however, the news from Europe came again to the foreground. Austria-Hungary's declaration of war against Serbia on July 28 was not, on the whole, received with the approval of the press, and American sentiment was visibly pro-Serb. It blamed the war on Emperor Franz Joseph and made no mention of the Vatican in this regard. The press also voiced the popular notion that England and France were fighting for the liberation of the rest of the world. When the German armies swept across Belgium and northern France, American public opinion, including the highest-ranking members of the Democratic administration, expressed their sympathies and readiness to help those in distress.

President Woodrow Wilson, despite his sympathy and esteem for Great Britain and its political system, showed remarkable restraint in voicing his views about the war in public. However, the diversity of opinions and suggestions coming from his closest advisers could have hardly left him unaffected. William Jennings Bryan, the secretary of state, considered American neutrality to be a religious duty and tended to disregard strategic, political, and economic considerations in the American approach to the European war.

Robert Lansing, a counselor in the State Department and an expert in international law, was much more aware of these factors and their importance in the formulation of American policies. Lansing, in fact, was the only one in the Wilson circle who knew and did not disdain the principles of *Realpolitik.* He also sympathized with Great Britain and France.

"Colonel" Edward M. House was especially influential in foreign policy. Wilson trusted House's opinion and judgments, which were pro-Ally from the beginning of the war. House disliked German militarism and aggressiveness since he found them to be dangerous for American security and international peace. He worked diligently to assure that Wilson would have the leading role in mediation for peace; to do so, he helped eliminate all the neutral powers as possible partners of the president.

After the news of the Austrian mobilization reached Washington, Wilson told reporters at the White House conference on July 27, 1914, that it was the traditional policy of the United States not to take part in political affairs outside of the Western Hemisphere.[18] The next day he was confronted with a message from Paris asking him to make a plea for mediation and delay of hostilities. At the same time, Bryan and the U.S. ambassador in London, Walter H. Page, another pro-Ally official of the administration, offered the good offices of the United States for peace.[19] On August 1, Bryan informed the ambassador that Wilson would like to know whether there was the "slightest intimation" that this suggestion might be acceptable elsewhere. He added that Wilson was "anxious to do everything in his power to avert the war."[20] Two days later, Page replied that "there is not the slightest chance of any result if our good offices be offered at any continental capital." U.S. action in this regard could have a chance only "after the war has reached a breathing space."[21]

House was not enthusiastic about Bryan's desire to persuade Wilson to offer his mediation. Back from Europe, House advised Wilson not to let Bryan "make any overtures to any of the Powers involved," since this could "lessen the weight of your influence if you desired to use it yourself later."[22] Wilson was not ready to follow House's advice. Instead, on August 4, he informed the European governments that he was ready to "act in the interest of the European peace, either now or at any other time that might be thought more suitable."[23] Nothing came of the offer, as the European powers' reply was to justify their respective positions. The fighting continued.

The Catholic hierarchy in the United States encouraged and supported Wilson's attempt at mediation. Its leader, James Cardinal Gibbons, archbishop of Baltimore, urged the president to act. Through Senator Blair

Lee of Maryland, the cardinal let Wilson know that he "heartily approved of the mediation." Wilson seemed pleased with this, since he wrote back that "it is most interesting and satisfactory," assuming that Catholics might support his policy in the future.[24] Gibbons was able to approach Wilson, directly or indirectly, throughout the war. Thus, he became the means by which the Vatican was able to convey its views. Besides Gibbons, several other clergymen encouraged Wilson to offer his services for peace. Early in September 1914, Thomas McCaffrey, in behalf of Catholics, Rabbi Henry Berkowitz, in behalf of the Jews, and John Sutherland, in behalf of various Protestant denominations, urged Wilson to "appoint a day to offer prayers for the restoration of peace in Europe." After the election of Pope Benedict XV, it was suggested to Wilson that the "Pope would aid the President in bringing about peace in Europe"; the press in Minnesota, for example, was full of articles designed to show the "close relationship between the Pope and the President."[25]

Wilson was not enthusiastic about acting jointly with the pope for peace. The clash over Mexico was intensified after Benedict XV was elected, primarily because of Wilson's personal views about the role of the Catholic church in general and the Vatican in particular. Moreover, since a significant number of Catholics were recent immigrants or descendants of recent immigrants, many tended to divide their allegiance between the old and new countries. Because of their allegiance to the Vatican and growing political strength, Catholics were considered by certain groups as convenient channels for meddling in the internal affairs of the country. Predominantly Protestant America, and Wilson as well, assumed, rightly or not, that Catholics were trying to influence the administration's policies and stands on a variety of subjects.

In fact, however, many Catholics were confused about the war. They were torn between America and the lands of their ancestors. Irish Catholics and German Catholics, the most influential groups in the Catholic church, were the most active in determining its policies and attitudes. Both groups had anti-British sentiments and thus a basis for close collaboration during the period of U.S. neutrality and afterward.[26] Amounting to sixteen million faithful, the Catholic church in the United States was, according to an observer very close to its hierarchy, "isolationistic, neutral, and pro-German by sections."[27]

The Irish Catholics had little sympathy with the aims and efforts of Great Britain and wasted few words in its favor during the war. Shortly after the outbreak of the war, the German Catholic Central Verein held its fifty-ninth annual convention and pledged its members to work for

Germany—since "blood is thicker than water," insisted Joseph Frey, the president.[28] For three years both groups acted to preserve American neutrality and to counteract Allied agitation and propaganda. A plethora of newspapers, reviews, journals, and occasional publications voiced Catholic views and opinions. Many articles and editorials, however, tended, despite cautious hesitation, to lean openly toward the Central Powers.[29] In fact, the U.S. Catholic press fully reflected the Vatican's preoccupations and intentions in regard to the United States. Like the Holy See, the U.S. Catholic hierarchy and press assumed at the outset of the war that the most desirable course for the U.S. government was strict neutrality.

The U.S. Catholic hierarchy ill served the Vatican, however; that is, it failed to provide accurate and unbiased information about the sentiments and disposition of the majority of the U.S. population and the U.S. government. "All information," wrote Shane Leslie, "described a neutral and isolationistic republic, the old hereditary enemy of Britain and nothing else. There was no American France as there was an American Ireland. American Germany was lodged in places of wealth and influence."[30] Speranza made an even more unflattering remark about the conservatism of the American Catholic church. Late in 1916, he wrote that "there is such a difference between American Roman Catholicism and European Roman Catholicism that you might call them intellectually distinct sects." He found that "any attempt to present to American Catholics the extremely frank and rationally liberal views of Italian Catholics may easily appear as an attack on the Church."[31]

The U.S. Catholic press generally reflected the Vatican's attitudes about the belligerents and America's duties in the war. It impressed upon its readers the war's terrible destruction and sacrifices, and its brutality. Similarly, it stressed the need for Christian ethics, the blessings of peace, and the danger of spreading the war. On occasion, the church press and church dignitaries publicly reflected about the responsibilities for the war, though they also warned that quick judgments should be suspended until the end of it. In the press, the Allies were accused of, and the Central Powers absolved from, the responsibility for the outbreak of the war. The war was sometimes presented as God's punishment of European nations for persecuting the church and trampling on its rights. France, England, Germany, and other countries were explicitly mentioned. The government and the president were frequently reminded that the United States should keep out of the war.[32]

Wilson's inner thoughts and feelings about Catholicism and the Vatican determined in many ways the administration's attitude toward the pope. His stand is sometimes difficult to depict. Initially, on the basis of his past experiences, Wilson did not expect Roman Catholicism to succeed in America.[33] Later on, however, he seems to have changed his opinion and showed a veiled distrust of Catholics. In his *History of the American People* (1902), he made several infelicitous and unflattering comments about the immigrants, predominantly Catholics, who came from southern Europe after 1890: "Now there came multitudes of men of the lowest class from the south of Italy, and the men of the meaner sort out of Hungary and Poland. . . . They came in the numbers which increased from year to year, as if the countries of the south of Europe were disburdening themselves of the most sordid and hapless elements of their population."[34] Though it was not explicitly anti-Catholic, this statement may well imply an anti-Catholic bias.

Wilson's remarks in his *History* were a definite hindrance to his political career. When he campaigned for governor of New Jersey in 1910, his opponents spread rumors that he hated Catholics. During the 1912 campaign for the presidency, he was again accused of being inimical toward all immigrants, especially Catholics.[35] Wilson had to work hard to repudiate his remarks in the *History* and to deny rumors about his anti-Catholic bias. In fact, he countered these accusations by lavishly praising the Poles, the Italians, and others.[36] Despite appearances and statements to the contrary, however, Wilson distrusted Catholics. Although certain historians claim that relations between the hierarchy and the White House were excellent and boast that Cardinal Gibbons had free access to the president, Wilson almost always turned a deaf ear to the Catholic hierarchy's suggestions.

Early in 1913, Wilson's problems with the Holy See became more acute. He came under attack for allegedly recognizing Archbishop John Bonzano, apostolic delegate to the United States, as the pope's official representative to the American government. Bonzano was linked with Tumulty, "thus making it possible for his [Bonzano's] foreign master to be advised of the secret councils of the President." Protests came in from various parts of the country, one from Iowa claiming that "an effort is being made to control our politics and make America a great Catholic country."[37] The Bonzano affair burst out into the open after *Outlook* published an article describing the pope's alleged intentions to move from Rome to Washington. Its author warned Wilson how dangerous it might be for the country to "ignorantly coquette with the oily agents of the Papacy," and insisted that the Catholic church possessed "the most commanding sites in and around the capital" and that Bonzano had become a "full-fledged ambassador of the Pope toward this government."[38] These protests were not a happy beginning for the new democratic administration. Since feelings were running high, Wilson took the warning seriously. He realized that his moves were being closely watched and that any cooperation with the Vatican might create troubles for his administration.

From the beginning of the war until its end, American views about the Vatican and its activities became both more sophisticated and hostile. Various observers and the administration's officials commented on the Holy See's aims and position, influence and policies, during the war. On the whole, their impressions were more or less unfavorable, and as the war progressed, many people came to despise the Vatican and the pope for the methods and policies they were pursuing. Speranza's evolving views are characteristic. Early in the war, he suspected that Benedict XV wanted to make the papacy a recognized influence in the world. In order to achieve this, he wrote, the pope "has relinquished the idea of temporal dreams and fallen back on an earlier position of the Pope, that of quasi-spiritual advisor to Kings and nations."[39] Later, after the United States entered the war, Speranza assessed Vatican policies toward the United States as "vacillating between friendliness and unfriendliness; this policy serves to assay and test public opinion and enables the Vatican to swim with the tide."[40] For his part, House was sure that Benedict XV was inclined toward the Central Powers. In the spring of 1915 he reminded Wilson that "I suppose you know that the Pope was elected through Austrian influence and that he is largely guided by it."[41] Thomas N. Page, ambassador in Rome, who became well acquainted with the Vatican's activities, was scornful of them. He wrote to Wilson late in the war: "If I had the least idea of favoring such a thing [sending an American mission to the Vatican] it would have been dissipated by what I have seen of Vatican policies since I have come to Rome. I must separate in my mind the idea of the Catholic Church from that of the hierarchical political organization of the Church here."[42] The temporal ambitions of the pope and the Vatican's assumed unfriendliness toward the United States and sympathies for the Central Powers did not inspire much enthusiasm among the administration's officials and observers.

Wilson and the Curia quickly realized the extent of their mutual distrust. Yet in certain instances, both Wilson and the pope had to act toward each other with the utmost courtesy and politeness. On August 20, 1914, Page cabled that Pope Pius X had died. Wilson instructed Bryan to forward his condolences to the college of cardinals. His message expressed his sense of "the great loss which the Christian world has sustained in the death of His Holiness Pius the Tenth. By his pure and gentle character, his unaffected piety, and his broad and thoughtful sympathy with his fellow-men he adorned his exalted station and attracted to himself the affectionate regard of all who felt his worldwide influence." The message was transmitted to the dean of the college of cardinals and was received with deep gratitude.[43] Two weeks later, after the results of the voting in the conclave became known, Page reported that Cardinal Della Chiesa had been elected to St. Peter's chair. Bonzano conveyed the official notification to Wilson on September 23. In it, Benedict XV expressed his belief in mutual cooperation and the president's favorable disposition toward the Holy See. He prayed to God that "He lavish his bounty upon and unite Thee and Thy Confederation with us in generous affection." On October 2, Wilson replied to the pope, congratulated him upon the election, and wished him "many useful and happy years under the guidance and blessing of Almighty God."[44]

This exchange of telegrams between the Vatican and the White House did not pass unnoticed, and protests were once again dispatched to the president. A certain Reverend William Horne expressed his "unhappiness and surprise" over Wilson's message to the Vatican on the death of Pius X and accused Wilson of "catering to the Catholic support." A more important protest came from the American Federation of Patriotic Societies several days later.[45] A Kansas newspaper attacked Wilson for his message of August 20, insisting that it "clearly commits our government to an acknowledgment of the Papal pretension to spiritual and temporal authority." It also expressed doubts as to whether Wilson really "believed that the departed Pope was a man of broad sympathies."[46] Wilson was reminded to stay away from the Vatican and not make a common front with the pope in his eventual action for peace.

On August 18, 1914, Wilson warned all concerned that the United States "must be impartial in thought as well as in action, must put a curb upon our sentiment as well as upon every transaction that might be construed as a preference of one party to the struggle before another."[47] He made similar exhortations during the months to come. Wilson's proclamation of August 18 was enthusiastically greeted by the Catholic as well as other churches throughout the country. The official Vatican newspaper published the proclamation on the day Pius X died, thus giving it wide circulation among Catholics in Europe.[48] Many interpreted it as Wilson's pledge to work with the Vatican for peace and to preserve a neutral and impartial America. Wilson's subsequent actions, as the Curia saw them, constituted a breach of his word, and they were condemned as such.

In the beginning, Wilson concealed his private beliefs and views about the war behind this public appeal for neutrality and impartiality. However, he soon voiced his disapproval of Germany and its conduct of its military operations. House found him willing to go "even further than I in condemnation of Germany's part in the war." Wilson termed German philosophy as "essentially selfish and lacking in spirituality" and was indignant at the German chancellor's "designation of the Belgium Treaty as being only a scrap of paper."[49] The German army's burning of Louvain provoked Wilson's wrath and evoked some harsh words about Germany, as House noted that Wilson "felt deeply the destruction of Louvain." Ironically, Wilson spoke out about Louvain, although in private, but the pope kept silent rather than protest against German acts. Wilson's and Benedict XV's approaches to the war were running in altogether opposite directions, with no chance that their views and policies might coincide.

Despite Wilson's efforts to maintain reserve and keep America's passions toward the belligerents under control, the impact of the war was evident in different forms and degrees of intensity. The situation was becoming tense, economic problems were multiplying, and pressure from abroad was increasing in intensity and scope. A campaign initiated by different ethnic and religious groups and denominations uncovered substantial cleavages over the policy to be pursued, and the propaganda of both the Allies and Germany seemed to be tearing the country apart. The U.S. Catholic church contributed, in various ways, to this development, and the administration was either unwilling or unable to take more determined measures to prevent it.

CHAPTER 3
EFFORTS TO MEDIATE, 1914 – 1916

President Wilson's offer to mediate between the belligerents in August 1914 was the earliest move to end the war. Subsequent overtures and proposals were made both to the Allies and to Germany. Numerous conferences were held, and representatives met and corresponded in order to gain perspective and assess the situation. Some of these moves were sincere; others were shams devised for internal and external propaganda. Numerous intermediaries—states and individuals—appeared on the stage, only to fade into the background. Real plans and designs for peace were conceived, only to have mutual hostility reconfirmed. It became evident that American sympathies lay more with the Allies than with the Central Powers, even though Wilson realized that both sides were waging the war for reasons of revenge, military mastery, and economic domination.

It was an awareness of these factors that prompted the U.S. policy of nonintervention. Neither the British blockade nor Germany's submarine warfare, each of which threatened America's rights as a neutral, had been able to draw America into the conflict. Isolationism and formal neutrality increased Wilson's determination to avoid war, and crusaders such as Bryan kept reminding him that it was America's duty to work for peace. The exhortations of pacifists and liberals throughout the world strengthened Wilson's desire to act for peace whenever there seemed to be some prospect of success, and he came to be viewed as a rallying force for peace, a major spokesman for the uneasy conscience of humanity.

The timing of any attempted mediation was important, however. Both sides would have to accept it, since rejection by one side would threaten America's usefulness in the future or, even worse, might lead the country into the war. Since Wilson was also the principal spokesman for the neutral nations, it was assumed in the Vatican that he would be anxious to enlist the support of the pope, who also hoped to end the war. Such cooperation seemed all the more likely in view of Wilson's and Bryan's appeals to Christianity. Also, both the United States and the Vatican assumed initially that peace should be reestablished on the basis of the status quo ante bellum. The Vatican, indeed, was prepared to devote considerable energy toward the success of this joint effort.

Was such an expectation realistic? Were not the American and the Vatican approaches similar in appearance only? Were both sides sincere? These and other questions figured prominently during the two years of U.S. mediation efforts. It appears that the Vatican and American approaches to mediation and peace were diametrically opposed. The basic element in U.S. policy during this period was the preservation of Anglo-American friendship; the achievement of peace was secondary. Since the German government tended to discourage U.S. mediation and had introduced submarine warfare, the ties between London and Washington were strengthened.[1] The Vatican, though careful in voicing its views, came to believe that the Central Powers were not responsible for the outbreak of the war. It regarded the Allies as the more aggressive and their program as overly ambitious, among other reasons.[2] As the war in Europe progressed, the differences between the United States and the Vatican became more and more apparent and, therefore, mutually exclusive.

The pope continued his efforts to end the war, and, paradoxically, his moves somewhat paralleled American actions. That is, although both sides' moves were not coordinated, their timing seemed to coincide. The Wilson administration acted to make use of German Ambassador Johann von Bernstorff's statement to Oscar Strauss on September 8, 1914, that Germany might accept Wilson's offer to mediate. The pope moved boldly, and in his exhortation *Ubi Primum* published that same day, he announced his intention to intervene in every way possible, as soon as an opportunity arose, to bring the war to an end.[3] He insisted that "we are firmly and deliberately determined to leave nothing that is in Our power undone to hasten an end of so great a calamity," and he urged "those who rule the affairs of peoples, that they now turn their minds to forget all their discords. . . and initiate councils of peace and reconcile themselves."[4] The invitation was clear enough, but the chances of having it accepted by the belligerents were slim, indeed. The pope was as yet an unknown, the war was only several weeks old, and, most important, the Allies came to believe that the German influences were dominant in the Vatican.

The pontiff, thus, could not find an attentive audience among the rulers and governments. Even among Catholics, the response was limited. The Allied governments refused to entertain the Vatican's suggestion, and Wilson did not consider it politically feasible. Even Secretary Bryan did not accept it, his burning Christianity and his distress over political developments in Europe notwithstanding. Although he insisted, in a letter to Wilson on September 19, that the United States should take the initiative for peace, he neither mentioned the pope nor indicated that the pope's views were to be solicited as to the terms upon which a stable peace could be made.[5]

The pope had also asked the faithful to pray for peace and implore God to take away the awful scourge. On October 4, Wilson proclaimed a day of national prayer for the restoration of peace in Europe. Bryan wrote afterward that "care was taken that nothing should be said of a non-neutral nature, the trend of speeches being that God might so direct those in authority in the belligerent nations as to hasten the restoration of peace." The similarity was remarkable, indeed, but nobody was anxious to follow the pope's advice.[6] This was only the beginning; as time went on, the exclusion of the pope from American peace efforts became even more obvious.

It was at this time that the administration took the first step to bar the pope from acting together with Wilson for peace. Bryan informed Wilson that the neutral states in Latin America, as well as Spain and Denmark, insisted that America ought to mediate for peace and that they were anxious to participate. Pressed by House to postpone any action and thus thwart Bryan's plans, Wilson was reluctant to act. He did not believe that America would be called upon to choose partners in mediation or to invite participants. He expected that it would become clear when such action was acceptable. "I think, speaking confidentially," Wilson stated, "that it is very desirable that a single nation should act in this capacity rather than several. The difficulties and complications would be many and the outcome much more doubtful *if there were several mediators.*"[7] Collective mediation was not to be considered, and the Vatican, implicitly rather than explicitly, was ruled out as a partner. Wilson would mediate under his conditions, at the time most convenient to America. This explains, at least in part, why the White House did not entertain the Vatican's suggestions and proposals throughout the war.

The Vatican, unaware of this momentous decision, proceeded to appeal for peace, although the pope was not apparently thinking of acting jointly with Wilson. In the middle of October, Thomas N. Page, U.S. ambassador in Rome, wrote about rumors that the pope intended to take some steps toward mediation. Page connected this with the pope's efforts to restore his temporal power, but admitted that "no one quite knows how the matter stands at present."[8] The pope made a far more important statement in his encyclical *Ad Beatissimi,* dated November 1, 1914. In it, he plunged into an examination of the causes of the war, a task many statesmen avoided at that time. He found the major reasons for the war to be lack of mutual love among people, disregard for authority, unjust quarrels among the various social classes, and material prosperity, which was becoming the focus of human behavior. Although the pope directed his words ostensibly to the faithful, he also intended them for governments and rulers, which he felt were neglecting the dictates and rules of Christian wisdom. He again asked rulers to achieve for their peoples the blessings of peace. The pope's pronouncement gained an immediate response in America.[9] On the whole, however, it seemed to be a voice in the wilderness; it was ignored in Europe as the war grew more ferocious and brutal.

On December 1, Bryan again tackled the sensitive question of U.S. mediation. He found that the war was inflicting losses on American business, dislocating trans-Atlantic traffic, and disturbing neutrality. America ought, "as the leading exponent of Christianity," wrote Bryan, to help neutrals and belligerents to compose their problems and settle their differences on the basis of justice and friendship.[10] The similarity with the pope's reasoning was obvious, although not surprising. Wilson, however, again chose to follow House's advice. On December 3, House and Wilson discussed Bryan's letter. Wilson was warned that the Allies would consider it an unfriendly act and, further, that peace would not be wise until Germany was subdued. They agreed that House should go to Europe to discuss peace with the belligerents.[11] Later in December, House was informed that mediation was not feasible as far as Germany was concerned, and he advised delay.

In America, pressure for peace was mounting as the activities of the Vatican continued and became more visible. On November 26, Gasparri advised the belligerents of the pope's decision to propose suspension of hostilities through Christmas, and, in an allocution to the College of Cardinals, the pope complained that his efforts to bring about peace were not "crowned with happy success." Although there was a great deal of pretension and self-righteousness in this statement, he promised to continue to work for peace and to preserve complete neutrality and impartiality.[12] The proposed armistice was rejected by the belligerents.

The pope, his attempts frustrated, acted to get Wilson's support in his struggle for peace. He made the decision with hesitation and qualms in view of the unpleasant clashes over Mexico and the Vatican's evident disapproval of American trading with the Allies. As usual, the Vatican's campaign began with rumors in the Italian press that the Vatican desired to move toward intermediation. The rumors persisted as it became known through the press that the American cardinals had presented a memorial asking Wilson to cooperate with the pope in his efforts for peace and that it was favorably received. The Vatican news agency also reported that the U.S. government had decided to send an envoy extraordinary to the Vatican to congratulate the pope on his accession to St. Peter's throne. In sending this news to Washington, Page warned that "the whole affair is a very intricate and delicate one, and so far as outside countries are concerned required a most careful handling."[13] The Vatican's suggestion stood no chance of being accepted, and, furthermore, it did not jibe with the facts. It was simply a way of ascertaining Wilson's reaction without officially committing the Vatican to anything. Wilson personally composed a reply to Page, saying that "nothing has been as yet brought to our attention officially which would sustain the press reports of which you speak concerning suggestions by Cardinals to the President." Bryan authorized Page to say that Wilson "did not think of acting upon such suggestions" without previous agreement with the Italian government.[14] It was tantamount to refusal: Wilson excluded joint action with the pope by refusing to interfere in what he considered Italy's internal affairs.

On January 30, 1915, House boarded the *Lusitania* on a peace mission that was to take him to London, Berlin, Paris, Nice, and Biarritz. He arrived in England in time to witness the initiation of Germany's submarine warfare and to hear angry outbursts on the part of France and Russia against U.S. mediation efforts. The British joined its allies in order to fight off any settlement unfavorable to their aims, a fear that proved groundless, however, since House was not inclined to press mediation and seemed to approve of the Allies' plans and designs. This altogether changed the initial character of House's mission. Amid discussions and entertainments, House was urged to go to Berlin, where, despite British efforts to keep him from making that trip, he arrived on March 19. The Germans were not encouraging about peace talks either; they pressed the question of America's munitions exports to the Allies and made the question of the freedom of the seas a condition for peace discussions.

House left Berlin on March 30, going on to Nice and Biarritz for informal talks with Nelson Page and Ambassador Joseph E. Willard. The question of Vatican mediation was not raised during House's first tour of the Allied and German capitals. The pope's offer to mediate was not welcome, both because House did not expect Wilson to mediate and because the Allies opposed it. But when House arrived in Nice and Biarritz, the question entered onto the agenda for discussion; he knew of the pope's constant efforts to act with Wilson in bringing about peace,

and the State Department had similar information.[15] The American
Catholic press, prompted by Gasparri's letter of January 15, 1915, to
Reverend J.T. Roche of the Rockford Diocese, heartily seconded the
pope's peace efforts, and the grand master of Knights of Templar
implored Wilson to act for peace and promised his help "in taking the
question with our fratres in Europe."[16] As awareness of Vatican
ambitions was growing, the administration was becoming openly
hostile to the pope's interference.

While in Nice, Page explained Italy's situation to House in detail,
especially the chances of Italy's joining the Allies. He also intimated that
Italy would not consent to the pope's mediation or to his playing any
important role. House agreed, suggesting that the Central Powers might,
if the pope became the mediator, use him for their own aims. He advised
Wilson that he was doing everything *"to make sure that the Allies never
accept him."*[17] A few days later, House defined more clearly his reasons
for excluding the pope and King Alfonso XIII of Spain from mediation
efforts. After a dinner with Ambassador William G. Sharp in Paris, he
confided to his diary: "My purpose is to set the Pope and the King of
Spain aside as peace makers so that Woodrow Wilson may have a clear
field. I desire to see the President become mediator by a process of
mediation and if the Pope and the King of Spain are safely out of the
way, there is no one else I can think of in sight. I am gathering information every day which will have a tendency to put the Pope and the
King out of the running." The next day House informed Wilson of his
decision, quoting almost verbatim the diary entry.[18] Wilson accepted
House's decision—and frank explanation—without question. He never
commented on it or made any elaborate analysis in writing.

The elimination of the pope as mediator was a direct consequence of
an interview Lansing had with Gibson Fahnestock, a close personal friend
of Cardinal Farley of New York. On March 29, Fahnestock came to the
State Department with the cardinal's approval in order to discuss Italy,
the Vatican, and other related problems. Talking about Italy's entrance
into the war and the Vatican's reaction to it, he said that Cardinal Farley
claimed that the Holy See was in a most difficult position because of
"the devotion of Austria-Hungary to the Holy See and the predominance
of the Italians in the Roman Hierarchy," that the pope's most earnest
desire was to preserve the Dual Monarchy, and that Italy's entry into the war
would defeat this desire. Russian domination was a major fear of the
Vatican, Fahnestock explained, and if Italy became an ally of Russia,
Catholic power would be weakened: "The hope lay in peace coming

before the Austro-Hungarian Empire was crushed by Russia, which would in all probability be the result if Italy entered the war." For this reason, Fahnestock said, the pope was doing everything he could to restrain Italy and to bring about peace before it was too late for Austria. Lansing then inquired whether the Curia favored Germany and expected it to succeed. Fahnestock again quoted Farley as saying that "the Vatican was pro-German and, for the sake of Franz Joseph, desired the success of Germany and Austria," adding that "the Roman Church would do nothing which would assist in the defeat of Germany and Austria and would probably exert its influences to suppress hostile feeling against them."[19]

Suddenly everything became clear: the Vatican's inner disposition toward the belligerents; its motives for leaning toward the Central Powers; the reasons for its drive for peace; its sympathies for Austria-Hungary and Germany, on one hand, and its fear and distrust of Russia and Great Britain on the other. All of these things were contrary to Wilson's recent thinking and arguments about European peace. In December 1914 he had expressed his belief that "the government of Germany must be profoundly changed and that Austria-Hungary will go to pieces altogether—ought to go to pieces for the welfare of Europe"; in January 1915, he told Chandler Anderson, the legal adviser to the State Department, that the Russian conditions—control of Constantinople and the Dardanelles—pleased him. He did not see in them any conflict of interest with Great Britain.[20] Wilson thus chose to disregard completely the Vatican's trepidation and concern for the Central Powers. He advised House not to visit Italy in order to avoid the accusation that Italy was being pressured to enter the war; yet there is no evidence that he objected to the Allies' trying to win Italy to their side. These facts explain convincingly why Wilson gave his approval for House to eliminate the pope as a mediator and came to consider himself as the only person qualified to carry out this duty. Wilson's plans were temporarily thwarted when, on May 7, 1915, a German submarine torpedoed the *Lusitania* off the Irish coast.

While Wilson and the State Department were forced to cope with the mounting tension that brought the United States to the brink of war with Germany, the pope and other neutral aspirants could proceed unchecked with their plans and designs through May, June, and July 1915. Wild rumors circulated that the pope was being asked to act for peace alone or in cooperation with other neutrals. There were also voices of disappointment at Wilson's hesitation to act. King Alfonso XIII complained to Ambassador Willard that he was unhappy that "our government had not responded more cordially to his offers of cooperation

toward peace."[21] A day after, Page reported that the leader of the Dutch
Catholic party arrived in Rome to ask "the Pope to use [his] influence
to have [a] peace congress met at The Hague." Page used this to suggest
that Wilson propose the congress instead.[22] The rumors were cut short
after the sinking of the *Lusitania,* but were circulating again by the end of
May and into June. On May 23, the State Department took note of the
withdrawal of the Austrian and Prussian ambassadors from the Vatican
as Italy was about to declare war on Austria-Hungary.[23]

In June, another attempt was made to break the deadlock and
encourage neutrals to act jointly for peace. In early spring of 1915, a
group of American women, led by Jane Addams, Emily Balch, and Alice
Hamilton, actively promoted the cause of peace through the International
Congress of Women, which was held in The Hague. After the congress
voted its program, which included prohibition of war without previous
arbitration between the belligerents, self-determination, disarmament, and
the voiding of secret treaties, its delegates visited various European capitals
in order to present their conclusions. A delegation led by Miss Addams
visited London, Bern, and Rome. While in Rome, the delegation was
received by the pope and Gasparri. During the interview with the pope,
the question of the war was discussed, as well as "the possibility of some
action on the part of the neutral nations to initiate negotiations between
the warring countries." The pope was receptive to the idea but insisted
that "it was for the United States, the greatest of neutral countries, to
make a move in which he would gladly cooperate if it seemed best."[24]
The pope obviously felt Wilson was in a position to do something effective
if he wanted to; the pope himself was disheartened by his failure to keep
Italy neutral and did not think that it was proper for him to act when the
clash between America and Germany was at its peak.

While the delegation was in Rome, rumors intensified that papal action
was pending, namely, that the pope would decide to hold a peace congress
over which he would preside, and that the Vatican was about to publish
a "white book" that would reveal the pope's efforts to bring about peace.
Since this news came from Switzerland, where the Austrian and Prussian
ambassadors to the Vatican were residing, it may have been planted by
the Central Powers. The pope lent credence to the rumors, however, by
telling Miss Addams that he would send a representative to such a
congress. This disturbed the Allies and the Americans, but Page seemed to
discard the rumors as irrelevant. Instead, he considered them a hint that
the Vatican wanted to have a seat in the peace congress if one occurred.[25]
House also seemed not to take Miss Addam's activities seriously, insisting

that "she has accumulated a wonderful lot of misinformation in Europe." Not so the French ambassador, however, as he complained to Lansing about "Jane Addams's activities."[26] The pope was actually bidding Wilson to act, testing his goodwill and determination to step in as a peace-maker. However, there was no reaction from Washington.

Far more negative in its ultimate consequences was the pope's inter-view with Louis Latapie, a correspondent of the conservative French newspaper *La Liberté,* which was published on June 22, 1915. The pope, in commenting on a variety of subjects, questioned the opening of the Vatican's mail by the Italian authorities, the internationalization of the Law of Guarantees, and the continuation of submarine warfare. He indicated that the time had not yet come for a peace initiative, but promised to do his best to put something into motion and to act at the first convenient opportunity.[27] The interview was very embarrassing for the Italian government and the Allies, and it created a great deal of excite-ment in Italy. The reaction was so strong, in fact, that the Vatican had to deny it officially as inaccurate. Page believed that the interview showed that the pope would "align the Vatican against the Allies," which was a serious matter "under the extraordinary conditions now existing in connection with the intricate relations of the Vatican."[28] Page's letter of June 30, describing the imbroglio, arrived in Washington on July 23 and was forwarded to the White House. It offered Wilson another oppor-tunity to voice his distrust of the pope. As he commented to Lansing, "the information he [Page] gives us from the inside viewpoint of the recent indiscretion of the Pope is most interesting and *shows where many currents are running.*"[29] The pope's slip, whether intentional or not, only confirmed Wilson's belief that the Vatican was the tool of Germany, and he felt justified in ignoring further hints.

At the height of the furor over the *Lusitania* notes in July 1915, which coincided with the anniversary of the outbreak of the war, the pope made another appeal for peace. In a widely distributed statement, he implored all concerned to start both a direct and an indirect exchange of views in order to realize the rights and aspirations of the peoples involved. He seemed to be moving closer to the American views, spoke harshly of militarism, and insisted upon maintaining equality among the states. "The balance of the world and the prosperous and secure tranquility of nations rest upon mutual good will and upon respect for the rights and dignity of others far more than upon the multitude of armed men and upon the formidable girdles of fortresses."[30] The French, and to some extent the Italians, vehemently denounced the pope for his failure to distinguish between the aggressors and the states who took up arms only to defend themselves. As a result, the pope started wavering about his initial action and even conceded that at the moment he had no intention to work for peace—"as such a step would be useless."[31] The pope's utterance did not attract any attention or reaction in America; it seemed to be another tactical and political blunder on his part.

In frustration the Vatican decided to change its tactics. If asked, it remained ready to step in tactfully. That would be a more propitious way of keeping itself in the midst of the activity and of reminding those in authority of its views and influence. As Vatican activities usually attracted wide attention, the propaganda effects were obvious, forcing the governments concerned to counteract them. These tactics, which became evident in the fall of 1915, have been practiced consistently ever since.

On September 1, 1915, Germany promised, at the insistence of Wilson and Lansing, not to torpedo passenger ships. Thus, the administration successfully closed the incident that arose over the torpedoing of the *Arabic*. The next day, Wilson and Lansing, in separate audiences, received Cardinal Gibbons, who made the visit to express the pope's satisfaction with the outcome. After the audiences the cardinal informed newspaper correspondents that the "détente between the United States and Germany places the former country in an advantageous position for putting an end to the European conflict." This statement indicated that the pope and Wilson might have discussed a joint peace initiative. The European and the American press went wild. Italian, French and British newspapers claimed that Cardinal Gibbons had handed Wilson a message from the pope about the restoration of peace in Europe. The German press insisted that the meeting had taken place in order to suggest the convocation of a peace conference. The British were the most excited and demanded that Vatican authorities either confirm or deny the information. The Vatican chose to deny that Gibbon's visit had anything to do with a peace conference, and the whole incident was closed.[32]

This affair accomplished two things. First, the pope was successful in reminding Wilson that he was the leader of the greatest neutral country and should act accordingly; second, the Vatican drew U.S. public opinion to the subject of peace and represented the Allies as being opposed to it. It was no accident that on September 5, 1915, a convention of German-Americans was to open at Chicago.[33] Although it was a shrewd move, the ultimate result was not what the Vatican had expected. The Allies rose to the occasion, and the Vatican's image and influence came out shattered and diminished. The extent of the Vatican's dilemma and its growing concern over the future were clearly revealed: it was unable to accomplish much by itself and therefore longed desperately to be accepted as a partner in striving for peace. The ever-increasing influence of the United States disturbed the Vatican and prompted the pope to look for Wilson's cooperation, only to be ignored or rejected outright.

The failure of the House mission to Europe, the subsequent crisis over the use of submarines, and the growing uneasiness in America over the future could not have left Wilson undisturbed. House still remained Wilson's agent in arranging peace, and he still hoped to bring America and the Allies together. He worked hard to secure an Allied invitation asking Wilson to mediate, and he tried to eliminate anything that might threaten this. This was not enough, however. It was necessary to secure the cooperation of the Central Powers as well. House, in his frustration, believed that the United States should build and use armed force in pressing for peace. He was prepared to go to war with Germany if necessary, which Wilson refused to sanction. Wilson did approve House's proposal to start negotiations with the French and British governments in the fall of 1915. They were to be told that the U.S. concept of peace was the same as theirs. Such thinking was encouraged by Grey himself, who in August 1915 appeared to believe that U.S. mediation was possible provided the United States promise to join a league of nations and help to enforce the peace settlement to be made.[34]

By the fall of 1915, the Vatican's policymakers tentatively suggested what they considered to be a program for future peace. Limited in scope and unacceptable to almost all the belligerents, it contributed nothing to the solution of broader questions such as freedom of the seas, disarmament, arbitration, or the creation of a league of nations. In fact, the pope told Mgr. Alfred Baudrillart, rector of the the Institut Catholique de Paris, in September 1915, that peace could be restored if Germany evacuated Belgium and returned occupied territories to France, except for Alsace-Lorraine. The Habsburg Monarchy would be preserved, with small territorial recompense to Italy. An independent Polish kingdom could be carved out of the part occupied by Russia. Finally, Russia was to be eliminated from the Balkans, the Dardanelles, and Constantinople.[35] The Vatican's peace program, as defined here, was modest and conservative, demonstrating an evident preoccupation and concern for Catholic nations: Austria-Hungary, Poland, Italy, and Belgium. The pope did not insist upon indemnity for Belgium, since this might be displeasing and objectionable to Germany. It was felt that peace would come more readily because the belligerents were exhausted and willing to negotiate.

This program countered what Wilson defined as America's program for peace. Besides material differences, there were differences in sentiment as well. The elimination of militarism and navalism, freedom of the seas, disarmament—these were also to be resolved in peace talks. In his correspondence with House, which laid the groundwork for his trip to Europe, Wilson clearly indicated that he regarded Germany, its system and objectives, as the most serious impediment to peace; at the same time, he did not believe that Allied demands constituted a similar obstacle. Wilson tacitly accepted and approved of the general aims of the Allies and believed that peace ought to be established on those lines. Thus, his program came to differ substantially from that of the pope, both in its broader implications and in its detail. Wilson did not believe in a peace based on crushing military victory by either side, and the prospect of a German victory, which seemed an anathema to him, eventually led to U.S. involvement. He also maintained that national control of munitions, equality of nations, national self-determination, and Russian access to the sea were essential for future peace. His attitude toward Austria-Hungary did not change much after December 1914. Belgium, he believed, should be evacuated and indemnified by Germany. He knew about the French desire to regain Alsace-Lorraine but did not give his approval to it as yet; here, his views were close to those of the pope.[36]

Wilson assumed that the belligerents wanted security—as France, Germany, and Great Britain had stated. But they all wanted security achieved through military victory. Although Wilson was not inclined to accept this, the pope appeared reconciled to German domination, both military and political. The differences between the program of the pope and that of Wilson were thus enormous: except for certain changes, mostly favorable to Catholics, the pope was intent on preserving the status quo ante bellum in Europe. Wilson and America favored more substantial changes in international relations and the institution of an international organization bound to work for international peace and cooperation on a more equitable footing. America forecast the dawn of the new era, but the Vatican tenaciously clung to the old, nineteenth-century outlook on international relations.

While House was preparing for a new trip to Europe, corresponding with Grey and Bernstorff in order to get certain points straightened out, rumors of an impending peace offensive by the pope circulated again. Early in November 1915, Lansing was informed about "the peace movement among the neutrals."[37] A few days later, Pleasant Stovall, the U.S. minister in Bern, reported the arrival in Switzerland of Count Bülow, former German ambassador to Italy. Stovall indicated that the object of his trip was to try to "associate the Pope with a league of neutral nations, Sweden, Netherlands, Switzerland and Spain in joint action for peace."[38] The arrival of Cardinal Hartmann, archbishop of Cologne, in the Vatican confirmed this; as Page indicated, the cardinal's arrival had to do with Bülow's stay in Switzerland, "where he is said to keep in close touch all [the] time with the Vatican representatives, and relates to peace proposals to be made by Germany."[39] At the same time, General Wille, the chief of staff of the Swiss army, invited the Vatican and America, "the two great powers not engaged in the war," to act. "They should proclaim," he added, "that [the] time had arrived for a cessation of hostilities with a view of peace."[40]

All these biddings had made an impact upon the pope. Observers of Vatican activities came to believe that the German government had brought great pressure on the pope to intervene. This proved to be correct. On December 6, 1915, the pope addressed an allocution, *Nostis Profecto,* to the College of Cardinals. More than ever before, he pleaded against the fatal war "by land and sea" and against spreading it to other nations; he urged all belligerents to act "to prepare the way for peace . . . a peace just, lasting, and not profitable to only one of the fighting parties." His method for achieving peace was, however, an old one: an exchange of ideas, with goodwill and serene conscience, "eliminating all that is unjust and impossible and taking count of all that is just and possible." He found it vital that "on one side and the other of the belligerents there should be concession on some point and renunciation of some hoped for gain."[41] The pope thus earnestly urged negotiations but did not offer the program that was developed in the Vatican. Incidentally, at the time of House's stay in England, that is, in January 1916, even Wilson seemed to be encouraging negotiations in general, leaving details to a later time. Whether the pope's message was intended to support Wilson is hard to say; it may have been. Its echo was widespread, but the reactions were again contradictory and discouraging.[42]

Early in January 1916, House again went to Europe. In conversations with Grey and other British leaders, he repeated what Wilson had already committed himself to, namely, to cooperation in bringing about and maintaining peace. The pope's address, the persistent rumors about his intervention, and the implications must have been present in the minds of House and his British counterparts while they were exchanging their respective views. They were unanimous in their determination to avoid having the pope as a mediator: House still insisted on having a clear field for Wilson. On January 14, 1916, House met Lloyd George, Lord Rufus Reading, Lord Chief Justice, and other British leaders. While covering the wide range of topics, House described Wilson in detail, telling of "his capacity for staying put, of his courage and of his statesmanship." Then, he wrote somewhat ruefully, "I spoke of the Pope and of how impossible it would be for him to act as mediator." Ultimately they agreed that Wilson's intervention for peace should come in the fall, after "the big battles of the summer would have been fought." The next day House informed Wilson about his discussions of the previous day: "We agreed that the war could only be ended by Your intervention. *We discussed other mediums, none of which were satisfactory.*"[43]

The pope's role as mediator was sealed off during House's stay in France. House arrived in Paris on February 2, after a brief stay in Berlin at the end of January. He did not mention the decision about the pope's elimination but found the German leaders insistent upon gaining indemnities from Great Britain and France and having control of Belgium and Poland. This was unacceptable to Wilson, the Allies, and the pope as well. In Paris, House discussed the problems raised in London with Aristide Briand and Jules Cambon, the prime minister and an official of the Foreign Ministry, respectively. He found the conversation satisfactory and "along the lines of my conversation with Lloyd George in London."[44] This meant, in fact, that the French leaders agreed to the exclusion of the pope from mediation efforts.

House and Wilson could not accept the mediation of a person who was disliked and distrusted by the Allied governments and who was considered close to the Central Powers. That would have violated the basic intentions of Wilson's mediation, as outlined by House. Neither did the pope's program for a peace settlement, as known to the Allies, commend itself: it insisted upon the status quo, demanded cessation of military operations, and did not provide for indemnities. The United States, therefore, hoping to secure the Allies' and Germany's consent to mediate, would not risk cooperating with the Vatican. Besides House's ego, which seemed insatiable, practical considerations induced him to act as he did. The pope, it seems, had realized this. He did not dare to broach the subject of peace for quite some time.

On February 22, 1916, after another series of conferences with the British, House and Grey initialed a memorandum embodying the conditions of Wilson's intervention for peace. It provided that Wilson would cooperate with the Allies in securing a reasonable settlement and the establishment of a league of nations. If Germany refused and the Allies accepted the proposal, the United States would probably enter the war against Germany. However, Grey was careful to stipulate that the timing of the proposal depended upon the Allied decision.[45] This was a gigantic case of self-delusion. House returned to Washington early in March and reported to Wilson and Lansing about his mission. As a result of this, Wilson decided to reorient administration policy, abandoning a century-old isolationism and even risking war with Germany. This was of no avail, however, as the British never meant to take the memorandum seriously; they intended to use it as a last resort, an alternative to military defeat. All Wilson's and House's proddings that the machinery provided by the memorandum be put into motion fell on deaf ears in London.

On March 24, 1916, the German submarine torpedoed the British packet *Sussex*. This caused a serious confrontation between Berlin and Washington, which lasted through April. It ended on May 5, when the German government accepted the responsibility for the destruction of the boat and expressed its readiness to provide satisfactory compensation to injured Americans. The next day the German note was published in the newspapers, and it was received with mixed reactions. Wilson sounded satisfied with Germany's reply but insisted in his answer that there would be no clashes in the future over the submarines.[46]

This protracted crisis and the possibility of a breakdown in relations between Germany and the United States greatly worried the Vatican. It took time for the slow-moving Vatican bureaucracy to decide to act, and by the time the pope's personal letter to Wilson was delivered, the crisis was over. The press in Germany, Italy, and the United States was familiar with the Vatican's intentions, but interpreted them as a move to mediation.[47] On May 6, Mgr. Francis Russell, Gibbon's representative in the national capital, delivered to Lansing the pope's letter to the president.[48] In the letter, the pope pleaded with Wilson not to break off relations with Germany over the *Sussex*, but did not suggest that they act together for peace. Wilson was eager to proceed and demanded the British cooperate on the basis of the House-Grey memorandum. U.S. public opinion and Congress were becoming more restive about the blockade and the submarines, and Wilson advised the British that he would have to move for peace. He urged House to tell Grey that American sympathies might be alienated, as peace sentiment was growing stronger. He even went on to warn the British that it would be "much better for Great Britain that we should initiate the final movement for peace than that the Pope should."[49] House's letter to Grey did not mention Wilson's remark about the pope's services but insisted that the British should support Wilson. Grey refused, replying to House that it was premature to move for peace.

Wilson's reference to the pope did not mean, however, that he was ready to change the administration's stand and embrace the Vatican in order to get British consent. Such an argument would have been useless, since House realized that, in dealing with the Allies, it was the U.S. leaders who had forced the pope out of the game.

Allied and German diplomats in Washington seemed very curious about the contents of the pope's message. Bernstorff asked House about it, saying that peace talks in Germany had been revived by "the alleged message from the Pope." On May 14, he asked House how much truth there was in the rumor that "the Pope was urging the President to use his good offices to make peace." House professed not to know the details, but thought that "such things were absolutely of no value." "When peace came," he insisted, "it would have to come by the insistence of the President," since he was the only one in the world who could bring it about.[50] Bernstorff's inquiry might have been an indication that the Vatican did not keep Berlin well posted about its move.

The Allies could not remain idle either. Confronted with Wilson's pressure, they did everything they could to eliminate the additional pressure that could have mounted if the pope had decided to intervene. Macchi Di Cellere, the Italian ambassador, told Polk that Mgr. Bonzano told him that the press reports about the pope's representations to Wilson were erroneous and were never made. Spring-Rice had the same news but believed that it was an election maneuver and that the whole action had originated in Germany in order to force Great Britain to accept mediation.[51] The French, though not implicating the pope directly, warned the administration that they could not accept the peace. "Anyone suggesting peace now," wrote the French ambassador, "would be considered by my people as a friend of Germany."[52] The allusion was clear enough to everyone familiar with the situation. The Allies agreed that the pope should not mediate, though they could not agree about the wider implications of Wilson's presumed action at the moment.

Early in May, while awaiting Grey's reply to House's letter, Wilson was confronted with the invitation from the king of Spain to act together toward securing arbitration. Ambassador Willard was told by the king that in asking this he had "the assurance of the Pope's full cooperation." The plan provided that the king take the initiative with Germany and Austria-Hungary, where his influence was perhaps stronger, and that Wilson do the same with England and France. The Vatican would support the move on human and moral grounds. The king asked Wilson to express his views as soon as possible.[53] Early in June, there were signs that Alfonso XIII was doing his best to get Austria-Hungary to agree to the proposal. Robert Penfield, the U.S. ambassador in Vienna, wrote that "some members of the Imperial family . . . are doing their utmost eventually to have the King of Spain as sole mediator; and failing this, then as joint mediator with America's Chief Executive." He added that the pope did not have a chance, since Austria-Hungary preferred as peacemaker "a potentate whose influence is more than spiritual."[54] There was no information about the king's activity in Berlin. The proposal was not taken seriously and was answered only three months later. Wilson's refusal to act was explained by the Allies' unwillingness to cooperate for peace and by his reluctance to approach any neutral to act jointly so that the Allies would not be responsible for prolonging the war.[55]

The pope was clearly excluded from working jointly with America for peace. The determination to exclude him grew stronger with time, as the military and political developments of the war turned against the Allies. Neither Americans nor Allies trusted him. This exclusion eased tension and tended to smooth relations between Wilson and the Allies, but the pope was frustrated and later outraged as he found himself secluded and powerless. His ambition was sapped, and the interests of the Catholic church could not be protected. He deplored this stigma imposed upon him and the hampering of Vatican movements. After a lengthy ordeal, he protested openly. "Our grief is the more increased," he wrote to the German bishops in September 1916, "at seeing how Our incessant appeals for peace have given rise to unworthy suspicions among some people, and have provoked expressions of discontent among others, almost as if Our exhortations were not prompted by a wish for the public good, but by some design for Our own interests."[56] There was nothing he could do to change the situation, however, as long as the Allies and the Americans saw in him a potential enemy, opposed to their designs and ambitions.

Pope Benedict XV

CHAPTER 4
SUBMARINES AND THE EMBARGO, 1914–1916

The efforts of the Vatican and other neutrals to mediate between the belligerents were seriously hampered, if not completely disrupted, by the ever-growing economic ties between the United States and the Allies. The British maritime blockade affected Germany's trade with neutral nations and cut vital supply lines both for war production and for wide consumption. The German government had to find a way to counteract the blockade.

All three powers—the United States, Great Britain, and Germany—had strong and valid reasons to insist upon their respective positions. The U.S. government was intent on using this opportunity to bolster the sagging economy at home; furthermore, trading with belligerents was not prohibited by international law and was in accord with the public will. Great Britain used its superiority on the high seas, invoked international law, and instituted a form of warfare practiced earlier, one that had proved very congenial to its tastes and ability. Germany, as a continental power confronted with the blockade and what it considered American leniency, introduced U-boats. This proved somewhat disadvantageous, since U-boat warfare tended to inflict indiscriminate human and material losses and interfered with the rights of neutrals to travel and do business. Above all, it threatened to provoke American entry into the war, a factor that loomed large before Germany's leaders. The German government and public bitterly resented what they considered to be U.S. favoritism toward the Allies in business transactions and U.S. readiness to avoid clashes over British maritime policies. This was the problem that divided the civilian and military leaders in Germany.

The Vatican, confronted with this steadily deteriorating situation, gradually developed views—on various issues—that came close to those of Germany. It felt (and said) that American export trade tended to favor the Allies and discriminate against the Central Powers. The Vatican's decision makers, in formulating their attitudes, exhibited an amazing ignorance of international law. They accused the British government of bringing suffering, starvation, and poverty to masses of people. They considered the U.S. attitude nonneutral and, as such, condemned it. They regarded submarine warfare as a cruel and inhuman means of waging war, but at times they believed that the circumstances justified it.[1] Submarine warfare could have compelled Great Britain to give up the blockade and consider peace; it might even have brought about its military defeat. It was believed in the Curia that Germany risked provoking American entry into the war. The Vatican did not want this since it might contribute to the defeat of the Central Powers and diminish its chances to mediate for peace.

The Vatican, therefore, considered the export trade, the blockade, and U-boat warfare as being interconnected and interdependent. These were questions with expressly political significance and implications that could have had far-reaching consequences. This explains why the pope asked the belligerents and neutrals to abstain from anything that might prolong the ordeal of the Old World.[2] In doing so, it initially paid little attention to the U.S. internal situation.

In view of the Vatican's ambitions to work for peace, any intensification of the seaborne trade, the blockade, and U-boat warfare could have been detrimental. Therefore, the pope appealed to the neutrals to stop selling food, munitions, arms, and raw materials, to stop granting loans and credits, and to stop traveling aboard ships bound for Europe.[3] The Vatican also assumed that mutual exhaustion would make the belligerents more amenable to peace proposals or the conclusion of an armistice. The Allies in turn believed that the Vatican's attitude in this respect favored the Central Powers, especially Germany, which was better prepared and supplied for a war of attrition. The Allies, by contrast, were dependent upon imports, mostly from overseas, either from the British dominions or America. They also had to provide money and supplies to a number of lesser states (Italy, Belgium, Serbia, Montenegro), which Germany did not have to do, at least at the beginning of the war.

The outbreak of war in Europe caused considerable confusion in the United States. Germany's adherence to the Declaration of London of 1909, which prohibited placing food and raw materials on the list of contraband items, forced the Wilson administration to settle the problem with Great Britain. The British government, by an Order in Council of August 20, 1914, tightened up its control around the Central Powers. By the end of 1914, the British had almost complete control over neutral ships sailing to Germany. The U.S. government, confronted with the British refusal to sanction the Declaration of London, ceased its objections and acquiesced in the British maritime war. Yet Grey wanted an informal understanding, and Wilson reciprocated by indicating that there were "no important questions in principle" to discuss between the United States and Great Britain.[4]

Another problem that was settled in a satisfactory way was the question of loans by U.S. banks to the belligerents. In August 1914, the French government asked J.P. Morgan and Co. to float a $100 million loan in America. But the U.S. government refused to approve the French request; to do otherwise would have violated the spirit of neutrality. By the fall of 1914, however, the initial restrictive policy was modified, and the ban on loans to the belligerents was partially lifted. The extension of commercial credits came next. In the spring of 1915, when U.S. exports rose enormously and exceeded imports from aboard, the total revocation of the ban on loans to belligerents was announced. Soon, the submarines appeared on the scene and attracted some attention. Both sides used U-boats, but during the fall of 1914, only against warships. Several skirmishes between the U-boats and British cruisers were reported in the American press during October and November.[5] These ominous developments indicated that the war on the high seas was spreading and that it would probably spread even more.[6]

The growing U.S. trade and financial operations materially helped the Allies, but hurt Germany. The German government, perfectly aware of American rights to trade with belligerents, began to contend that the United States, by selling munitions to England and France, was prolonging the war.[7] German-Americans loudly protested in an attempt to force the Wilson administration to establish an embargo. As time passed, this campaign grew to include other ethnic groups and religions opposed to the Allies in general and Great Britain in particular. German Catholics all over the country, but mostly in the Middle West, campaigned vigorously; organized into the German Catholic Verein, this group played a significant role in the National German American Alliance.[8]

The Catholic church and its leaders in America tended to lean toward the Central Powers. Their motives varied: sympathies for the old countries, Irish hostility toward England, dislike of French and Italian Freemasonry and anticlericalism, fear of Orthodox Russia, and concern for Catholic Austria-Hungary. The Catholic press voiced other grievances, mostly directed against Great Britain.[9] It criticized the U.S. policy toward the Allies for favoring Great Britain and berated Wilson for tolerating the British blockade.[10] It is unlikely, however, that the initial Catholic reactions were the result of promptings from the Vatican. Rather, they reflected the more specific views of certain religious and ethnic groups or wider observations on the state of the Catholic church in the belligerent countries.

The Vatican decided to voice its views only after long observation of political developments. In his encyclical of November 1, the pope mentioned "the lamentable state of civil society," "the latest weapons devised by military science," "the paths of commerce blocked," and "the poor made destitute," among other things. He invited Catholics around the world "to lift up our voices in prayer to God in Whose hands are the hearts of princes, and of all responsible for the continuance of the scourges now afflicting us, and to cry in the name of all mankind: Give peace, O Lord, in our days."[11] Similar exhortations were repeated in the pope's subsequent pronouncements.

The pontiff's concern was reflected in the U.S. Catholic press, which was genuinely disgruntled with the growing U.S. trade with the Allies. Newspapers attacked the selling of military materials to England, calling them "the hateful missiles of death."[12] Still others branded this traffic as immoral, since it brought "destruction to Europe and prosperity to America."[13] Some questioned the hypocrisy of "a nation which preached peace while providing the instruments of war."[14] The U.S. Catholic press frequently voiced the opinion that Americans should refrain from traveling aboard the ships of the belligerent nations. In asking Americans to make these sacrifices, the Catholic newspapers stood in open opposition to Wilson's policies.[15] The Catholic hierarchy obviously had understood the pope's utterance of November 1 as a signal to promote, if possible, a total embargo on U.S. exports to Europe.

The Catholic campaign in the United States received support from Grand Admiral Alfred von Tirpitz, German secretary of state for naval affairs. He urged the initiation of the U-boat campaign against British commerce in an interview given to Karl von Wiegand, an American journalist, and published in the New York *Sun* on December 23, 1914. Tirpitz warned that the U-boat campaign might hit the Americans as well.[16] Simultaneously, the German-American Alliance tried to get Congress to pass laws imposing an embargo. During the congressional hearings, representatives of the alliance emphasized that "an embargo would hasten the advent of peace in Europe."[17] Catholics attending the gathering of the American Neutrality League at St. Louis on January 10, 1915, overwhelmingly endorsed the demand made by the alliance in Washington.[18]

The Vatican moved warily in developing its attitude toward the British blockade and U.S. trade. But its attitude seemed to grow more and more specific; it recognized that British control over the seas was becoming stronger and that U.S. acquiescence was almost complete. An opportunity to voice its views occurred early in 1915, after an exchange of notes between London and Washington relative to the British warships' intercepting neutral vessels and searching them for contraband.[19] The official

Vatican organ, after mentioning the skirmishes over the blockade, pointed out that the problem should be treated strictly as a practical matter, not as a theoretical question.[20] The U.S. government was expected to lodge a more energetic protest and see that its demands were accepted. This became even more evident when, on January 11, 1915, Grey defended the British right to visit and search. *L'Osservatore* published the British reply two days later, commenting that U.S. acceptance of the British position "might favor one belligerent bloc against the other."[21] The U.S. position did not satisfy the Vatican.

On February 4, 1915, the German government announced a new maritime policy, declaring all waters surrounding Great Britain and Ireland to be a seat of war—a decision that set off new developments.[22] The German decision had been made on February 1 and the Vatican informed about it. Two days later, the Vatican daily had published news that the German embassy had advised the U.S. government that the U-boats would not interfere with American vessels carrying food for the civilian population of the Allied countries.[23] The Curia was much upset when the U.S. note advised the German government that it would be held to "a strict accountability" for illegal destruction of American ships and lives. In order to soften the effects of its new maritime policy, the German Ambassador Bernstorff, who was directing German propaganda in the United States, decided to ask the Vatican to help. At the end of February, he cabled Berlin that "Roman Catholic circles here are very warmly disposed toward us, but not very active in so far as agitation is concerned. The influence of the Catholic church could do very much here. *For that instructions from Rome [would be] very desirable.*"[24] This was an open admission of Catholic support for Germany's policy, of mutual cooperation, and of the desire to continue it in the future. Bernstorff had in mind papal intervention to secure an embargo on munitions trade.

The German government was receptive to Bernstorff's suggestion. It believed that the pope would act—and the pope did so. Meanwhile, the British liner *Falaba* was sunk by a German submarine on March 28, 1915, an incident that lost more support for Germany in the United States. Spring-Rice found relations between Germany and the United States "in a dangerous condition," although German propaganda, supported by the pacifists, was actively in favor of imposing an embargo. The attitude of the Catholic clergy he found to be "problematical," since they were for Austria-Hungary and against England.[25] As the U.S. government delayed taking a stand on the *Falaba* case, Germany decided to ask the pope to act in order to avoid full responsibility.

The German government charged Erzberger with the sensitive task of inducing the pope to act on this question. In the first week of April, Erzberger arrived in Rome, and on April 3 he had a long audience with the pope. On that occasion he arranged that Karl von Wiegand "will have an audience with the Pope and Cardinal Secretary of State . . . *concerning American shipments of war equipment to the Entente."* Wiegand's interview took place on April 5 in the pope's private library.[26] It was published in the *New York World* several days later and created quite a stir in Europe and the United States. In the course of interview, the pope told von Wiegand to transmit the following message to the American people:

> Work incessantly and disinterestedly for peace, to the end that this terrible carnage and all its attendant horrors and miseries may soon cease. Through this, your country and your press will be rendering service to God, to the world, to humanity, the thought and memory of which will live through ages to come.
>
> *If your country avoids everything that might prolong this struggle of nation against nation, in which the blood of hundreds of thousands* is being shed and misery untold inflicted, then America, by its greatness and its influence, will contribute much toward the rapid ending of this terrible war.

The pope further asked Wilson to take the initiative toward peace, promising his utmost support. On the same page, readers were informed that the president was much impressed and deeply moved by the pope's plea.[27] The aim of the statement was clear: it was to show that the pope favored a U.S. embargo on arms and munitions. Germany confirmed that the pope acted with this aim in view. On April 4, 1915, Bernstorff handed Bryan the note demanding that the U.S. government stop exporting munitions.[28] The British Foreign Office instructed Sir Henry Howard, the British minister to the Holy See, to find out whether the Vatican stood behind the published text of the interview.[29] Gasparri confirmed its authenticity but argued that the pope could guarantee neither his words nor phrases of the published text. In an audience with Howard several days later, however, the pope admitted that he had said all that von Wiegand had quoted in the interview.[30] As the pope's statement demonstrated, the Vatican was confused and ignorant of the fact that the selling of the war material was perfectly legal. The pontiff himself admitted this to Cardinal Gasquet, after realizing the implications of his statement.[31]

The pope's statement almost had disastrous consequences for the Holy See. House read the interview while in Paris. On April 13, he saw Théophile Delcassé, the French foreign minister, and read to him the part "of the interview von Wiegand had written for the *New York World* which laid emphasis upon the intimation that if the United States stop selling munitions of war to the Allies, the war would probably cease." House found that it was consistent with what the Germans had argued during his recent stay in Berlin and that the pope was being "used by the Germans." He promised Delcassé; that "no amount of pressure brought to bear upon the President would make him change his determination concerning the sale of munitions to the Allies." A day after, House cabled to Wilson that the pope's interview "was not altogether friendly."[32] Wilson approved of House's promise to Delcassé; it confirmed Wilson's friendship for France and readiness to proceed with his policy undeterred by the pope's appeal.[33] The interview discredited the pope before the administration, confirming its belief that the Vatican was close to the Central Powers.

Why did the pope go so far to conform to Germany's demand? Besides ignorance of international law, there were other, more practical reasons for his step. It was a political deal, a quid pro quo between the Vatican and Germany. The Curia had been in desperate financial circumstances since the death of Pius X, and Erzberger had helped collect money in Germany. The pope was thus repaying Germany for its aid and hoping, at the same time, to serve Catholic and German interests. His interview with von Wiegand was a service that appeared to do both.[34]

The emotions stirred by the sinking of the *Falaba* and the pope's interview had not yet calmed when a new and most serious incident occurred. On May 7, 1915, a German submarine sank the British liner *Lusitania;* 1,198 persons were aboard, 128 of them Americans.[35] Americans were shocked and enraged at what appeared to be the deliberate murder of noncombatants. Some urged that the United States should declare war. Wilson remained calm and did not allow himself to be pressed into hasty action. Yet in a note to Germany on May 13, the administration demanded that submarine attacks against unarmed merchantmen be stopped.

For the Vatican, the sinking of the *Lusitania* came as a sudden and unwelcome surprise. The Curia was weary and fearful of voicing its views. The sinking of the *Lusitania* could not be sanctioned by the Vatican or the pope. It was barbarous and inhuman; besides, it could provoke American entry into the war. The pope, however, was still relunctant to vindicate international law. When asked to state his views, the pope refused to do so: "The wise reflections of the Consultor do not encourage an immediate protest from the Holy See, but instead I intend to accelerate the date of the holding of a Consistory . . . so that I may have occasion to renew the condemnation of all methods of barbarism . . . which have caused the deaths of so many victims, such as the barbarous sinking of the *Lusitania.*"[36] In public, however, the pontiff was more moderate and circumspect in making his own views known, since the Vatican was teeming with German agents.

American Catholic reactions to the *Lusitania* incident were mixed at best. The cardinals, it seems, tried to set the general tone of the Catholic press. Cardinal Gibbons believed that Americans should give up traveling on belligerent ships, since a "true lover of America should sacrifice personal whim when the honor and peace of the nation hangs in balance."[37] Cardinal Farley expressed his satisfaction with U.S. restraint in view of "the greatest tragedy I have known in my life."[38] Cardinal O'Connell, in praising Wilson's speech of May 10 in Philadelphia, insisted that "all America, every human being must feel reminded of a first duty—a duty clear enough yet so easily clouded by self-interest."[39] The cardinals' restraint, however, was not shared by Catholics around the country. The Catholic press in Illinois, for example, did not consider Germany's submarine activities objectionable and demanded that the United States energetically defend its neutrality rights against British interference. This represented the feeling of most American Catholics, although there were some exceptions.[40]

In May 1915, after Italy had entered the war and as the diplomats and other personnel of the Central Powers were leaving Italy, the pope decided to fulfill a promise made to Cardinal Gasquet. On May 25, he published an open letter on the existing political situation, actually addressed to the cardinal dean of the Sacred College. In it, he referred to the sinking of the *Lusitania:* "The war continues to deluge Europe with blood and not even do men recoil from means of attack, on land and on sea, contrary to the laws of humanity and international law."[41] Although the pope's letter was vague, there can be little doubt that the rebuke was aimed at Germany. Besides the *Lusitania,* the pope condemned the German use of asphyxiating gas as well. Although the English and French appeared dissatisfied with the vagueness of the pope's statement, it did show that Germany's influence was not as strong as before and that the Vatican would criticize certain practices. The pope had learned international law quickly.

The pope's protest against the blockade was voiced in an interview granted to Louis Latapie. The interview caused great excitement everywhere: it implied, in the form of a question, that Britain's starvation of the German people was as inhuman as the sinking of a large passenger liner on the high seas. The British were outraged at the comparison, since the pope had promised Howard not to combine consideration of the blockade with the sinking of the *Lusitania*. This was a very sensitive matter in view of American Catholic opposition, since every pontifical pronouncement on the blockade seemed to cause considerable embarrassment for Great Britain. The British government exerted all available pressure on the Curia to correct the impression that the pope had on purpose connected the blockade and U-boat warfare. Its efforts were rewarded when *L'Osservatore Romano* published a statement by Gasparri that the pope had intended to ascertain the opinion of his interviewer—"not to pronounce against lawful blockade." Gasparri also personally assured Howard that the pontiff "had never censured or condemned blockade as being contrary to either natural or international law."[42] The pope's poorly defined statement clearly indicated the strain the Vatican was under in presenting its views to the world; it also diminished the pope's influence with the belligerents.

The Catholic press campaign received additional impetus from the news that an Anglo-French financial mission was about to arrive in the United States. The aim of this mission was to get a consortium of American banks to float loans totaling many millions of dollars. By this time, of course, the Wilson administration had completely reversed its stand on loans, and such an operation was now possible. On September 25, it was announced that a banking syndicate would undertake to float a purchase of $500 million in bonds, as a joint obligation of the British and French governments. German-Americans and Catholics strongly protested. On September 15, the German-American Alliance denounced the "money trust" and the Anglo-American "finance combine." It exhorted German-American depositors to protest to their bankers against appropriation of their money for Allied war purposes. The Catholic newspapers voiced widespread disapproval of the transaction, insisting that "we hope that they [the Allies] won't get it . . . Uncle Sam is not going into the gambling business." The Vatican newspaper was not happy, either, as it ruefully informed its readers that the Anglo-French commission had concluded a loan in New York for one billion dollars.[43]

The Vatican was very concerned lest the United States declare war on Germany over the submarine issue. Germany refused to accede to U.S. demands over the *Lusitania,* and mutual distrust lingered throughout the summer. The pope decided to intervene in order to prevent disaster. On August 24, he sent a message to Chancellor Bethmann-Holweg, through

Erzberger, asking him to settle the question of the *Arabic* peacefully. The chancellor, in turn, declared that if investigation proved that a German submarine had sunk the *Arabic,* he would be ready to render full satisfaction to the United States. On September 1, Bernstorff informed Lansing that submarines would not attack passenger liners without warning and gave an assurance of safety for noncombatants. The pope was credited by some for this concession on Germany's part.[44] On August 29, Gasparri also instructed Gibbons to advise Wilson about the action in Berlin and to express his belief that the Germans would follow the pope's suggestion. Gibbons visited the White House and the State Department on September 2, the day after Bernstorff had made his statement to Lansing. The pope was thanked for his action.[45]

Germany's reckless use of submarines against unarmed merchantmen was actually becoming more annoying to the Vatican, which admitted the right of neutral nations to trade with belligerents. Submarine warfare was considered detrimental to the Holy See's eventual action for peace, destructive in itself, and an excuse for the Allies to go on fighting. Mgr. Francesco Marchetti-Selvaggiani, the Vatican's representative in Switzerland, summed up this view after the *Arabic* crisis was over: "Zeppelins and submarine warfare against merchant shipping are bellows with which the otherwise faintly glimmering enthusiasm for the war is continually kindled into new life; they are thus Lord Kitchener's best allies. If Germany . . . insists on her point of view that the world must be razed to the ground before there can be any idea of peace, the Entente will— *sauf l'imprevu*—remain true to its program of letting the Central Powers go on fighting until they have conquered themselves to death."[46] German stubbornness was castigated, but there was no sympathy for the Allies either. Both obstructed Vatican endeavors to stop the spread of the war.

This was the desperate voice of one lost in the jungle of world politics. There was no room for the Vatican, as the pope slowly came to realize. At times he sounded very discouraged, yet he continued to make his voice heard and to register his protests. The Curia found the behavior of the belligerents, as well as that of the neutrals, at times incomprehensible. It could not approve of actions that threatened to extend the war or the folly of submarine attacks on neutral shipping and innocent civilians. As the Vatican still tended to look more benevolently upon Germany than upon the Allies, it could not but feel bewildered at the prospect of America's joining the Allies.

For one brief moment, it seemed that this danger might be eliminated: Admiral von Tirpitz was relieved of his post, and Admiral Henning von Holtzendorff replaced him on the German staff late in September. Bernstorff announced a change in submarine policy on October 5, 1915, and confirmed the intention of the German government to settle the *Arabic* issue.

But the submarine truce was brief. On November 7, 1915, an Austrian submarine sank the *Ancona* in the Mediterranean, which prompted the U.S. government to send a strong protest to Vienna demanding disavowal and indemnity. The Austrian reply, made on December 15, was evasive and truculent, and created rumors of an immediate break between the two states. Finally, on December 29, the Austrian government admitted responsibility for the destruction of the *Ancona* and offered to pay an indemnity. The following day, a submarine sank the British steamer *Persia* in the Mediterranean, which brought another protest from Washington, insisting upon the assurance of early action in accord with the *Ancona* pledge. Germany quickly complied with the U.S. demands for the Mediterranean area, although it categorically denied responsibility for the destruction of the *Persia*. In fact, however, Germany's military and naval leaders concluded by the end of 1915 that U-boat warfare ought to be intensified in order to achieve final victory.[47]

The Vatican was filled with anxiety over developments in the fall of 1915, especially over the outcome of the *Persia* and *Ancona* incidents. The pope, in addressing an allocution to the College of Cardinals on December 24, insisted that "we are confronted today with the savage spectacle of human slaughter," and complained about "the wider spread, the greater pertinacity, the excess, which, with their terrible consequences have turned the world to an ossuary and a hospital, and the progress of human civilization to an anti-Christian retrogression."[48] A few days later, Gasparri condemned Germany's U-boat actions to Mgr. McNally (a Canadian bishop received by the pope), insisting that it was contrary "to humane and divine law."[49]

Wilson's preparedness campaign in the United States was sharply criticized in the U.S. Catholic press, which maintained that it brings in itself "the seeds of war." On the whole, however, American Catholics seemed divided on the issue; Cardinal Gibbons, for example, approved of it, since he came to believe that it would make for peace rather than for war.[50] The Vatican press carefully watched Wilson's tour through the country late in January 1916, publishing bits of information about his speeches. It refrained, however, from making extensive comments about the campaign.[51] Wilson's preparedness campaign, despite all its idealistic and humanistic motives, could not but sound ominous to the Curia, since it might possibly extend the world conflict. The Curia most likely came to believe that preparedness was America's reply to Germany's U-boat warfare.

The U.S. Catholic press continually waged a vigorous campaign against the administration's increasing economic and financial ties with the Allies. U.S. exports grew rapidly through 1916, to the great chagrin of German-Americans and Catholics.[52] The German Catholic party in the Reichstag seemed to be cooperating in this campaign. In March 1916, it approved the use of submarines as a bargaining weapon in negotiations with foreign countries, meaning the United States, and in April its representative in the Reichstag insisted that "the American nation had signally failed to observe the admonitions of the President in his proclamation of August [18, 1914] to be neutral in spirit and act."[53] The U.S. Catholic press also accused the administration of inconsistency in allowing Americans to travel on armed merchantmen. One newspaper charged that "our neutrality must be practical, not theoretical; and our interpretation of international law must take into account circumstances that put an altogether new aspect on things. . . . We cannot consistently with our national honor pursue any course but that of non-friendship, non-enmity for either side." There could be but little doubt that the Vatican was behind this press campaign, encouraging Catholics in America and Europe to act as they did.[54]

The Catholic campaign in general and the pope's interventions in particular in the question of U-boat warfare irritated State Department officials. Early in May 1916, the pope sent a personal message to Wilson asking him to refrain from taking rash steps against Germany after the sinking of the French packet *Sussex* on March 24, 1916. In fact, the U.S. note of April 18 had indicated that unless Germany abandoned submarine warfare, the United States would be forced to sever diplomatic relations. Early in May, the German government accepted the U.S. demand but insisted that England should honor the U.S. stand as formulated in December 1914 and October 1915. If the United States could not induce England to do this, Germany reserved for itself freedom of action.[55] The pope's appeal was received with suspicion; it was thought to be a way of gaining publicity for the Vatican. The composition of the U.S. reply to the pope's message was entrusted to Alvey Adee, second assistant secretary of state and a veteran bureaucrat. In a covering letter, forwarding the text of the reply, Adee wrote plainly: "I don't much like the tone of the Pope's message. He seems to ask the President to get out of the way and let him settle the matter."[56] Adee's brief comment undoubtedly reflected the growing impatience over and disapproval of what was considered the pope's inadvertent intrusion into Wilson's domain.

In the presidential campaign of 1916, Catholics got a chance to express their resentment over a wide variety of subjects. Catholic rank and file and Catholic leaders disparaged Wilson's Mexican policy and sharply criticized the administration's European policies. Irish-Americans and German-Americans strongly objected to what they termed Wilson's "leniency toward Great Britain and much too strict and biased policy with Germany." Wilson's neutrality policies were savagely criticized, and the blame for munitions trade was laid directly on him. Wilson's frequent references to his "hyphenated" critics alienated many Catholic immigrants, since such allusions tended to emphasize their divided loyalties to the United States and their European homelands. This, of course, smacked of the anti-Catholic strains of the nativist tradition and an ill-concealed bigotry.[57] In the summer of 1916, James M. Cox of Ohio sent a letter from a Democratic Catholic politician who wrote about the "poison" emanating from the Catholic press and its impact on the anti-Wilson campaign.[58] German-Americans of all denominations, including the representative of the Roman Catholic Central Verein, voted against Wilson's candidacy at their meeting in Chicago in late May 1916.[59] Wilson seemed to have little chance of being reelected.

Yet when the election returns were analyzed, it became clear that the majority of Catholics had voted for Wilson's reelection. The Catholic working class had not ignored the administration's pro-labor record, and the Catholic electorate could not disregard Wilson's efforts, so far successful, to keep the United States out of the war. In analyzing Wilson's victory, both the *Gaelic American* and the *Irish World* admitted that the administration's foreign policy was a crucial factor in his reelection.[60] Characteristically, this explanation was not seriously entertained by the Vatican press. In commenting upon the outcome of the elections, the Vatican official newspaper argued that "President Wilson's present foreign policy did not play an important role in the elections." It also expressed its belief that this policy might be continued in the future as well.[61] This, in fact, was an admission of the Vatican's disappointment with the outcome of the elections; it had fervently hoped that the Republican opposition and the Catholic voters would elect Charles Evans Hughes and bring about change in U.S. policies toward the European belligerents. Wilson's reelection prompted the pope to increase his mediation efforts and to plunge the Vatican even more energetically than before into the arena of world politics. The growing possibility of America's entrance into the war was, indeed, clearly perceived by the Curia.

The Vatican well understood the increasing importance of American commercial and financial ties with the Allies, as well as the eventual implications. These ties had made the United States, it was believed, even more concerned with the ultimate outcome of the war. And they were not conducive to peace, either. The U.S. course was contrary to the Vatican's position that the United States ought to impose an effective embargo as the first step toward peace. The Vatican's assumption in this regard was utterly unrealistic and impractical, and it tended to favor the Central Powers. In order to carry it out, however, the Vatican, at Germany's instigation, was willing to use the Catholic hierarchy and the Catholic press in the United States. This was not welcomed by the Democratic administration and tended to deepen already evident cleavages among various ethnic groups and to stir up agitation and antagonism among certain voting segments of the party.

Vatican involvement in the negotiations on U-boat warfare, the embargo, and the blockade was not well received by the U.S. government. It was as unpopular as the Vatican's attempted mediation. Since Vatican views ran against the prevailing beliefs and practical needs of the Wilson administration and the U.S. business community, they had but slim chance of ever being entertained. After the pope inadvertently expressed views that were interpreted as pro-German, his suggestions were all the more ignored.

The pope intervened personally, both in Berlin and Washington, only when it appeared that Germany and the United States would go to war over the use of submarines. After the sinking of the *Lusitania* and the *Sussex,* the Curia came to believe that Germany's reckless attacks on passenger liners and merchantmen were self-defeating—both morally and politically. Although U-boat warfare was considered inhuman and as such, reproachable, its consequences were viewed as being even more disturbing. Namely, it could bring neutrals, most likely the United States, into the war. This specter greatly disturbed the Vatican.

CHAPTER 5

WILSON'S PEACE PROPOSALS AND THE VATICAN'S
COUNTERPROPOSALS, DECEMBER 1916–APRIL 1917

By the fall of 1916, agitation for peace received fresh impetus in the United States, and Wilson's desire to mediate appeared stronger than ever. But maintaining U.S. neutrality became more difficult than ever: the British intensified their economic war against the Central Powers and refused to consider the peace proposals of Wilson and the German chancellor. Wilson, for his part, appeared to mistrust Britain and disregard its position. On the other hand, there was increasing evidence that the German navy was considering the inauguration of unrestricted submarine warfare. For a short time, Wilson considered asking the belligerents to state their peace terms. He was ready to cooperate in the search for peace, with or without prior agreement with either side, at the moment most convenient for the United States.

This approach had obvious risks and perils. There was a chance that Wilson's effort might end in complete disaster, which would have been a fatal blow to his prestige and influence. If the British refused to entertain such a proposal, relations between the United States and Great Britain would be strained or even broken. Refusal of the Allies would worsen the situation for America, since Wilson would be forced either to insist upon or to withdraw his proposal. This would further compromise chances for getting the belligerents to negotiate and further threaten U.S. interests abroad.

As the October 1916 electoral campaign drew to an end, and especially after the November presidential election, which gave Wilson a second term in the White House, the stage for action was set. The German government had indicated earlier that Wilson's action should come promptly. He was also ready to offer his mediation because of pacifist agitation within his own country. At the same time, he was sure that House's old plans were no longer applicable. House and Lansing demonstrated their contempt for the idea of a negotiated peace of any kind. Both seemed to accept the British contention that the peace proposal would be resented by the Allies, and they foresaw its ultimate rejection.[1]

In the fall of 1916, the Vatican authorities watched the situation very carefully. With the rejection of their earlier hints, they did not think it was an opportune time for a new Vatican initiative. Signs of discord between Vienna and the Holy See put the pope further on the defensive; Jesuit General Vladimir Ledochovsky indicated that Emperor Franz Joseph was "displeased with the Pope who shows himself to be too much of an Italian."[2] The British were told that there was no truth to rumors that Austria-Hungary wanted the Holy Father to propose an armistice. Yet it was obvious that the pope "has an aspiration to play the part of peacemaker in some nebulous future." The British, however, warned the Vatican that the "Allies wouldn't dream of making peace until their objects had not been attained."[3] Lloyd George's pronouncements in late September further persuaded the Vatican to stand aside, if only for the time being.[4]

The pope, eager to help in promoting peace, was ready to act upon the intimations coming from Germany and Great Britain. On October 14, 1916, Bethmann-Holweg sent an urgent message to Wilson, asking him to intervene to stop the European war. As encouragement, the chancellor added in a cable to Bernstorff, Wilson should communicate "with the Pope, the King of Spain and European neutrals. Such an action, since it cannot be rejected by the Entente, would insure him [Wilson] re-election and historical fame."[5] The chancellor tried to draw the Holy See to Germany's side, directly opposing Lloyd George's and Gaisford's warnings to the pope against his involvement. Though the invitation was dangerous for the Vatican, the pope could not remain a disinterested observer. On October 20, he informed Ambassador Rodd that Germany wanted peace and was willing to restore Belgian independence, evacuate occupied French territories, and probably give up Alsace-Lorraine in return for some compensation (Madagascar). He repeated that he had nothing to do with these proposals and would not do anything unless it was indicated that his action was expected.[6] The pope showed his interest in and support of Germany's initiative. This strengthened an assumption, already widely held, that he was encouraged by the German government to act.

During November 1916, rumors of peace efforts continued to spread. On November 14 Wilson told House that he intended to demand an end to the war.[7] By the end of November, he had drafted a message to be sent to European capitals. He insisted upon the futility of war and its baneful effects on western civilization, but seemed uninterested in the war's origins. Wilson found that the neutrals were in an intolerable position, and in order to avoid further suffering, he decided that future U.S. policy would depend upon the goals for which both sides were fighting. For this reason, he asked the powers concerned to formulate their objectives at an early conference.[8] In the debate that followed, House and Lansing induced Wilson to delay publication of his message.

An appeal for the pope's support for peace action came from another quarter, much closer and more important to the Vatican. Late in November, 1916, Archduke Charles, heir-apparent to the Habsburg throne, forwarded a personal letter to the pope through Nuncio Valfre di Bonzo, asking him to use his influence among the belligerents to induce them to end the war. At the same time, Charles disclosed that the German peace demand would be announced shortly.[9] When the German proposal was finally forwarded to the governments of neutral states, and through their services to the Allies, Gasparri assured the Austrian government that the "Holy Father has done and will do everything he can to get Germany's proposal for peace negotiations accepted."[10]

On December 12, 1916, Bethmann-Holweg informed the Reichstag that his government had decided to negotiate for peace. Contrary to the pope's expectations, however, he did not explain what Germany's war aims were. That same day the Spanish ambassador, the Swiss minister, and the U.S. chargé d'affaires were handed invitations for peace negotiations, to be forwarded to their respective governments. The U.S. chargé d'affaires, Joseph Grew, informed the State Department that a special note had also been sent to the pope.[11]

On hearing this, Wilson decided to revise the earlier draft of his note. The revised text of the note was then sent to all belligerents. Wilson simply invited them to define the goals for which they were fighting. Although dissenting voices were heard, U.S. public opinion overwhelmingly endorsed Wilson's proposal.[12]

The Vatican tried to generate support in the United States for the German proposal immediately after its publication. Monsignor Francis Russell visited Lansing and told him about the "Pope's request to urge for peace."[13] On December 15, Gasparri cabled Vienna about the "enormous importance of securing American support for the idea of general disarmament."[14] On the following day, Gasparri strongly urged Count Salis against a flat refusal of the German note and the proposals made in it. "In case these were impossible," insisted the cardinal, "the moral advantage would rest with the Allies in continuing the struggle." He believed that Germany's terms would be moderate.[15] But he was mistaken, the German terms were quite ambitious.[16] Salis, for his part, believed that Gasparri had neither put his heart into Germany's offer nor given it the expected support. Here he was in error. On December 18, Gasparri asked nuncios in Vienna and Munich to appeal to both emperors, to let them consider what immortal glory they would obtain in the eyes of their fellow men.[17] But Germany had different plans and would not be deterred by the pope's assurances of glory and immortality.

After Wilson's note of December 18 was published, the Vatican seemed convinced that peace was in the offing, despite the obvious dangers in the situation. The Vatican press published Wilson's note along with a lengthy editorial, which stated that the Holy See could not express strongly enough its satisfaction with "this most important document in which such a distinguished man asked the belligerents to end the war," and applauded its sensible timing. The editorial did not, however, miss the opportunity to point out that the pontiff had been trying to do the same since the beginning of the war.[18]

Ambassador Page quickly perceived the dual nature of the Vatican's ambitions and thought. On December 25 he wrote that the Italian press was generally hostile to the president's proposal. The clerical press, however, was "partly favorable, though a part of it refers to the Pope as the true intermediary." He also pointed out the insistence in the clerical press that both the United States and Switzerland represented Protestantism.[19] In writing to Wilson, Page noted that despite general acceptance of his note, the Vatican papers had been lukewarm, trying to "keep before the public the suggestion that the Pope is the natural mediator as representing the higher, moral principles of peace which the better elements in all countries recognize."[20]

The pope's aspirations to play a critical role in efforts toward peace soon became apparent. On December 24, 1916, he formally addressed the cardinals in the Curia, but did not mention Wilson's proposal in his reference to peace. This created certain suspicions and uneasiness. Salis interpreted it as a sign of distrust of Wilson and his action, and further maintained that it was done intentionally to discourage the president's initiatives in the future.[21] Whatever his motive, the pope was not happy to let Wilson have the responsibility of establishing peace, since he believed that he himself should be one to whom the world would turn as a guide for peace. In any case, his efforts were purely academic, for neither Wilson nor the German government intended to heed him.

Wilson's note seems to have been well received only by certain members of the Catholic hierarchy in America. On December 23, 1916, Cardinal Farley wished Lansing "every success in the very critical negotiations in which you are engaged."[22] Spring-Rice, however, suspected the sincerity of the Catholic hierarchy who came to regard Wilson's note as a hindrance to Vatican peace efforts. Late in December he insisted that American Catholics would much prefer that the pope be mediator and rather seemed to hope that Wilson's attempt would break down. He went so far as to argue that the pope had a better chance than

Wilson of being accepted as intermediary.[23] Although the pope expressed his approval of Wilson's peace efforts, the "Catholic clergy, as a whole," wrote Spring-Rice, "have greeted the German peace declaration with enthusiasm and have been constantly working in order to ensure peace."[24]

Spring-Rice well described the prevailing mood of Catholics and confirmed the conclusions received by Page and Salis from Rome. The Vatican was playing, whether intentionally or not, directly into Germany's hands. The German leaders wanted to draw out Wilson's intentions and eliminate him from the discussions at the future peace congress, and the Vatican decision makers, for their part, maintained that the pope had a moral right to initiate peace talks. If German and Vatican plans had worked, Wilson would have been deprived of a seat at the peace congress.

Still, the Vatican wanted to support Wilson's invitation to the belligerents. In order to do so, the Curia decided to use Spain. In December 1916, Ambassador Willard wrote from Madrid that Spain hoped to play a "joint and equal role with the United States in urging peace."[25] Willard's letter was a preliminary to the step initiated by the Spanish ambassador in Washington, Juan Riano. On December 26, Riano informed Lansing that the pope had asked the king of Spain to "felicitate, through me, the most excellent President of the United States on the peace note addressed to the belligerent nations." Riano was received by Wilson on January 12, 1917, but did not accomplish much. By seeming to act in accord with Wilson, the Vatican wanted, most likely, to force Germany to announce its plans. The Vatican's demarche may have also been a part of a plan to reserve a place for itself in any future peace talks.[26]

Germany's reply to Wilson's invitation to present its war aims was noncommittal and restrained. The German government expressed its hope for a direct exchange of views with the Allies. By admitting that neutrals might assist in preventing wars in the future but not in ending the present conflict, Germany's reply automatically excluded the Vatican from the game. In comparison, the second Allied reply was more precise. It insisted upon evacuation of occupied territories, liberation of national minorities, autonomy for Poland, reparations, the return of Alsace-Lorraine to France, and the creation of a league of nations. In a covering letter of reply to Wilson, Balfour pointed out the Allies' firm belief that these goals could be accomplished only through ultimate victory.[27]

Balfour's reply to Wilson's note created a good deal of excitement in the Vatican. Its protests were conveyed confidentially to Page. The Vatican's main grievances were directed against Balfour's explanation of the Allied decision to expel the Turks from Europe. It emphatically denied

Balfour's argument that the Turkish cruelties against the Armenians were the real cause for this decision; instead, it argued that the real reason for giving Constantinople and the Straits to Russia was the promise that French President Poincaré had made to Russia in 1913. If the Ottoman Empire were expelled from Europe, it was believed in the Curia, Russia would have a more secure position in the Mediterranean as well as in Central Europe and would seriously threaten the Catholic position and interests. "Reuniting under Russia," Page was told, "the whole of Poland, the Dardanelles, Kurdistan, Armenia, Bukovina and Galicia . . . will almost bring [the] Cossacks to [the] gates of Vienna and Berlin and with an enlarged Serbia under her orders will impose Russian hegemony on all Europe and give her preponderant influence in [the] Orient." The Vatican considerably exaggerated the Russian threat and virtually accused the Allies of neglecting the future of Europe. It further argued that a new war against Russia was not only possible, but also inevitable after the general war was over.

The next day, Page explained the Vatican protest more fully. He suggested that the Vatican was working with all its powers for Austria; and he seemed to accept the contention of the Vatican memorandum about Russia, since the cession of all territories mentioned above would "give to her tremendous, if not overwhelming, power in Europe and make her very strong in the Orient." He was also aware that the Vatican was blaming Britain for this development.[28]

Essentially, the proposed Russian control of Constantinople and the Straits after the end of the war was a major cause of the Vatican's distrust of the Allies. Only when Russia quit the war and the Soviets denounced the secret treaties did the Vatican feel relieved. From November 1917 relations between the Allies and the Holy See improved markedly, and a good deal of useful work was accomplished.

By the end of December 1916, the Vatican came out with a new peace program. As outlined in a memorandum handed to the German ambassador in Vienna, Count Odo Wedel, the program coincided at certain points with the terms presented in the Allied note to Wilson. It insisted upon the following: (1) freedom of the seas; (2) general disarmament; (3) evacuation of French territory and of French-speaking Lorraine; (4) evacuation from and complete independence for Belgium; (5) irredenta to Italy and freedom of action in Albania; (6) restoration of Serbia, Rumania, and Montenegro, though without territories they acquired in the Second Balkan War; (7) England to return German colonies; (8) Russia to make Poland independent; and (9) Turkey to receive compensation for the loss of Armenia.[29]

The program was impressive and more specific than that from the belligerents. It was not simply a return to the status quo ante bellum. It provided for certain territorial changes and included several very sensitive points, points that did not correspond with the views expressed by the Allies in their note to Wilson on January 12, 1917. However, the fundamental problems—freedom of the seas, general disarmament, and reparations—were not settled by the Vatican's proposals. Although the Allies insisted upon reparations, the Vatican plan did not mention them. On the other hand, the Allied note included neither freedom of the seas nor a general disarmament clause, both of which were prominent in the Vatican plan. In forwarding this memorandum to Berlin, Wedel contended incorrectly that the Vatican plan originated with the Allies and was only handed to Gasparri for transmission to Berlin and Vienna. Wedel was not encouraging. Since Germany did not want neutrals, including the Vatican, involved in its plans for peace, their proposals were deemed unacceptable and their mediation useless.

At this point, the Vatican started a new and very risky game with the United States. Proposals such as those advanced here were repeated with tenacity and increasing urgency during the most critical period of U.S. neutrality. On December 29, 1916, Page forwarded what he termed a "curious report" of the Vatican's suggestion about America's way to work for peace. Page had received a visit from a man of "high character," who transmitted to him a message from Gasparri about "America's power to make peace within twenty-four hours" if it would act as a neutral in fact as well as in theory. The anonymous visitor pointed out that if the United States dealt with the Allies as it had dealt with the Central Powers—that is, if it stopped trade—the war would come to an immediate end. The Allied protests could be discarded, Gasparri suggested, if the United States declared its intention to settle certain problems with Japan. In this way, the Americans would be able to stop sending food and munitions to Europe and at the same time make Japan more attentive and less aggressive.[30] But Wilson and Lansing did not consider the offer seriously.

Such a message, it was obvious, was the Vatican's reproach of American trading with the Allies and toleration of the British naval blockade. It was a continuation of earlier efforts, this time on much larger and more ambitious scale. The motivation for such action at that particular moment is difficult to find. It is probable, however, that the Vatican had received some hints that the German government was reconsidering the renewal of submarine warfare. If Germany reverted to an unrestricted U-boat campaign, the war would receive a new impetus, and the Vatican peace initiative would come to nothing. If Germany did so, furthermore, the United States would almost certainly be brought into the war. The Curia was afraid of just such a development and went to great lengths to prevent it. The questions of blockade and submarine warfare quickly became the main focus of the Vatican's activity.

At the end of December 1916, House and Bernstorff held another round of secret conversations. The German and U.S. positions toward peace seemed to be far apart. Wilson wanted to get Germany's pledge of future cooperation for peace and did not show much interest in terri-torial adjustments. Germany, for its part, promised to sign an arbitration treaty, to join a league of nations, and to discuss problems of disarma-ment after the war.[31] It also intimated that a prompt and efficient move by Wilson could forestall a resumption of unrestricted U-boat warfare. This meant, in substance, that Wilson had to demand that the Allies make peace. Spring-Rice believed that new steps were imminent: "There is a strong pressure from a peace party and Catholics upon the President" to make such a demand. He also confirmed the existence of strong pro-German and Catholic influence in Congress: "It cannot be doubted that Catholics here are hostile [to the Allies] mainly on account of Ireland and Russian Uniats. They do not want mediation by President Wilson but peace with the Pope as mediator."[32]

Before Wilson made his new peace initiative, Marchetti expressed his views to Lord Acton of the British embassy in Bern. He indicated that although the Allied reply had left the door open for mediation, Germany was not ready to announce its reply for fear of adverse public opinion. However, it might announce it privately in Washington if the Allies did the same. Marchetti insisted that Wilson was hated in Germany because he was forcing the government to state its war aims while Britain was not yet defeated.[33] Marchetti thus seemed to be justifying Germany's hesitation to commit itself to peace. The pope obviously decided to leave no stone unturned in looking for a joint solution for peace and for a way to keep the United States from joining the Allies.

Before Wilson delivered his "peace without victory" speech, the pope had undertaken a new step by making a personal appeal to the Kaiser. He wanted to show the Kaiser that the Vatican had given full support to Germany's peace action and would continue to do so in the future. At the same time, he was asking the Kaiser to go one step ahead and indi-cate general terms for immediate discussion, especially those that could be settled quite easily. More specific and difficult issues would be left to future negotiations in which all would participate. The pope informed the Kaiser that he had sent a special note to the Allies recommending Germany's proposals as acceptable and open to discussion, but admitted ruefully that recent events did not support Germany's peaceful intentions. Finally, he made a moving appeal to the emperor's sagacity and broad generosity, insisting that the world needed peace after the lengthy and bloody trials of the war.

The Kaiser's comments on the margin of the pope's note clearly reveal his attitudes toward both the pope and Wilson and suggest the shape of future events. The German government was not only determined to refuse all peace initiatives, but it had also just decided to renew submarine warfare on February 1, 1917. As for the Vatican's recommendation of Germany's peace proposal to the Allies, the emperor asserted "this note was disputable; it is believed that it was never sent." He coldly refused all suggestions that the war be ended by peace negotiations and wrote contemptuously that peace ought to come through "German victory, accomplished with the help of God." He blamed the pope for this course of events when he insisted that since "the Holy See was not able to bring about the peace, Mr. Wilson had a priority in pacifistic activity." In commenting upon the proposal that Germany announce a general program for peace, the emperor wrote: "Wilson did exactly this sort of thing and got himself in a splendid trap. The Vatican and Wilson are both far from reality, in all probability, and utopians." He could not resist making a final remark: "*Sancta simplicitas*" and "very persistent and poor for Christ's regent on earth."[34]

The German emperor disregarded the pope, his activities, and his proposals. He decided upon a course that was to extend the war and bring new nations into the conflict. He rejected the alternatives suggested by Bethmann-Holweg and openly sided with the military, who insisted upon renewing full-scale submarine war. After publication of the Allied note, he decided that Germany had to fight the decisive battle, since the generals insisted that the "military situation is such that unrestricted U-boat warfare can begin on the 1st of February and for that reason should begin."[35] But the military ignored the possibility of U.S. involvement and its consequences.

On January 22, 1917, Wilson delivered his "peace without victory" speech. He informed the world that the future settlement must be a peace "among equals, without humiliation, victors and vanquished." He also proclaimed equality and self-determination for all nations, freedom of the seas, and disarmament.[36] Wilson also noted that he was perhaps the only person in high authority who could speak freely. He saw himself as the spokesman for the "silent men of mankind everywhere who have as yet had no place or opportunity to speak their real hearts out concerning the death and ruin they see to have come already upon the persons and the homes they hold most dear."

By making such a pronouncement, Wilson seemed to eliminate the right of other persons "in high authority" to speak out in behalf of mankind. The pope, who was suspected of "holding something back," was not excepted. Significantly, a comparison of Wilson's and the Vatican's proposals reveals substantial similarities in their basic assumptions about freedom of the seas, proportional disarmament, and the equality and freedom of small states. The only major difference lay in Wilson's insistence upon the "right of peoples now under alien domination to govern themselves." Wilson contemptuously ignored the pope's views and all the Vatican's suggestions. Although this last point was neither absolutely clear nor a real commitment, the Vatican used it as proof of Wilson's desire to restructure the Central Powers.

The official Vatican newspaper published the entire text of Wilson's speech as well as lengthy editorials. One editorial praised the importance of the "document through which Woodrow Wilson wants to make a new proposal for peace. It is a fine expression of good sense and humanistic strivings, told openly." Praising Wilson's act as a step toward achieving a long-desired peace, the editorial insisted that Wilson was impartial toward both sides.[37] Yet the Vatican authorities found certain points of disagreement with Wilson's program. On January 25, 1917, Page cabled that he had been told confidentially that the "Vatican was supporting Austrian contention against any reduction of her Empire." In another cable he indicated the Vatican's preoccupations with the desire of the Allies to "reduce adversaries to insignificant entities politically."[38] Page was reminded by the occasional Vatican "representative" that "America should, as [its] best course to stop the war, place [an] embargo on [the] exportation of all supplies to the Allies."[39] The Vatican considered this true neutrality.

The British, independently from the Americans, had the same information about the Vatican's views. At the end of February 1917, Broderick Jones, the head of intelligence at the British embassy in Rome, forwarded to Lord Cecil several extremely important pieces of information coming directly from the Vatican. The first, dated January 24, 1917, was Gasparri's observations upon Wilson's speech. The cardinal commented that the message was warmly received in the Vatican because it was in complete accord with the pope's own views. In referring to Wilson's phrase "a peace without victory," Gasparri suggested that this was a "misunderstanding maintained by the Entente." The Central Powers, he insisted, did not want war to ultimate victory. It was the Allies who demanded the dissolution of Austria-Hungary, the restructuring of Germany, and the transformation of both into small, insignificant states. Gasparri also repeated that the United States should stop exporting money, food, and munitions to the Allies. It would be not only in conformity with neutrality, but also prudent in regard to Japan. Jones was informed that this message had been conveyed directly to Wilson.[40]

The contents of Page's cables confirm virtually every point made in Jones's memorandum; they disclose the Vatican's preoccupation with the Central Powers and the ways in which the war might be brought to an end. In a rather blunt way, Gasparri let Wilson know that the Holy See did not think that his policies of neutrality could bring about peace; he advised Wilson to stop the flow of goods and money to the Allies. The Allies were blamed for their ambition to destroy the Central Powers, and the United States for supporting the Allied ambition and thus continuing the war. Germany and Austria-Hungary, accordingly, had been forced to defend themselves against annihilation.

Little time was left for mediation and suggestions from the Vatican, and events moved swiftly in directions that left few opportunities for the Holy See. On January 31, 1917, the German government informed the United States of the terms upon which it would be ready to negotiate. To these terms were appended a communication that, after February 1, the German submarines would sink all ships without warning, belligerent and neutral alike, found in a zone around Great Britain, France, Italy, and in the eastern Mediterranean. One passenger ship, however, was allowed to sail between New York and Falmouth weekly, provided it was painted red and white and carried no contraband.[41] The German decision to reopen an unrestricted U-boat campaign shocked Wilson. He was confronted with an enormous dilemma over America's duty in the pending crisis. Although he was not yet ready to commit the country to war, he quickly realized that a definite step had to be taken. He decided immediately to sever diplomatic relations with Germany.[42]

The Vatican press and its Secretariat of State quickly took notice of the impending submarine war and the severance of diplomatic relations between the United States and Germany. The official Vatican paper, however, did not publish any editorials on the matter, though the Vatican voiced its disapproval of Wilson's action.[43] Ambassador Rodd informed the Foreign Office that the "Holy See was enormously upset . . . by the President's action," and rumors began to spread around that it was a "put-up" job between Wilson and Germany. He added that the pope's hopes in Wilson and the United States were gone.[44] Broderick Jones forwarded two messages from the Vatican that recorded similar dissatisfaction. The first indicated that the renewal of submarine warfare did not surprise the Vatican. It was a decision made in self-defense, against the intention of Britain and its allies to ruin Germany and Austria-Hungary. "Peace or war," it was maintained, "are in the hands of Your Excellency [Wilson], who can, if you will, impose the end of the conflict by forbidding the exodus from America of money, food, munitions, which, it is judged, would be in conformity with perfect neutrality, so that no one can complain." It went on to say that if Wilson "has recource [sic] to these means, peace will be certain[ly] to the advantages of all humanity, not excluding the belligerent powers, and to the immortal glory of America and Your Excellency." This message, it was reported, was forwarded to Wilson.[45]

Thus, the Vatican virtually made Wilson responsible for the escalation of the war. It justified in principle the German resort to submarine warfare and blamed Britain for this action. Insisting, although discretely, that the Allies were completely dependent upon the United States for money, food, and munitions, the Vatican refused to see that a policy of strict neutrality would have led to a grave economic crisis and depression in the United States.

The breaking of diplomatic relations, not submarine warfare, caused even more bitterness and criticism in the Curia, which viewed the United States as more deeply involved with the Allies than ever before. The Vatican did not want to admit that its attempts to make peace had been dealt a severe blow, and its reactions were unusual. A week after Wilson's speech of January 22, Page cabled that in accord with his confidential information, the "Vatican seems to be interesting itself in creating [the] fantastic impression that the President's step in rupturing relations with Germany was taken in accordance with the latter." The Vatican believed that Wilson wanted peace, but that he had chosen a strange way of achieving it unless he was acting with Germany to prevent further exports to the Allies. Page added that to the "European neutrals this action shows disapproval of America's interference in European affairs." Nevertheless, the Vatican believed that Wilson would have a seat in a peace conference. Page interpreted this to mean that the "Vatican is conducting propaganda to prevent America uniting with the Allies."[46] Three days later, in a lengthy letter to Wilson, Page commented that a "good deal of misapprehension has been carried by the propaganda which has been made by the Vatican." After mentioning the campaign to place an embargo on exports, Page explained the reasons for this agitation. He found that great "apprehension exists there that Austria may be reduced to insignificance in the European equilibrium and that England and Russia may obtain an over-preponderant power" and that the master key to Vatican policy is its desire "to get itself placed under international protection and released from dependence on the Italian Law of Guarantees." The pope's eagerness to have a seat in the peace conference was no longer a secret, for it would be the first step toward internationalization. It was believed that the pope was to receive support from the Central Powers and the South American republics.[47]

The British also had news from their source of information. Broderick Jones forwarded memorandums showing that Gasparri considered Wilson persona non grata in Europe generally because of his mentality and philosophical point of view. The cardinal realized that Europe, especially Britain, was doing all it could to keep the United States from meddling in its affairs and that Wilson, like the pope, wished to participate in a peace conference. In order to do so, Gasparri believed, Wilson may have decided to become a belligerent, if only by firing but a single shot.[48]

The Vatican's displeasure was evident and increasing. In the general excitement, it made several substantial errors in judgment. There were, it admitted, significant differences in outlook between Wilson and the Vatican, differences that if carried to the extreme, could have unforeseeable consequences and dangers for the European political system. It was also certain that the United States would ultimately drift into the war and participate in the future peace conference and that Japan's presence at the conference was a motive behind the U.S. action. The Vatican still clung to its unrealistic and unattainable hope of securing a place at the peace conference.

The Vatican's concern over Austria-Hungary was increased with the proposal for a military offensive from the south. The proposal of a combined thrust of English, French, and Italian armies, although rejected by the French and British generals, added to Austria's difficulties. More important, however, was the problem of submarine war. Despite a great deal of hesitation, Austria-Hungary had to join Germany and form a common front on the high seas. The court and the government in Vienna turned to the pope for help. On February 6, 1917, Czernin handed Bonzo a memorandum for the pope asking him to work for peace. It explained that the empire had been forced to join in the submarine war: "It was not done for cruelty [of the war], but as an extreme step in defending its [the empire's] existence, as well as to hasten the peace." Czernin expressed the hope that the Holy See would not disapprove of the step, since the monarchy wanted peace without victors or vanquished.[49] But the Curia did not accede to Czernin's appeal. Several days later, Gasparri replied that at the present moment the "Holy See does not intend to express its views on such a complex question, even less to approve or disapprove, the use of submarines."[50] The Vatican, although very eager to help the monarchy, did not think it advisable to voice its views openly about the problem.

The U.S. government considered it worthwhile to induce the Dual Monarchy to break up its coalition with Germany. At the end of January 1917, House reported to Wilson that Wiseman had told him that there was "some ground to think that the Pope might be able to get Austria to consent to a separate peace," and that such an endeavor should be made. Wiseman also told House that a peace conference ought to be held in Spain—an idea that House tended to reject—and commented that the "Allies were looking to the holding of the peace conference in a Catholic country and a country favorable to Austria, and perhaps with Alfonso as a sponsor." House, interested in this suggestion, promised to watch events closely.[51] On February 8, Wilson instructed Lansing to ask for British approval to offer Austria-Hungary a separate peace with assurances that the empire's structure would not be changed. With support from the Vatican and the empire's urgent need to quit the war, such a proposal was very attractive. On February 11, Walter Page announced that Lloyd George accepted the suggestion, on condition that every precaution be taken to insure the utmost secrecy, implying that if the Germans found out about it, they would stop it.[52] Two days later, Wilson asked Austria-Hungary to consider the possibility of a separate peace that would not be discussed with Germany.[53] He pledged not to dissolve the empire. But Czernin turned down the offer, and Wilson did not pursue the matter further.

The Vatican quickly realized that a secret Allied communication had been conveyed to Vienna. On February 23, Gasparri wrote to nuncio Bonzo, *sub secreto sancti officii,* that he had been told that France and England had proposed a separate peace to Vienna. Bonzo was ordered to make inquiries through Cardinal Czernoch, archbishop of Strigonia, about the nature of the proposal and then to travel to Rome in the strictest secrecy.[54] The Vatican quickly developed ideas as to how Italy could benefit from it. If Austria-Hungary withdrew from the war, Italy would no longer have to fight since its main goal—unification of the *irredenta*—would be attained. This peculiar reasoning was characteristic of the Vatican way of thinking; no doubt it was inimical to the Allies and their unity.

The Vatican was still ignoring the problem of Belgium. By the end of January 1917, there were rumors that the German government would agree to an independent Belgium, subject to specific guarantees for Germany's security.[55] Gasparri refused to be drawn into the discussion. He thought that whatever the proposal, as long as it did not embody the complete independence of Belgium without any limitations imposed on Germany, it should be rejected. But he had seen some chances for attaining this "after eventual failure of the pending offensive of the Allied troops."[56] What Gasparri actually envisioned is a matter of conjecture. Perhaps he thought that Germany might, after the defeat of the Allies, be more willing to allow Belgium some measure of political freedom and compensate itself elsewhere.

In the weeks after the break in U.S.-German diplomatic relations, German submarines struck several British and U.S. steamers. More Americans were being killed, and the public resentment was growing. It was a period of general uncertainty, confusion, and exasperation. The Vatican seemed to ignore German acts. Ambassador Rodd was told by the Spanish ambassador in Rome that Gasparri "regards the German submarine blockade as justifiable in International Law." The British were disturbed. Drummond commented that the Vatican was utterly ignorant of international law, and Salis was instructed to explain informally to the cardinal that the Vatican's attitude was not in accord with international law.[57] The Vatican made no more statements on International law.

The Vatican reacted swiftly when the contents of the telegram sent by German Foreign Secretary Zimmerman to von Eckhardt, the German minister in Mexico, were made public. The Germans proposed an alliance with the Mexican government. Mexico would enter the war against the United States and regain the "lost territories of Texas, New Mexico and Arizona." President Carranza was asked to invite Japan to join in the coalition.[58] Wilson acted immediately. What was strange was the fact that the Vatican was constantly referring to Japan as a possible threat to the United States. Wilson's natural question was whether the Vatican was au courant with German plans or whether it was conveying warnings to the U.S. government? The answer to the first question is hardly possible. It was felt, however, that the Vatican was doing all this on purpose, as Ambassador Rodd commented that "there has been more than due

attempt [in the Vatican] to get up a scare in America." This was interpreted as proof that the Vatican was cooperating with the Central
Powers.[59] It did not occur to either Rodd or Page that the Vatican may
have sent these messages in order to gain favor in Washington.

When Wilson asked and obtained authority to arm American merchant
ships, the Vatican was quite upset. The pope and Gasparri acted swiftly.
Late in the evening of February 27, 1917, Gasparri summoned Salis to
the Vatican. He informed the minister that the pope was about to propose
to all belligerents, especially Britain and Germany, a simultaneous
cessation of hostilities "by means of starvation; neither blockade nor
submarines in respect of anything serving for food." The proposal was
absolutely secret; only the pope, Gasparri, and Salis knew of it. If Britain
accepted it, the Vatican would ask Germany to consider it, without
indicating British approval of the proposal. Gasparri also told Salis that the
"Pope was much preoccupied at the course which hostilities were taking,"
meaning Wilson's latest action. Salis promised to send the proposal to
London, but indicated that Britain had more to gain than to lose by submarine warfare. After the pope's proposal arrived in London, the consultation immediately began. Charles Smith from the Contraband Division
suggested that the eventual reply should insist that the British were
enforcing the blockade as a legal and recognized means of ending the war.
Lord Dragheda advised that the proposal ought to be rejected. Lancelot
Oliphant and Lord Hardinge proposed that it be sent to the War Cabinet.[60]
On March 2 the War Cabinet discussed the proposal and the reply to be
made to the Vatican. The proposal was rejected, since the cabinet did not
think it was technically feasible or, even if it were to be agreed upon, that
Germany could be trusted. After accumulating substantial stock of food,
Germany might use some pretext to negate the agreement and resume
unrestricted submarine warfare. Furthermore, the British would have had
to abandon their whole military policy, of which the blockade was an
essential part; this would be tantamount to an admission of the success
of the submarine campaign and of England's weakness.[61]

Balfour's cable to Salis also contained explanations to be given orally
to Gasparri. Salis was to argue that the British acted legally and exercised
due care for the lives and property of neutrals. German actions, on the
contrary, violated international laws and neutral rights and threatened
property and life. After dwelling upon numerous examples, he was to make
the following conclusion: "Their [German] so-called blockade is nothing
more than the arbitrary destruction of a small percentage of shipping
cargoes and lives, neutral and belligerent, found within certain areas of the

open sea. The one [British] action is legal in its character and humane in its execution, the other [German] is illegal and murderous."[62] When Salis submitted the British reply, on March 3, Gasparri did not discuss it.

The British rejected the pope's arguments, for the latter supported an impossible compromise between blockade and submarine warfare. The Vatican's reaction to the mounting dangers of submarine warfare was not well thought of, especially since Gasparri had refused to discuss it only three weeks before. The pope's proposal, hastily drawn, was doomed by Germany's opposition. It sounded more like a trial balloon, a piece of risky diplomacy characteristic of the Curia. England, for its part, flatly refused the proposal because of favorable developments in the United States. On the whole, this proposal resembled, in its urgency and scope, other proposals made to Page at the time. As a result, the pope lost some of his moral position and influence during the following weeks.

Early in March 1917, Page reported the start of judicial proceedings against Monsignor Gerlach and several others involved in activities that allegedly threatened Italian security. Gerlach was accused of bribing several Italian newspapers to publish German propaganda. Page suspected that he had supported anti-American propaganda as well. Another American observer in Rome, Gino Speranza, praised highly the restraint, tolerance, and skill of the Italian government in allowing freedom of action during the war to a "political power of such an influence as the Papacy and which was clearly pro-German and pro-Austrian." He regarded Gerlach's activities in Italy as conspiracy.[63]

At the same time, Page informed the State Department that the pope was considering the publication of an encyclical. By the end of March 1917, the press reported the pope's proclamation in the Consistory of March 23, 1917. He did not speak about peace, but urged the neutral powers to act in order to calm feelings between the United States and Germany.[64]

In the middle of March 1917, the Vatican press and agents began a new campaign. They acted to induce the U.S. government to impose an embargo, or at least to allow other belligerents to trade freely. When this proved to be unattainable, the Vatican increased its pressure. It virtually accused the United States of carrying out non-neutral policies. On March 20, Page wrote that he had been visited by someone from the Vatican who spoke to him of another "Delenda est Carthago." Page was told that the position of "President Wilson relative to the belligerent powers is not sustained from the point of view of International Law." By allowing only one group of belligerents to trade with the United States, Wilson found himself in an illogical position. Namely, while pretending to defend the freedom of the seas, he was in reality violating it. By yielding to "England's injunctions not to navigate to the Central Powers. . .he is not neutral." The entire tone of the message was much sharper than in previous ones. Wilson was also reproached for having missed a unique opportunity to be a *deus ex machina* in the struggle for peace. The meaning of this was obvious. Convinced that the United States was not neutral, the pope could claim that the Vatican was the only true neutral.[65] In any case, it was an unusual intrusion into the domain of international politics on the part of the Vatican. This could be conveniently used in future efforts for peace.

The U.S. declaration of war against Germany was resented and condemned by the Vatican and its press. Wilson's speech of April 2 and the Senate vote of April 4, 1917, were the targets of sharp criticism: "The man who was in December past the bearer of the flag of peace now is the bearer of a more destructive war; he [Wilson] is the man who brings the new world to participate in the destruction of old Europe." This same editorial alleged that many people were to change their opinions about Wilson, and that his action in declaring war against Germany demanded new thinking about a "nebulous future." The two great events—the revolution in Russia and the U.S. entrance into the war—made the present war, in a real sense, a worldwide conflict, the editorial concluded.[66] These were, indeed, words of disappointment and criticism, since with the U.S. entrance into the war, fewer options were available to the Vatican as well.

In striking contrast to the Vatican, the Catholic hierarchy in the United States appeared to favor Wilson's action. This was another blow for the policy of the Holy See, one that came unexpectedly. Various Catholic newspapers in the United States endorsed the declaration of war, numerous proclamations were published, sermons were preached, and prayers were offered in churches around the country. The leaders of the Catholic hierarchy called for absolute unity in support of the war efforts. Archbishops and bishops from all over the country met in Washington on April 18, 1917, and drafted a petition to Wilson pledging the support and loyalty of Catholic citizens. Wilson replied to Cardinal Gibbons with a warm letter of appreciation for the petition forwarded to him in behalf of the hierarchy.[67]

The Catholic hierarchy, obviously, could have taken no other attitude. Catholics had too long been the opponents and critics of the administration and its policies. They could have been accused, if they had acted differently, of not showing patriotism and loyalty in supporting the national cause in the war. The hierarchy realized this danger and for that reason put the power of its organization behind the government. Through the words of their leaders, Catholics pledged their unswerving allegiance to America and prepared to meet every demand made upon their loyalty and devotion.

During the most critical period of U.S. neutrality, the Vatican had strived hard and energetically for peace. It had expected Wilson's full support in these efforts. The Vatican, as a result of its efforts, produced what might be called a program for peace, and it worked tirelessly to prevent the United States from entering the war. To achieve this goal, the Vatican used any means available, the most important being the persistent request that the United States stop exporting money and goods to the Allies. The Vatican's request proved highly inconvenient because it was interpreted as being unwarranted interference in the internal affairs of a foreign nation. U.S. trade with the Allies was characterized by the Vatican first as a nonneutral act, and later as open disrespect for international law. America's entry into the war was disheartening, and it presaged an increasingly unpredictable future.

The Vatican had wanted to be in the forefront of peace efforts and longed to play a role in any future peace congress. However, it was accorded rather shabby treatment, indeed. The U.S. government paid no attention to its proposals and initiatives. The British, too, were suspicious and reluctant to accept Vatican proposals. Germany, for its part, exploited the Vatican when its support was useful, but Bethmann-Hollweg ignored the pope on the question of a peace conference. Although Austria-Hungary enjoyed the Vatican's support, it could make little use of it because of its complete dependence upon Germany. Strangely enough, the pope and Gasparri did not see through the German strategy, and their confidence and hopes in Germany seemed long unshaken. This was particularly evident in the summer of 1917, when the pope decided to act on his own.

Eugenio Pacelli, Nuntius in Munich

CHAPTER 6
THE PEACE NOTE OF AUGUST 1, 1917

In the summer of 1917, the pope decided to offer concrete peace proposals which both sides appeared eager to consider. By then, antiwar sentiments and war wearinesss were widespread. Incidents such as the mutiny in the French army in the spring of 1917 revealed impatience with the war, and the Russian Revolution of March 1917 became a matter of concern for statesmen and politicians all over the world. Slogans such as "no annexations, no indemnities" reflected the feeling of the futility over further carnage, and demands for the formulation of war aims indicated a general disposition toward a negotiated peace. Suspicion among Catholics and the activities of the socialists seemed to be creating an air of hopelessness among the interventionists. The problem of Belgium and of Alsace-Lorraine seemed to be the only obstacle in the way of peace.

The Vatican regarded the circumstances of the spring and summer of 1917 as favorable to the initiation of peace discussions, and the military situation seemed conducive to a compromise peace. The Vatican found itself in a very convenient position, having enough authority to wield some influence and having a previous history of working for peace. At that moment, it was actually considered the greatest hope for mutual conciliation.[1] The Catholic church was inherently a conservative institution: its goal was the preservation of the existing social and political order. Its authority in the belligerent countries was badly shaken since the war had disrupted its unity and Catholic loyalty to the Holy See; these sentiments had tended to give way to nationalism. Therefore, the very interests of the Catholic church demanded that the pope act. There were other considerations as well. The pope's action would enhance, it was hoped, his position and influence in the future peace congress. Finally, it would demonstrate the universal mission of Catholicism.

The pope's position, however, was not entirely clear. For him, neutrality, impartiality, and the separation from the war aims of the belligerents did not necessarily mean cutting off relations with them. In order to prevent the church from being harmed, he had to act with both sides. However, since the Central Powers were in a position to make his action effective and were expected to announce their war aims shortly, the pope decided to work more closely with them. This placed him in a very delicate position: if he became identified with one set of belligerents, the Vatican would come to be looked upon with suspicion. This is exactly what happened. Vatican personnel and the nuncios worked hard to acquaint themselves with all aspects of the political situation and the internal as well as external forces and movements for peace.[2]

Besides general political, humanitarian, and ecclesiastical considerations, several very specific reasons made the Vatican anxious to act. Austria-Hungary was in trouble in early 1917 as a result of war weariness, exhaustion, and low morale. Early in 1917, Count Otokar Czernin, the foreign minister, wrote to Emperor Charles that the monarchy should start negotiations with the Allies to prevent its collapse. He warned Charles that "another winter campaign would be absolutely out of question" and that in the "late summer or in the autumn an end must be put to the war at all costs."[3] The nationalities were becoming very dissatisifed, and in several industrial centers there were signs of rising unrest.

Before taking any action, the Vatican demanded disclosure of the conditions upon which the Central Powers would be ready to negotiate. When approached by Cardinal Bisleti in May 1917, Emperor Charles, although asking the pope to act for peace, appeared reluctant to commit himself wholly.[4] On April 10, 1917, Gasparri, after being informed about the Mansdorf-Smuts conversations in Switzerland, instructed Nuncio Bonzo to tell the emperor that the pope was willing to give full support to Austria's proposals.[5] Not until June 30, 1917, did the emperor tell Nuncio Eugenio Pacelli that Austria-Hungary was willing to cede to Italy "all or part of Trentino." It was considered imperative, however, that Austria-Hungary receive some compensations in colonies for not disturbing public opinion.[6]

There was a simultaneous exchange of views between the Vatican and the German government. Viktor Naumann and Mathias Erzberger approached the papal representatives demanding papal action.[7] The German government was aware of Austria's dire needs and keen desire to make peace quickly. The Vatican decided to act promptly with Germany, since it was clear that only German acceptance of such an initiative could make their action for peace successful.

The appointment of a new nuncio in Bavaria, Pacelli, showed that the pope intended to go ahead with peace feelers. On his way to Munich, Pacelli stopped in Switzerland and conferred with Vatican diplomats about the prospects for peace. Erzberger informed Pacelli that the Kaiser would like to see him personally. He suggested that Pacelli bring the pope's personal letter to the emperor.[8] Gasparri took this suggestion to mean that Germany was inclined to support Vatican action, and the pope's autograph to the Kaiser, together with instructions for his work, were sent to Pacelli.[9] This was the beginning of a prolonged dialogue between the Vatican and Berlin, which eventually culminated in the pope's peace proposal of August 1, 1917.

Another question that caused great concern in the Curia, as well as in Germany and Austria-Hungary, was the general fear of a socialist peace offensive. The Vatican could not have remained silent while the socialists were working to bring about peace. Socialist groups were agitating for a general conference of all socialist parties to be held in Stockholm, the major purpose being agreement on what concerted action was necessary for peace. This Europe-wide socialist pressure naturally disturbed both the Central Powers and the Allies. Demands for action to prevent the socialists from taking the initiative came simultaneously with efforts to induce the Vatican to move for peace. Czernin had realized "the danger of revolution which is spreading around the European continent" and insisted that everything should be done to eliminate the propagandistic effects of the proposed socialist congress in Stockholm. "In a search for an organization," wrote Czernin, "which might be able to stop the defeatistic aspirations of the Socialists . . . the only power, strong and influential enough to do it in all states, is the Catholic church." If successful, Catholic action against the socialists would be considered the greatest service ever done to mankind.[10] Emperor Charles shared this belief. On July 30, 1917, he asked the pope to act for peace "in order that Socialism does not have merits for pacification."[11]

The German government and Emperor Wilhelm II were equally concerned with the possibility of socialist intervention. The German Social Democrats were very active, and their leader, Phillip Scheidemann, was talking about revolution if Germany continued the war with "aims of conquest."[12] On June 29, 1917, the Kaiser told Pacelli of the socialist menace and demanded explicitly that something be done to neutralize it.[13] Late in June 1917, Marchetti-Selvaggiani requested direct action on the part of the Vatican. He wrote to Gasparri: "Move, do something. Be aware that here [in Switzerland] everyone speaks about peace, everybody acts for it, but above all the Socialists are the most vociferous. The Pope's silence might spell a disaster for the future." After the publication of the peace note of August 1, Vatican personnel even admitted that "it was a convenient moment [to publish the note] since we did not want, by any means, this to be done by the Socialists or others."[14]

The Vatican, obviously, was not enthusiastic about the prospects of a socialist campaign for peace. It was aware of the pending congress in Stockholm and had to do something to make the action of the socialists for a mediated peace needless and meaningless. The pope, therefore, acted upon his own impulses and considerations, as well as upon intimations coming from Berlin, Vienna, and Bern. He did so because of a real political threat to the Curia. The pope was well aware that the war had brought about a new political coalition between socialists and Catholics. He regarded this development with horror, since it signified the entrance of the masses into active political life. At this particular juncture, Catholics and socialists had joined in a search for peace, which incidentally coincided with the expectations of Vienna and the Vatican. It was a convenient opportunity to forestall the worst, at least for the time being.[15]

The U.S. government and Wilson were blissfully unaware of what was going on between the Vatican, Berlin, and Vienna. The Vatican had no reason to keep Wilson informed about its action for peace, in view of the fact that its earlier appeals had been officially ignored. But U.S. diplomats stationed in Europe kept the State Department informed about the peace movement initiated by the German Reichstag early in July 1917. The Social Democrats and Erzberger, as a leader of the Catholic Center party, decided Germany's intentions to work for peace must be clearly defined if the government wanted to retain their support in the Reichstag. From their joint efforts came the resolution declaring that Germany fought the war only to defend itself and that the Reichstag favored the negotiation of a peace of understanding. The majority passed this resolution on July 19, 1917.[16]

The essential meaning of the movement in the Reichstag was known in Washington by July 12. Assistant Secretary of State William Phillips noted that the "clerical party" had left the government to go over to the opposition. Intrigued by this action, he wondered whether it had been done on the orders of the pope. He noted that "it is known that the Pope's highest ambition is to start the peace move."[17] The next day Polk inquired in Bern whether it was true that Emperor Charles had recently told the Kaiser that Austria-Hungary has to have peace on the best terms obtainable and that a strong peace campaign was expected to begin in the United States. Stovall confirmed Austria's desire to obtain peace.[18] Yet nothing significant was expected from the pope at that moment.

On June 26, 1917, Pacelli was received by Bethmann-Holweg in Berlin, who explained that Germany sincerely wanted peace in order to end this "useless carnage" but that people like Lloyd George presented a real obstacle to peace. Germany was ready not only to restore Belgium under guarantees for its complete independence from England and France, but also to discuss the question of arbitration and mutual reductions of armaments. Bethmann-Hollweg went so far as to intimate that the boundaries of Alsace-Lorraine might well be altered, with some compensation.[19] Pacelli's instructions, which he had received on June 13, coincided in their most important points with the chancellor's statement.[20] From Berlin Pacelli proceeded to Koblenz to see the Kaiser. The meeting took place on June 29 in Kreuznach and was discouraging and fruitless. The Kaiser refused to commit himself to anything of importance mentioned by Bethmann-Holweg. The situation was discouraging for the Vatican in view of its planned peace initiative.[21]

Despite this uncertainty and the Kaiser's refusal to commit himself to anything specific, the pope decided to continue his efforts. Bethmann-Hollweg's statement induced the Vatican to take definite action. There was hope that the Allies might be willing to listen to the proposals, since the U.S. armies were still unable to throw decisive weight into the battlefields. On July 4, Gasparri sent Pacelli a memorandum containing seven points for which he had to solicit German opinion. The memorandum included some points similar to those Pacelli had received on June 13. There were several new points: the question of the freedom of the seas, arbitration, return of the territory and colonies occupied by respective powers, and the problems of the Balkans and Poland.[22] On July 13, however, Bethmann-Hollweg resigned. The German army's domination of political decision making made it unlikely that the Vatican's initiative would succeed. Gasparri realized this and instructed Pacelli to make certain points more flexible and more congenial to the German leaders.

On July 24, 1917, Pacelli discussed with the new chancellor, Georg Michaelis, the contents of the memorandum received from the Vatican on July 4. Michaelis promised to give it careful consideration. However, Pacelli found the new chancellor a rigid bureaucrat, an uncompromising Protestant, and an admirer of Luther. Pacelli also observed that eventual German acceptance of the Vatican proposal might be interpreted as a sign of weakness. The two men met again on July 30, but Michaelis was unable to give a definite reply.[23] The stumbling block in any action toward a general peace was Belgium. Since the German government hesitated to give its approval in this regard, Pacelli advised the Curia to prepare the note for the German government and publish it without waiting for Germany's reply. He advised the German Foreign Ministry that the Holy See would issue the note without previously seeing

Germany's reaction to it. Without Germany's concurrence, however, the whole demarche was doomed.[24] The pope was in a hurry to publish the note, hoping that the forthcoming London conference of the Allied Powers might answer to it.

On August 8, the papal note was composed. On the following day, it was handed to the British, Belgian, and Russian ministers to the Holy See. The British government was asked to transmit it to Wilson and Poincaré, as well as to the Italian king. The next day the text of the note was telegraphed to Bonzano in Washington and, on August 11, to Pacelli, Bonzo, and Ragonesi in Madrid. The papal appeal contained five basic points considered essential to just and lasting peace. It included (1) the simultaneous and reciprocal reduction of armaments; (2) machinery for arbitration of international disputes; (3) freedom of the seas; (4) renunciation of reparations, restitution of occupied territories, and specific guarantees of the "political, military and economic independence" of Belgium; and (5) determination of the future of border areas to be made in accord with the "aspirations of the population" and the "general good of the great human society." The same principles were to apply to the settlement of other territorial and political questions: Armenia, the Balkan states, and the territories of the old Kingdom of Poland.[25] Pacelli received the note on August 12, when he was handed the German government's reply to the seven-point memorandum of July 4, 1917.

The German reply was a strange mixture. It professed willingness to discuss the issues raised by the Vatican, but it advanced new issues unwelcome to the Vatican and certainly repulsive to the Allies. It agreed, although in principle only, to the need for disarmament and arbitration, but it left the procedure and details to be determined by the future peace conference. It supported the restoration of Belgium, with the guarantees for Germany's security to be arranged in direct negotiations between Germany and Belgium. Belgian territory was to be evacuated only after the war. The reply also indicated the desirability of direct negotiations between France and Germany, left Austria-Hungary freedom to settle its problems with Italy, and admitted the possibility of re-creating an independent Poland. Finally, the German government proposed the creation of national states in the Ukraine, Finland, the Baltic provinces, Ireland, Egypt, and Persia and regulation of the questions of Serbia, Rumania, and Montenegro in such a way as to make European peace stable.[26] Germany's answer did not accord with Vatican expectations. It accepted certain solutions in principle, failed to make definite commitments, and raised questions that the Allied governments were certain to refute. For that reason, the Vatican asked the German government to return a "simple answer."[27] It was anxious that no obstacles should prevent the proposal from being used as the basis for discussion.

On August 9, 1917, Salis cabled to the Foreign Office the essentials of the pope's proposal for peace. Copies were forwarded to Washington, Rome, Paris, and Petrograd. The British were unhappy that the Vatican had proposed "unacceptable" terms, even if only as a basis for discussion. They feared that the note might have a pronounced effect in the United States. In the evening of August 11, Spring-Rice called at Lansing's house with the news, giving him the substance of the papal appeal.[28] On August 14, Cardinal Gibbons was informed about the pope's action and was asked to speak in favor of it. Bonzano suggested the cardinal intervene to pressure the U.S. government into accepting the pope's program.[29]

On August 11, Gasparri solicited Salis's opinion about the note, adding that there were great differences between the belligerents. But the most recent statements, insisted the cardinal, brought their aims closer. The pope therefore wanted to "see if they could not be brought into agreement on the basis of these recent utterances." Gasparri added that the Vatican used Wilson's words in respect to the freedom of the seas, but Salis did not see their real meaning. Gasparri informed Salis that "the clause respecting the special reasons in a certain case" was meant to apply to Belgium and pointed out that the proposal should be acceptable to Great Britain if it still maintained the premises of its entrance into war in 1914. The cardinal admitted ruefully that Germany was expected to state its terms. Salis said only that the pope's ideas were open to criticism and that he did not think they were practical.[30] The same day, Sir William Wiseman cabled House from London, insisting upon the need for consultations between the United States and England in responding to the pope, since it was clear that a response would "raise many questions of difficulty." He hoped that Wilson would let Balfour know privately of his opinion and attitude. On August 13, House sent Wiseman's cable to Wilson, fully endorsing Balfour's suggestion and expressing hope that the president would, indeed, give Balfour his private opinion.[31]

No comments could be made on the note until the complete text was studied carefully. Ambassador Page cabled the text on August 15, but it was not received and deciphered in Washington until August 17. When asked by Spring-Rice for his opinion, Lansing refused to say anything specific. He seemed inclined to believe that Austria-Hungary had done the prompting and that a carefully worded reply was desirable.[32] Allied representatives wanted to be kept abreast of the moves and intentions of the U.S. government. Numerous visits, inquiries, and suggestions kept the diaries and visitor lists of the State Department officials very crowded.[33] Senator Claude Swanson (Democrat, Virginia) visited Lansing on August 17, and inquired about the note. John Warner, Washington correspondent for the *Christian Science Monitor* also did so.[34]

The administration began to discuss the note's contents and to formulate its own attitude even before the note arrived in Washington. On August 15, House presented his views to Wilson. He expressed a belief that the problem was not simple and easy to solve and saw dangers as well as hope in the note. France and Russia were in trouble and would probably insist upon peace on the basis of the status quo ante bellum. For that reason he believed that it would be more important to help Russia to "weld herself into a virile republic" than it would be to beat Germany to its knees. House feared that Germany might have a preponderant influence in Russia, both economically and politically, if internal order was not established. The reestablishment of the status quo would also benefit the Allies in helping Austria-Hungary to emancipate itself from Prussia; Turkey could remain an independent state, provided that Constantinople and the Straits were put under some sort of international control. This would tend to solve the complicated problem of Asia Minor as well. House also insisted upon the difficulties of keeping a large army in France and of giving material and military assistance to the Allies on the scale they expected, unless the submarine danger was overcome. The war was unpopular in the United States, House warned, and would become even more unpopular with time and new victims. For these reasons, he suggested that the peace should be achieved during the coming winter. To make it possible, he advised Wilson to answer the pope's proposal so "as to leave the door open, and to throw the onus on Prussia." This ought to be done by saying that the U.S. peace terms are well known and those of Germany are not, and that no government can discuss "terms with a military autocracy—that does not represent the opinion of the people for whom they speak." The German people must be told that "a peace must be founded upon international amity and justice."[35]

House knew that his solution of the problem ran contrary to views prevailing in the State Department. He tried to convert Polk to his point of view. In a long conversation, House expressed his views and got Polk to agree: "I believe I talked him out of the position he had—a position, indeed, which I am sure Lansing holds." House considered his letter to Wilson "the important document of the day." "I know," he added, "I am running counter to the advice of Lansing, Phillips and others in the

State Department. I feel, too, I am running counter to the President's own judgment." "Nevertheless, I am willing to stand upon it," House boastfully concluded, "for I am sure I have a more complete picture of the situation than either the President or Lansing."[36] Several days later, House again indicated his concern against rushing the decision and, in order to gain time to exert his own influence, recommended that the British government cooperate with Wilson in drafting a reply.[37] On August 17, before receiving Wilson's reply to his earlier letter, House acted again to make Wilson aware of "an opportunity to take the peace negotiations out of the hands of the Pope and hold them in . . . [your] own." He advised Wilson that in his opinion "the Allies must succumb to your judgement and Germany is not much better off." Since the situation—internal, external, and military—in all belligerent countries was going from bad to worse, Wilson should act immediately: "A statement from you regarding the aims of this country would bring about almost revolution in Germany in the event the existing government dared to oppose them." House accused the Allied governments of prolonging the war "by doing all and saying the things that best helped the militarists. The German people are told, and believe, that the Allies desire not only to dismember them, but to make it economically impossible to live after the war. They are, therefore, welded together with their backs to the wall."[38] House wanted Wilson to announce U.S. war aims, force the Allies to get them accepted, get the support of pacifists all around the world, and strengthen whatever liberal sentiment might exist in Russia.

House's thinking did not, indeed, accord with Wilson's judgment and intentions. First of all, Wilson did not favor stating U.S. war aims publicly.[39] He was also aware of the military advantages of the Central Powers, whose armies were at the moment controlling vast European territories. In replying to House on August 16, Wilson even indicated that he might not make any reply to the pope at all. If he decided to answer, however, he would emphasize that: (1) there is no ground for the belief that the pope's action would meet the wishes of any belligerent, and for that reason they did not form a solid basis for negotiations; (2) the pope's proposals practically advocate the status quo before the war; (3) the enemy's utter disregard of international law makes it impossible to be confident about any agreements that might be made. Wilson ended his letter to House by saying: "The present German Imperial Government is morally bankrupt; no one will accept or credit its pledges; and the world will be upon quicksand in regard to all international covenants which include Germany until it can believe that it is dealing with a responsible government. I see no other possible answer."[40] Thus, the two men had substantially opposite views, and there was little hope that Wilson would change his views in order to reconcile House.

Wilson's schedule during the next several days was hectic, indeed. On August 16, Tumulty gave him his views about the pope's note and how the eventual U.S. reply should be made. He advised Wilson to go no further in explaining the peace terms, since further explanations could stir up conflict between the Allies and the United States. Tumulty also insisted upon the necessity of deepening the German people's distrust of and contempt for the Kaiser. The suggestion should also be made to the world that no trust should be accorded those who did not honor the treaties and that those who rule Germany must prove themselves reliable before they will be admitted into confidence.[41] On August 17, Wilson met a group of senators in the White House to discuss the pope's note. The senators suggested different ways of answering the note; all were more or less hostile to it. For his part, Wilson indicated that the United States could not accept any future peace on the basis of the status quo ante bellum, since that would be a crime toward the country. Although Senator Henry Cabot Lodge found Wilson "adrift and troubled" about the pope's note, he left the White House assuming that "we helped him with our various suggestions and stiffened him."[42] The same evening Lansing conferred with Wilson at the White House for an hour about the note.[43] On the next day an instruction was sent to all U.S. diplomatic representatives abroad to ascertain confidentially the views of respective governments in regard to the pope's note. Wilson also asked Lansing to analyze the pope's motives and proposals.[44]

House was very unhappy about Wilson's letter of August 16. On August 18, Franklin K. Lane, the secretary of the interior, and his wife visited the "Colonel" in Magnolia, Massachusetts. After a prolonged discussion, House found Lane sympathetic with his views. Lane informed Lansing about House's arguments in a long letter. He thought that the Central Powers should not be led to believe that the United States would carry out a "policy of annihilation." The opportunity should be used, instead, to make plain not so much the U.S. terms of peace but the things in Germany that tended to make peace difficult to achieve. However, Lane told the "Colonel" that he believed that the United States was not opposed to talking about peace provided "as a *sine qua non* that the Central Powers would assume that the government by the soldier was not a possibility in the XXth century." He also expressed to Lansing his fear that the government was going about it too mechanically, with too little emotion and passion.[45] Lane's formal endorsement of House's view did not make the "Colonel" happier and more tranquil. As he wrote in his diary, "The President's letter shows that his mind is not running parallel with mine . . . . The President, I feel, has taken a wrong position and I am as certain as I ever am these days that he will make a colossal blunder if he treats the Note lightly and shuts the door abruptly. I wish I could be with him." House considered it a tragedy that he was heatbound in Massachusetts at that moment.[46]

Lansing and Phillips, in the absence of Polk, got their chance and used it as best they could to express their respective views on the subject. Phillips, admitting that the pope's message was a principal topic, charged that it was a "Teutonic move for peace on the *status quo ante*." He also believed that the note's primary purpose was to "create a division of opinion in enemy countries."[47] On August 19, Lansing finished his "Comments on the Pope's peace appeal" and the next day discussed them with Lester Woolsey, the solicitor at the State Department. The same day he forwarded them to Wilson, together with a covering letter.[48] Lansing expressed his opinion that the note did not go further than the German peace proposals of December 1916, although there were some preliminary agreements differing from it. As to the suggestion for mutually condoning war damages, Lansing commented somewhat ironically that "it is carrying the Christian doctrine of forgiveness a long way, since the burden falls very heavily on one side and very little on the other." It also went no further than to suggest that future negotiations were to be on the basis of the status quo ante bellum. As for the methods of insuring the future peace, Lansing argued that they depend largely "upon the trustworthiness of the signatories to the peace treaty." In view of the experiences of the immediate past, however, "I do not see how it is possible to rely upon the good faith of that government as it is now constituted."

Most of Lansing's comments examined the motives that inspired the pope's action. Lansing saw several elements as crucial in this respect. He connected the issuance of the note with the military successes of the Central Powers, with the destructive effects of the German submarines, with Russia's internal instability, with the limited availability of U.S. forces in Europe, with the increase of peace propaganda, and with the meeting of the socialist international. These factors were, it was assumed at the Vatican, conducive to further negotiations and discussions among the belligerents. In other words, the Allies and the United States could disregard neither the situation on the battlefields and on the high seas nor the internal tensions and socialist agitation for peace.

In assuming that the pope's initiative came at the instigation of Vienna and Berlin, Lansing endeavored to uncover the reasons that prompted Austria-Hungary to ask the pope to act for peace. As the first reason, Lansing indicated "a sincere desire for the restoration of peace." Although he expressed some doubts about the note, he nevertheless found it sincere. Second, the desire for peace was motivated, at least to some extent, by "an earnest wish to preserve the Empire of Austria-Hungary from dismemberment." The reasons for it were the "jealousies and dislikes of the various nationalities, composing the Dual Empire," and the fact that the "Empire has been the main support of the Vatican for half a century, and has been always faithful to the doctrine of temporal power." Third, Lansing saw in the pope's action "a desire to preserve the Monarchy from the increasing danger of socialism and the irreligious tendencies of socialistic doctrine," Fourth, he saw it as an "effort at the preservation, if not the increase, of the influence of the Roman Church." Wilson was very impressed with the document's soundness and the strength of Lansing's arguments. The next day the two men met again and discussed ways of composing the reply to the pope.[49]

Although Lansing's emphasis on the role of Austria-Hungary in this respect was exaggerated, his estimate of the motives and reasons for making this proposal was correct. Lansing saw the Vatican's action as an expression of practical necessity. He did not see in it the pope's preoccupations with the Vatican's standing and influence or with the unity of the Catholic world. He considered neither the Vatican's notions of the universal mission of Catholicism nor its fear that the Catholic masses in Europe would want to stand behind their respective governments and parties and thus weaken the position of the Catholic church. In the future, the Vatican would be preoccupied with all these matters.

Although Wilson, House, and Lansing dealt with the major problems and issues, prominent public figures passed on to them their respective views and proposals as to how to deal with the pope's message. On August 18, Abbott K. Lowell, in behalf of the Executive Committee of the League to Enforce Peace, advised Wilson that although the peace proposals of the pope supported the principle of a league of nations to enforce peace and were thereby welcome, the Executive Committee "feels that a League of Nations which will guarantee the future security of the world can be made effective only by the abolition of the Prussian democracy." The war should therefore be fought to the very end.[50] Thomas B. Neely, bishop of the Methodist Episcopal Church in Philadelphia, wrote to Lansing that America moved to defend humanity against the "greatest military menace the world has ever known." He wondered why an "ecclesiastic and an ecclesiasticism meddle in the affairs of the nations." The bishop advised Lansing that acceptance of the pope's proposals would mean German victory.[51] Arthur Chapman of New York advised Wilson that an answer to the pope ought to be made but suggested that the "Pope is not a nation and that the great ship 'USA' sailed only yesterday for Berlin on a glorious mission."[52] Henry Demarest Lloyd qualified the terms of the note as "altogether too favorable to Germany in her present mood" and proposed that "Germany must be made either powerless or free not only of the Hohenzollern dynasty, but also of that thing called the German mind."[53] Sosnowski, in behalf of the Polish National Defense Committee, warned that the "chief object of the peace proposal . . . is to protect the interests of the Roman Catholic Church, to save the Roman Catholic States, to keep in power the Roman Catholic dynasties."[54] Bolton Hall, a New York attorney, advised Wilson that his answer be composed in such a way as to "strengthen democracy everywhere, [so that it] may not antagonize the Catholics at home and abroad, may not add to the difficulties confronting Russia, may not strengthen reactionaries here." Robert Kohn, another New York attorney, suggested that the U.S. reply indicate that the president was ready at any time to "discuss with responsible governments the measures and means whereby this war may be ended."[55] Judging by the contents of the mail received, it appears that most of Wilson's correspondents supported, in one way or other, his and Lansing's ideas as to how the pope's note should be answered.

Wilson's problem seemed to be now to reconcile House and avoid hurting his sensitivities. He did this by sending to House, on August 22, the draft of his note, asking him to "tell me exactly what you think of it." He explained that the reply had to be brief, centering on a single point: that "we cannot take the word of the present rulers of Germany for anything." Wilson assured House that he had tried to indicate the U.S. attitude on those questions that were discussed in the "socialistic and other camps." He justified his refusal to discuss certain questions more specifically by the fear that "it might provoke dissenting voices from France and Italy if I should—if I should say, for example, that their territorial claims did not interest us."[56] Nonetheless, House was deeply grieved by Wilson's refusal to take his advice. He perhaps calmed his feelings by writing in his diary; "I am thoroughly satisfied with the way he [Wilson] has done it, for he has covered all points I asked him to embrace, and has left out the dangerous points to which I called his attention." Still, he added at the same time, "While I am complimented, yet, if I were President I should take a different course, and have written somewhat differently myself."[57]

The Allied ambassadors, in bringing messages from their governments and inquiring about the contents of the U.S. reply, were kept in the dark while the reply was being worked out. The Russian ambassador, Boris Bakmetoff, kept both House and Lansing well posted on the Kerenskii government's attitude toward the pope's note. On August 19, he told House that in "view of the Stockholm conference, it will become a real menace if the Pope's overtures are not treated in the right way." He proposed that Wilson call an Allied conference in order to formulate peace terms and announce them to the Germans. The next day Bakmetoff told Lansing that the Russian government thought that the pope's proposal could not be accepted, since it did not end military autocracy. Lansing suggested to Bakmetoff that "similar but independent action seemed to be wise," thus indicating that Wilson intended to reply to the pope.[58] On August 21, Lansing told Di Cellere that there was no reason for rushing and that he was not familiar with the nature of Wilson's reply. For his part, Di Cellere told Lansing that the Italian government was not disposed to send a reply. Several days later, Lansing told Di Cellere that nothing would be said about the aspirations of certain powers.[59] Jusserand insisted that the French government should be consulted as to the contents of the reply.[60]

The British were kept in touch through House and Lansing. On August 21 Ambassador Page informed the State Department that the Foreign Office had told the Vatican that it had not yet consulted the Allies and was unable to say what reply, if any, would be sent to the pope.[61] The same day Lansing told Spring-Rice that he was unable to say what answer would be sent to the pope, but Spring-Rice guessed that Wilson would not participate in a joint reply.[62] The next day House wrote to Wiseman that if Wilson replied to the pope, he would ask the British government to make no answer except to state that they entirely agree with what he had to say.[63] On August 24 House cabled Balfour that the reply to the pope was completed and would be sent in a few days: "It will serve, I think, to unite Russia and add to the confusion of Germany." He asked the foreign secretary that the Allies stay firmly behind it: "If the United States are to put forth their maximum effort, there must be a unified people and the President has struck the note necessary to make this possible." Wilson was aware of House's efforts to win British cooperation, but the British refused to give carte blanche to Wilson, as House had expected.[64]

After receiving the reply from House, who had made a few small stylistic changes, Wilson went to see Lansing in his house on the evening of August 26. They discussed the text of the reply; Lansing accepted it. The next day the note was encoded and sent to U.S. diplomatic representatives abroad.[65] It was read and approved at the cabinet meeting on August 28, after it had already reached the Allied capitals. Late that evening, the text of the reply was handed to the press.[66]

Despite a certain uneasiness and certain qualms, expectations at the Vatican were great. The hope for a favorable response, especially from Wilson, pushed Vatican personnel into frenetic activity. The hopes of Austria-Hungary, who wanted to solve its most urgent problems, were equally fervent.[67] On August 18, the Vatican newspaper carried a long editorial explaining the origins of the pope's note and its meaning in the present crisis.[68] On August 20, L'Osservatore published a long article, giving new details and explanations of those questions that were considered vague and unclear. It commented, among other things, that the freedom of the seas was a "dream dear to President Wilson," and discussed questions of disarmament, Belgium, and forced annexations. It observed that the pope's note tended only to put together the elements of a "general character with regard to which the chiefs of the principal belligerent states were more or less in agreement."[69]

In his eagerness to give the note a better start, Gasparri went even further. On August 24, 1917, he called to the Vatican Dr. Rodolfo Foa, a respectable Italian journalist, and told him that he wanted to be interviewed. The interview was already prepared and was intended for American consumption. Dr. Foa was asked to pass the text of the interview to John Bass, the correspondent for the Chicago Daily News in Italy. Several days later the pope finally received Wilson's reply, which created consternation in Vatican circles. Gasparri immediately forbade publication of the interview.[70]

The interview was interesting in itself: it indicated how the United States, its place in the world, and its contribution in the struggle for peace were regarded. Gasparri began by referring to the unjust and severe criticism accorded to the note in the United States, saying that it was not properly understood there. The criticism was not justified in view of the fact that the United States had not entered the war in order to acquire new territories or make other gains. It had entered the war to "defend the principles of peace and justice throughout the world." For this reason, the United States could not regard the pope's note, inspired as it was by the same reasons and lofty motives, with contempt or hatred. In commenting upon the adequacy of the note and its validity in the struggle for peace, the cardinal argued that in issuing the note "the Holy See did not want to present the peace treaty and ask the Powers to put their signature on it." On the contrary, it wanted to exploit a convenient opportunity to put together a "basis for future peace." Certain questions seemed easier to solve, since the views of different belligerents were close. Others would have to be discussed and settled afterward. "The Vatican," Gasparri insisted, "only invited both sides to discuss their pretensions and clarify them." For this reason certain proposals in the note are better defined, and others less precise and detailed. "The Note had profited enormously by Wilson's declaration of January 22, 1917 . . . when he proclaimed the need for the limitation of armaments and the freedom of the seas."

The pope, Gasparri went on, clearly indicated that a spirit of conciliation was necessary in order to discuss certain problems—as, indeed, Wilson urged in his message. The aspirations of peoples, which the pope cherished, also coincided with Wilson's ideas and was one of the "cardinal principles of the future democratic development." In replying to the question of how peace was to be preserved and defended after the war, Gasparri argued that disarmament and arbitration would have to be accepted and fully supported by all of the world's nations. After achieving such unity, it would be difficult for any nation not to honor these in spirit as well as in letter. The Vatican was recommending boycott (sanctions)—economic and moral—of all those who in any way infringe on the treaties. If these were accepted, wars would not be possible. At the end of the interview, Gasparri expressed his confidence in sincerity and loyalty of the American people and their aspirations for justice, charity, and peace, all of which had induced the pope to make his appeal.[71]

Gasparri's interview contained scarcely veiled criticism of Wilson's lack of cooperation. Gasparri also made the best possible use of the arguments Wilson had developed during the period of U.S. neutrality, and he seemed unwilling to admit that with the United States now in the war, these arguments were no longer relevant. Furthermore, although Gasparri insisted that the pope's note had only suggested some basis for peace, not the conditions for peace, he expanded some of the note's basic elements in his interview. That is, disarmament, arbitration (forced, if necessary), and boycott were proper ways of preserving peace.

On August 29, U.S. newspapers published Wilson's reply to the pope, with lengthy editorials and comments. Exploiting the circumstances shrewdly, Wilson succeeded in avoiding all the pitfalls. His reply was a combination of suavity and crudeness, as John Snell has pointed out correctly. It also praised Benedict XV's intentions, his humane and generous motives. But in refusing the pope's proposal, Wilson insisted that it would not bring the desired peace and might lead, instead, only to a truce. The central idea of the pope's proposal—return to the status quo ante bellum—was unacceptable to the United States. The papal program could not be carried out unless it had a firm and satisfactory basis. Wilson believed that "the object of the war was to deliver the free peoples of the world from the menace and the actual power of a vast military establishment controlled by an irresponsible government." Since that government— the German government—planned the domination of the world, it was not possible to see how the world could deal.with it. "The plan proposed by His Holiness the Pope would, so far as we can see, involve a recuperation of its strength, and a renewal of its policy; would make it necessary to create a permanent hostile combination of nations against the German people, who are its instrument; and would result in abandoning the new-born Russia to the intrigue." Castigating Germany's rulers even more, Wilson insisted that the American people, though it had suffered intolerable wrongs at the hands of the Imperial German government, desired no revenge against the German people. All the world's people—small or large, weak or strong—should have a right to freedom, security, and self-government. The real test for every peace is whether "it is based upon the faith of all peoples involved or merely upon the words of an ambitious and intriguing government." Since the German government had committed intolerable wrongs, it would have to make amends. But this was not to be carried out at the expense of the sovereignty of any people, rather in vindication of the sovereignty of those that are weak and of those that are strong. The final passage indicated the heart of Wilson's attack: "We cannot take the word of the present rulers of Germany as a guarantee of anything that is to endure, unless explicitly supported by such conclusive evidences of the will and purpose of the German people themselves. . . . Without such guarantees treaties of settlement, agreements for disarmament, covenants to set up arbitration in the place of force, territorial adjustments, reconstructions of small nations, if made with the German Government, no man, no nation could depend on now. We must await new evidence of the purposes of the great peoples of the Central Empires."[72]

In essence, Wilson's message was an invitation to revolt, a contemptuous tribute to the German political and military establishment, and a plea to the Allies to follow Wilson's lead in creating a better, new world after the war. On August 31, 1917, since Gasparri was absent, the text of the reply was handed to Monsignor Federico Tedeschini, the under secretary at the Vatican. L'Osservatore Romano published the text on September 1, but refrained from making any strong statement or extended comments on it. Only later, when the Vatican realized that its whole campaign was badly timed and executed, did Gasparri admit that there were certain misunderstandings.[73]

The arguments Lansing put forward in his comments and the arguments Wilson advanced in his answer to the pope are similar. Both insisted that the Vatican was proposing a return to the status quo ante bellum; both advanced the same arguments regarding the territorial settlement; both believed that the pope's note was issued at the moment when the military advantages of the Central Powers were formidable. The phrase, "we cannot take the word of the present rulers of Germany as a guarantee of anything that was to endure," was in accord with Lansing's emphasis. There were, however, certain dissimilarities. The most prominent was that Wilson avoided mentioning the possibility of the "dismemberment of the Empires." Lansing, on the other hand, seemed to have begun his analysis and argued his case from that viewpoint. Furthermore, Wilson's rhetoric, rather than Lansing's sober style, was unmistakable—as well as effective.

U.S. newspapers and public opinion in general greeted Wilson's reply enthusiastically. The press paid due tribute to the pope, his exalted office, and the unique position he occupied. But it was equally unanimous in claiming that the pope's proposals could not possibly be accepted by the United States and the Allies. It repeatedly pointed out that Wilson's reply was an appeal to the German people to reject the predatory and aggressive policy of the bureaucracy that had started the war. It criticized the pope's note for its vagueness on many crucial subjects and its silence on such subjects as the submarine campaign. Editorials also announced that the United States was very much concerned with future peace and could not allow itself to be menaced by a "Mitteleuropa" stretching from Hamburg to the Persian Gulf, that it could not leave all problems to be discussed at the peace conference (since the Central Powers were morally bankrupt), and that the war must be ended with a permanent and just peace. Reparations were considered an indispensable part of such a peace.

The U.S. press also aired the belief that Germany and Austria-Hungary had prompted the pope's note; it praised Wilson for his skill in speaking to the peoples of Germany and Germany's allies. Because of this and because no reply was forthcoming from the Allies, several editors insisted that Wilson was acting as the Allies' spokesman. On the other hand, the German-American, Irish-American, and pacifist press maintained that Wilson's reply left the door open to a peace, since the idea of internal reform was popular in Germany. The Catholic press carefully refrained from anything beyond expressions of respect for the pontiff's motives.[74]

The French openly protested, and the British, too, disapproved of the way Wilson handled the pope's note. That is, he had replied without consulting the Allies. Wilson either was not willing to consult them or considered separate replies unnecessary; this confirmed suspicions that he considered himself the Allied spokesman. The Russian government fully approved of Wilson's reply in a letter of September 10. In returning this letter to Lansing, Wilson noted that Russia's position was very satisfactory to him: "I hope that they will see that it is not necessary for them to make any reply."[75] On August 30, the British War Cabinet discussed certain passages to which they "could not give unqualified assent" or with which they could not express official agreement. Lord Cecil was authorized to inform the Allies that it was thought that no further reply to the pope should be sent until the answer of the Central Powers about Belgium was received. The French government went along with the British about a reply to the pope.[76] On August 28, Jusserand visited Lansing and had quite a heated discussion with him over the fact that France had not been consulted. The next day, Jusserand told Phillips that the "Note would make a bad impression abroad"; Phillips found Jusserand "generally disgruntled." On August 30, when Jusserand was received at the White House, he was told that "regard must be had to the public opinion which was in some respects lukewarm." Jusserand had noticed Wilson's irritation each time some other person in high authority, the pope, for example, made a move to assume the role of peacemaker. "The President plainly showed me his ill-humor about Benedict XV's wanting to 'butt in' (his own words)," explained the ambassador.[77]

The reaction in Germany was pronounced. Wilson's reply was published on September 1 and was received with mixed feelings by political parties, individuals, and the press in general. The text was well publicized all over Germany and Austria-Hungary, since Lansing had, on August 29, 1917, authorized Ambassador Sharp, Minister Stovall in Bern, and Chargé d'affaires Langhorn in the Hague to spend the money needed for translation, printing, and distribution.[78] The conservatives attacked Wilson vehemently for his instrusion into Germany's internal affairs. On the floor of the Reichstag, members of several parties delivered long speeches attacking the reply. The moderates and the right wing of the Social Democratic Party (SPD) were very critical of the reply. But Wilson's reply also received a considerable positive response. Some editorials were very favorable to Wilson's recommendations, especially *Vorwärts*, the central organ of the Social Democratic Party. Curiously enough, Social Democrats of both the Left and Right attacked Wilson: the first considered him a bourgeois statesman; the second boasted their patriotism. Both, however, were unanimous in refusing Wilson's call for revolution.[79]

Wilson's closest advisers and collaborators greeted the reply with enthusiastic approval and predicted far-reaching consequences in the enemy bloc. Phillips found it a "magnificent document," in which the final passage was the most impressive. Auchincloss noted that it "met with universal approval," and Senator Owen complimented Lansing on it.[80] House commented that Wilson's reply was enthusiastically received by the press: "It is a culmination of an idea I have had for a long time. I am anxious to see whether the results will be as valuable as I have hoped." There was no trace of bitterness in House, although he seemed to ascribe to himself the mentorship of the whole idea.[81]

In his enthusiasm and eagerness for the complete success of Wilson's action, House took a further step toward influencing the pope himself. He thought that it would be enormously useful for the cause of peace if the pope could be induced to say something favorable about Wilson's reply. He therefore decided to convey to Benedict XV the notion that "the President had not closed the door but indicated a way by which it could be thrown wide." On August 29, House called Dudley Field Malone, the collector of the Port of New York and asked him to see Cardinal Farley or Cardinal Gibbons and suggest to them that a cable conveying this idea to the pope should be sent to the Vatican. House saw enormous possibilities in this move: "If we could bring the Pope to say this it would create a sensation in Austria and Catholic Germany. It would make them feel that there was but one way by which peace could be obtained."[82] Malone went immediately to see Cardinal Farley, who was not in. Therefore, he asked J. J. Dunn, chancellor of the Archdiocese of New York, to write a letter to Bonzano, making the following suggestions: (1) the Vatican need not reply to Wilson; (2) if it does, it should emphasize the liberal suggestions and avoid mentioning the criticism of the Kaiser; (3) the door should be opened for future discussion between the pope and the president; (4) the pope should point out similarities between Wilson's and his aims and politics. At the end, Malone insisted that this letter ought to go immediately, "as the Vatican should know the temper of the federal authorities." House was upset when he realized how far Malone went. He had certainly gone much further than intended, since House was aware that the whole idea was repugnant to Wilson. Bonzano refused to take Malone's suggestion and branded it as "anonymous"; it was not forwarded to the Vatican. On September 10, Wilson and House discussed the whole affair and agreed that it was "Malone's mistake."

Wilson seemed resentful of House's action, wondering whether it would "involve us" in any way. House did not think it would.[83] This was an idea that only House could have conceived, another inconsequential indication of his diplomatic amateurism.

Ambassador Page, Bryan, Senator John S. Williams of Mississippi, and others joined in the chorus of praise for Wilson's fine piece of work. Early in September 1917, Page wrote from London that the "reply expresses definitely the moral and the deep and clear political reason for the war— the freeing of the world, including the German people, from the German military autocracy—and it expresses this better and with more force than it has ever been expressed by anybody on this side of the world." After pointing out that the reply made acceptable peace terms clearer, Page added that it set forth the one "big thing worth fighting for—no revenge, no mere boundary rectifications, no subsidiary thing to confuse the main purpose. This gives moral leadership to the whole war . . . and the leadership of the war is now definitely and confessedly transferred to you."[84] Senator Williams thought that the reply was "one of the best state papers ever written to the world." On September 10, Bryan told Secretary of the Navy Daniels that Wilson's reply to the pope was like the saying of St. Luke that "you cannot put new wine into old bottles," referring apparently to the pope's efforts to preserve the status quo.[85]

Wilson himself was ebullient. He had no reason for hiding his feelings and reactions, although his reactions to the lavish praise revealed some uncertainty as well. More important still, he explained why he had not previously consulted the Allies in this very important matter. To Senator Williams, Wilson wrote that "there seemed . . . to be no other answer and, therefore, this one was comparatively easy to write." To Arthur Brisbane of the *Washington Times,* he admitted that "I wrote [the reply] almost as a matter of course, because the whole body of issues in this great struggle has assumed in my mind a great simplicity, and there seemed to me to be no other way of stating it."[86] On September 1, in a letter to Cleveland Dodge, Wilson did not sound so confident: "Whenever I write anything like the reply to the Pope my first and greatest desire is to know what men whose judgement I trust think of it, because I never entirely trust my own instincts and conclusion." Dodge's letter was "the reassurance which my heart craves," as well. The next day, in answering House, Wilson insisted that "I did not dare to submit it to our Associates across the sea more than twenty-four hours before I made it public." "I felt morally certain that they would wish changes which I could not make . . . . The differences of opinion will be less embarrassing now than they would have been if I had invited them beforehand," he concluded.[87] With a combination of boldness and luck, Wilson moved into the forefront as a spokesman for the Allies, although they by no means had authorized him to act as such.

The pope's peace note came to Wilson as a God-given opportunity to act upon his own. He exploited this opportunity very well; indeed, he demonstrated to the world that his diplomatic gifts and skills were substantially greater than had been generally assumed. His reply was not only an excellent piece of diplomacy, it also accomplished a great deal in the political sphere. In the United States itself, Wilson's reply solidified popular support and put Catholics on the defensive. Abroad, however, the effects of Wilson's reply were much more extensive. In Germany, his reply had sown internal divison and unrest and had also precluded the pope's eventual future intervention. It helped Chancellor Michaelis and Germany explain to the pope that Wilson was not ready to negotiate, although in reality Wilson had nothing to do with Germany's decision to make an unsatisfactory reply to the pope about Belgium. It also made Austria-Hungary at once hopeful of survival and dubious about the ultimate success of Germany's policy; it thus made the Habsburgs a wavering ally. It avoided, at that particular time, discussion of the war aims. At the same time, Wilson's reply did not arouse French, English, and Italian suspicions about carrying out secret plans and mutual obligations. It contributed to the failure of the pontiff's action, thereby removing all responsibility in this respect from the Allies. The Vatican clearly showed its intention to put all of the onus on Wilson. Surprisingly, Wilson did not shrink from that responsibility and seemed quite ready to take upon himself the brunt of the Vatican's dissatisfaction and criticism. His reply made it quite clear that neither the Allies nor the Central Powers nor, for that matter, the United States wanted a simple return to the status quo ante bellum—as the Vatican immediately realized. For his part, Wilson regarded the pope's action as interference in a domain that he claimed was exclusively his.

Finally, the lack of more definite agreements and the reluctance of the Allies to support his action openly gave Wilson the initial advantage. It put him instantly into the forefront, which he held for a long time, despite Lloyd George's efforts to snatch it away from him. At that moment, however, the Allies had given the impression of a voluntary retreat, particularly in view of the fact that the pope had not sent his note only to Wilson. There was thus sharp criticism of the Allies' subsequent silence.

L'EGLISE

Die Kirche im Krieg
Holzschnitt von Franz Masereel

The Church in the War. Drawing by Frank Masereel

Raphael Merry del Val, Cardinal Secretary of State

Cardinal Gibbons with Admiral Benson and Secretary of Navy Daniels

Francis Aidan Cardinal Gasquet, O.S.B.

Desire Cardinal Mercier, Archbishop of Malines

FOODSHIP

for BELGIUM

© 1915 N. WILLIAMS

HELP FILL THE
INDIANA SHIP
WITH
WHEAT, FLOUR AND EVAPORATED MILK
FOR THE NON-COMBATANTS IN BELGIUM

American help to Belgium

President Wilson leading a preparedness parade

The torpedoing of the *Lusitania*

President Wilson reading his war message to Congress

CHAPTER 7
NEW PEACE EFFORTS, 1917–1918

By the end of October 1917, it was evident that the pope's effort to achieve peace had failed. The Allies, unwilling to commit themselves to negotiations, much less state their war aims, covered their silence by publicly supporting Wilson's reply. They insisted that it was up to Germany to announce its aims, which it had consistently refused to do. Wilson's reply to the pope and the endorsement it received from the Allies seemed to provide the Central Powers with considerable opportunity for throwing discord into Allied ranks, but the Central Powers never exploited it.

The Vatican worked tirelessly to keep all avenues for further discussion open, encouraging all concerned to state their views and objections. It harbored the idea of issuing a new note, provided a new note would be effective. Even before Wilson's reply was published, Marchetti told a member of the British legation in Bern that the Allies ought to have interpreted the pope's note differently: "It was intended by the Pope to be the first of the series of notes, and he wished each side, or each belligerent country, to say how much of it they accept and on what points they wanted further information as to his proposals."[1] Ambassador Paul Cambon informed Balfour that the Vatican hierarchy, including the pope, was optimistic about the outcome of its peace efforts. Gasparri insisted upon providing further, more or less definitive, explanations and clarifications through the issuing of a new note, and he wanted to send a special note to the U.S. government, since he believed that Vatican proposals had encountered resistance and misunderstanding there. Others in the Curia advised restraint and prudence. A new note was to come out in September.[2] All of these hints implied that the pope's good offices were still available and that those who did not use them in order to bring peace must take responsibility for continuing the war.

The Allies dreaded the idea of a new note. In a lengthy memorandum, Harold Nicolson tried to explain the origins and inspirations of the pope's note and to forecast what moves the Vatican might yet make. He suggested that Gasparri's more dynamic approach would probably prevail in the Curia. If so, it was natural to expect either further proposals of an indirect nature, or a direct and supplementary rejoinder to Wilson's reply.

Nicolson also pointed out that papal diplomacy was actively seeking piecemeal adjustments of individual points so that the Vatican would be in a favorable position to issue further proposals.[3] On September 14, 1917, Cecil pointed out to the War Cabinet that the new Vatican move might be part of a game to get Britain to start negotiations with Austria-Hungary. The Austrian government, Cecil warned, could have passed this information on to Italy and France to try to eliminate them from the war. Since Russia could not be counted on, the United States and Britain would then have to carry the burden.[4] In order to prevent this, Lloyd George decided to ask Wilson to begin secret negotiations to remove Austria-Hungary from the war.

Spring-Rice also had information that the pope's new peace note was to be issued soon. In this new proposal, Lorraine would be returned to France, and Alsace would remain with Germany. Constitutional changes might also be expected in Germany. On the whole, the pope's proposal was to be so moderate that neither the Allies nor the Americans would be able to reject it lightly. Bonzano's office encouraged this expectation.[5] Page wrote that the Vatican anticipated good results from the note, since the British government made inquiries as to which points were referred to the Central Powers. The reply from Germany and Austria-Hungary, crucial for the outcome of the pope's action, was eagerly awaited.[6]

The pope and Gasparri struggled to get the basic elements of the note, especially the point referring to Belgium, accepted by the German government. The major protagonists in this dramatic struggle were the German military and Michaelis on the one hand, and Pacelli on the other hand. The odds were overwhelmingly against Pacelli, who fought a losing battle from the beginning.[7] After forwarding to Michaelis the British suggestion that a German declaration on the independence of Belgium was necessary, Pacelli awaited the German decision. Although he had done everything to elicit a favorable response from Germany, the Crown Council held in Potsdam on September 11, 1917, could not reach a definite decision, since the army opposed issuing any explicit statement about Belgium's independence. On September 13, Pacelli informed the Curia that Germany's reply would not contain a favorable statement on Belgium. He was told that Belgium has "high value for Germany, which she may lose if she puts her cards on the table."

Gasparri immediately realized that it would be "inconvenient" if no mention of Belgium were forthcoming. He suggested that Germany "accept the proposals of the Holy See as a whole, while reserving for herself the right to solve all pending problems at the peace conference."[8]

This suggestion was unrealistic, since the Vatican could not expect Germany to accept its proposals in toto. Evidently, Gasparri was more concerned with formal acceptance of the pope's proposal than with solving the pending problems. He obviously did not have much faith in the practical value of the note itself, but he tried to preserve the prestige of the pope and the Vatican by getting Germany's approval of it.

The Germans ignored Gasparri's statement that the Vatican would never have issued the note if Chancellor Bethmann-Holweg had not indicated a favorable reply on the Belgian question. On September 14, Pacelli was told that the German reply would avoid general acceptance of the note, would refer to the Reichstag resolution of July 19, and would be published on September 20. Gasparri asked Pacelli to urge the chancellor and the emperor to insert an explicit statement about Belgium. "In case they refused to do this," he wrote, "you should warn them that the war will continue to the end. The Holy See denies any responsibility for future misfortune, as it would be ascribed to the German government. If the reply is positive, public opinion will be on Germany's side, and the war will not last long."[9] What sort of responsibility was Gasparri talking about, and to whom would the Vatican be responsible? On September 17, Gasparri made clear who would ultimately be responsible. "A single, satisfactory, and definite reply," he wrote, "would bring the enemy [the Allies] into a difficult situation and make continuation of the war impossible."[10] But the Germans and the Austrians remained unresponsive.

On September 20, Pacelli made a final attempt to secure Germany's reply on Belgium. He wrote to Michaelis that the "Holy Father desires to receive a clear interpretation of Germany's intentions with reference to points 3 and 5 [indemnities and Belgium]." This made a separate reply about Belgium unnecessary, but the demand was rejected: the German Foreign Ministry replied on September 22, 1917, that "they had nothing more to add."[11] On September 20, *Giornale d'Italia* published news from Bern that the German reply had been made public. The same day the reply was handed to Pacelli in Munich; the Austrian reply was given to Bonzo by Czernin in Vienna. Gasparri was upset, and although he did not have the complete texts of the replies, he instructed Pacelli to announce in Berlin that the Central Powers had committed three errors: (1) they had made only a general reply; (2) Germany had explicitly had to accept points 3 and 5 if negotiations were to continue, and (3) if Germany accepted the Vatican's suggestion, therefore, it need not make a separate reply on Belgium. Gasparri asked the German government to heed his advice and said that the Vatican press would not publish the German reply until the government in Berlin had given its final word on points 3 and 5.[12]

Germany's reply was very unpleasant for all concerned. Georg Hertling, the Bavarian prime minister and a prominent Catholic, decided to sooth the Vatican. He told Pacelli confidentially that the Holy See might consider that the expression "in accord with the manifestation of peace of the Reichstag" constituted the acceptance of points 3 and 5 of the pope's note. He also indicated Germany's willingness to start secret talks about the peace, so that the Holy See need not view the existing situation so pessimistically.[13] The Curia was sufficiently encouraged to continue peace efforts for weeks to come.

On September 22, Germany's and Austria's replies were published in the Italian press. The German reply was couched in general terms, as had been expected. It recognized that the pope's action was in accord with the Reichstag resolution, greeted with "particular sympathy" the pope's conviction that in the future "the material forces of arms must be replaced by the moral forces of right," and admitted the need for a simultaneous limitation of military forces and the organization of an arbitration system that would be compulsory in international disputes. It also fully supported the pope's request for "true freedom and community of ownership of the seas." The Austrian reply was couched in more genuine phrases, but it was not fundamentally different from the German note, although Vienna was ready to "enter into negotiations on an obligatory tribunal of arbitration" as well.[14] Though Germany had not been much impressed with the pope's proposal, it hoped to use the Vatican for eventual contact with the Allies. The question of Belgium was relegated to another note. This, as well as the silence on indemnity, made Germany's reply useless for advancing Vatican peace efforts.

The U.S. government carefully watched for the publication of Germany's reply. On September 28, Lansing instructed Hugh Wilson, chargé d'affaires in Berne, to telegraph the full text of Germany's and Austria's replies to the Vatican peace proposal.[15] On September 20, Page reported that the Vatican had made every effort to induce the Central Powers to accept the pope's note in toto, "but it seems to fall unsuccessfully."[16] Two days later, Page suggested that the replies were considered a "mockery." He was told that Germany would amplify the papal suggestions regarding the three important points and "encourage the Pope to proceed." This, he believed, was an indication that the pope had received private assurances on other points.[17] In a letter to Wilson,

Page indicated that the Catholic press discussed the Allies' ability to continue the war and that the "Pope's note appeared to be a good basis for this propaganda." He added that an editorial in *L'Osservatore Romano* of September 22, 1917, insisted that the Kaiser had answered the three principal questions of the pope's letter affirmatively. "Therefore, it is said, the Pope would continue his efforts."[18] On September 27, the news came from Rome that Germany's supplementary reply had been received the previous day, saying that it remained firm on the Reichstag resolutions.[19] Germany's reply did not elicit much comment in the State Department. Phillips thought that it was "very vague and deals only in general terms. It is susceptible to various interpretations and the Germans themselves do not agree on its meaning."[20] Polk appeared anxious to get the reaction of the Belgian government to Germany's supplementary note, which was intended for publication in the U.S. press.[21]

The Vatican may well have acted to drive a wedge between the Allies and the United States. On September 26, 1917, Marchetti pleaded with Alen Savery that the Allies, especially Britain, answer the pope. A statement to the effect that the Entente was willing to consider peace proposals, insisted Marchetti, would enormously strengthen the nonmilitary elements in Germany and help resolve the Belgian question. He blamed Wilson's cry of "no peace with the Hohenzollerns" for making the Germans more stubborn, and he was opposed to American intervention in European affairs. The "Old World" ought to be able to settle its own problems "without calling in for help from another continent," he felt, and if the Allies defeated the Germans, the Americans—such was their character—would declare that they had won the war. The Vatican was worried about an unpredictable future and about Wilson's ideas and concepts for a new world. Cecil commented that Marchetti's jealousy of the United States was "very curious."[22]

On September 29 the pope asked Salis whether the door for negotiation was still open. He did not mention the United States explicitly, but was apparently soliciting British opinion and action. Salis let the pope know that he was "badly served by his press" with such anti-British articles as that published in *L'Osservatore Romano* on September 27, 1917.[23] He told the pope, and later Gasparri, that such writings were absurd and made a hearing in England impossible. Gasparri handed Salis a personal letter for Lloyd George in which he expressed his willingness to provide "further explanations and more precise definitions with respect to such points as might be indicated by them." Gasparri also explained in more detail the Vatican's view on disarmament—which he termed a "basis for peace"—and even ventured to suggest that one way to resolve that problem might be the "simultaneous and mutual abolition of compulsory military service." As an example, Gasparri pointed to the voluntary armies of Great Britain and the United States. Once the question of the army service was settled, "disarmament would be brought about almost automatically and without disturbance of public order." Compulsory military service was considered a "real cause of innumerable evils; in the simultaneous abolition thereof, by mutual consent, lies the true remedy." It was felt that the solution of this problem would bring about international peace and restore the exhausted finances of various states.[24]

Page was kept informed of the Vatican's stand on the question of disarmament, and he was told that the Curia believed that Wilson's idea of enforcing treaties and international arbitral judgments by an international force was quite impractical. Instead, "Gasparri will urge, I hear," wrote Page, "suppression everywhere of compulsory military service."[25] The Vatican, obviously, did not think much of Wilson's concept of an international organization or its role in the postwar world. Instead, it advocated the formation of a court of arbitration to decide on international disputes, the penalty of universal isolation (or boycott) being provided against any state that refused to submit an international question to the court of arbitration or to accept the decision thereof. Salis's criticism of how the Vatican press wrote about the freedom of the seas bore fruit. No articles appeared afterward on the subject, which was quickly noticed in Great Britain and elsewhere.

This was risky diplomacy on the part of the Vatican. While asking for British cooperation in its peace efforts, the official organ of the Curia was accusing Britain of domination of the seas. The similarity between arguments advanced in the Austrian reply and those used in Gasparri's letter is revealing. Emperor Charles insisted upon the "suppression of armed forces," only to receive the Vatican's support in the abolition of compulsory military service. The Vatican proposal was vastly expanded, however, portraying the pope as a crusader against militarism. The Vatican took this step with undue optimism, since it had been resolutely rejected by the British government. After the letter was considered in the War Cabinet, Salis acknowledged its receipt. By making such a proposal, the Vatican endeavored to remain in the midst of the diplomatic activity after the failure of the note. The exchange of views continued, and rumors about a new papal note did not subside for some time.

Sonnino knew about Gasparri's letter to Lloyd George. Much disturbed, he let the British know that the pope was preparing to issue a new note.

He indicated that the Vatican was cooperating closely with the Central Powers and wanted to get the Allies to agree to an exchange of views with them. Sonnino was intent on preventing this, since it could prove "irresistible to the great mass of the people in Italy and France and would arouse such opposition to the war as to render us into this position where they would be able to dictate their own terms." He advised prudence on the part of the British and rejected the idea of announcing war aims. He considered Wilson's reply to the pope a mistake, the "only result of which had been to cause the German people to rally to their government." The British agreed with Sonnino and acted accordingly.[26] Incidentally, Marchetti believed the same.

Sonnino, apparently, did not trust the British. He decided to approach Wilson and warn him about the dangers involved in entertaining the Vatican's proposal favorably. On October 9, Macchi Di Cellere submitted to Lansing a memorandum to that effect. He told Lansing about the contents of Gasparri's letter to Lloyd George, which Lansing had not known about. Sonnino argued that the Vatican was evidently endeavoring to make itself essential in eventual peace discussions and that Gasparri's letter indicated the pope's desire to serve as a medium for transmission of peace proposals and counterproposals. He believed that the Central Powers had endorsed this, since they were speculating upon the "alleged dissatisfaction for the war of some parts of public opinion in the Allied countries and upon the possibility of breaking up the Entente." Sonnino voiced deep concern about the possibility of trouble among the civilian population. Such weakening of morale, Sonnino forecast prophetically, might have "the same influence on the morale of the armies and would make in all events a resumption of hostilities very difficult if not absolutely impossible." The beginning of any peace discussion with the Allies, without any binding pledge from the Central Powers for the integrity of Russia, would immediately be used in Petrograd to obtain a separate peace or to increase internal dissension in Russia and thus paralyze any Russian action. "It would, therefore, be dangerous to encourage all these intrigues by answering now to the Holy See and letting the warring peoples believe that negotiations of some sort are being conducted. The imprecise and vague references made by Germany in regard to Belgium and to the other fundamental points of any peace...show that the Central Powers are not inclined to negotiate. Any answer to the Holy See or a promise for an answer would irremediably compromise the general situation," concluded Sonnino.[27]

It was clear that the U.S. government would not encourage the pope to proceed. Like Sonnino, Wilson was aware of the general war weariness and of the destructive effects of the pacifist campaign. Since he did not want the pope to get mixed up with the war and other temporal problems, he easily accepted Sonnino's views. At that moment, further-more, the United States appeared ready to take a more active part in the war. Wilson, House, Lansing, and Lord Reading were discussing the question of U.S. representation on the Supreme War Council. Wilson's concurrence with Sonnino's views was communicated orally to Macchi Di Cellere by Lansing. When the British communicated Gasparri's letter to Washington, it was quickly forgotten.

The German government, for its part, suspected that the Vatican was plotting with the Allies and demanded to be informed about the outcome of its efforts. Pacelli was bluntly told that the German government firmly believed that "England has submitted the Allies' proposals for peace to the Holy See." Surprised and skeptical, Pacelli asked Gasparri whether this was so. He wanted to inform the Foreign Ministry, since he believed that cooperation between Berlin and the Vatican was essential for future action on the part of the Holy See.[28] Gasparri avoided making any reply. At the same time, the Holy See acted energetically to prevent any initiative on the part of the clergy to work for peace.[29]

Sonnino's warnings about the dangers of allowing the Vatican to make its peace proposals proved to be accurate and appropriate. In Italy both Catholics and socialists stirred up agitation with a subsequent decline in fighting morale among the soldiers. Inadequate care for the soldiers only added to the popular dissatisfaction and the desire for peace.[30] On October 18, 1917, Deputy Guido Miglioli, a well-known pacifist, proposed in the parliament a resolution accusing the government of not replying to the pope's note. The influential *Corriere della Sera* published a lengthy article criticizing the Allies for not replying to the pope on October 20, 1917. It argued that Wilson's reply could not be taken as a collective answer and that the pope's note should be accepted. Walter Page detected a rising pacifism in England and all over Europe. "What is called the Catholic conspiracy exists and is strong throughout Roman Catholic Europe . . . . Devout Roman Catholics of all nationalities are influenced by the Catholic wishes." Even English and French Catholics, he perceived, "find their loyalty divided between their countries and their church, and the resolution of many good men is weakened unconsciously."[31]

The U.S. Embassy in Rome acted to ward off this threat. Speranza, on Page's order, was charged with collecting information on and analyzing (1) the worldly influences to which the pope is subjected regarding his peace proposals; (2) the question of Catholicism in Germany, especially in Bavaria, and the relation of Catholicism to German political unity; (3) the extent and vitality of Catholicism as a political factor in Austria-Hungary and Spain for and against the Central Powers; and (4) the extent and vitality of Catholicism as a political factor in France and Italy.[32] The Vatican's activities attracted much attention and suspicion among Allies and Americans, and they were carefully scrutinized and reported.

The battle of Caporetto confirmed the Allies' concern. On October 24, 1917, German General von Below launched the Austro-German attack on the Italian front. The battle ended with the Italian divisions in full retreat and enormous human and material losses. By the middle of November 1917, the new front was established along the Piava River, and the German-Austrian armies controlled a substantial part of Italian territory. On October 30, a new Italian government was formed under Vittorio Orlando. On November 5, the prime ministers of Great Britain, France, and Italy met at Rapallo and agreed to form the Supreme War Council in order to coordinate their military operations.[33] On November 16, Wilson decided that the United States should join the Supreme War Council.

It was an almost unanimous consensus that the Vatican and the socialists had contributed to the Italian debacle. This opinion was voiced freely in the press and became a subject of discussion in political circles. Sonnino was the first to accuse the Vatican of mischievous dealings. On October 25 he reminded the deputies, while defending Italy's war program, that the "Pope's peace note of August 1, 1917 was inspired by the enemy." Although this accusation was not entirely true, it was accepted by the majority.[34] Rodd put the responsibility for the Italian defeat squarely upon the Vatican and the socialists.[35] Page was most vociferous in accusing the Holy See. On November 2, he cabled Washington that "all depends on whether the insidious propaganda based on Socialist's [sic] literature and the Pope's peace suggestions have undermined . . . [the] Third army, on which rests hope of immediate defense."[36] A week later, he issued another indictment of the Vatican, demanding that the U.S. government counter German, socialist, and Vatican propaganda for an immediate peace by establishing effective propaganda on "our part." "The entire Allies' cause is imperiled by the Vatican peace proposals which contributed to cause the present situation by undermining Italy's defensive forces."[37] The accusations leveled against the Vatican were partially justified. After the Caporetto debacle, many people in Italy and abroad seemed to believe that the new Italian government should look for peace through compromise with Austria-Hungary.[38]

The Vatican quickly sensed the dangers of this Allied campaign. It could have exposed the Holy See to other inconveniences and jeopardized its chances to work for peace. Benedict XV sent his friend and an unofficial liaison between the Vatican and the government, Baron Monti, to see the prime minister. Monti told Orlando that the accusations leveled against the Pope were not "just," since the demand for the peace note came from England.[39] Gasparri instructed the nuncios in Berlin and Vienna to ask the respective governments to withdraw their troops from Italian territories. He was worried about the "pacification of the peoples" and requested that the Central Powers renounce any idea of annexation in Italy "in accordance with the principles expressed in the note of the Holy See." Emperor Charles told the nuncio that Austria had no intention of annexing occupied territories, but did not consider it possible to cede irredenta to Italy either.[40]

The Allies and the Americans were worried lest the Vatican use this opportunity to issue a new peace proposal similar to that of August 1. They could not refuse to consider it—in view of Russia's withdrawal from the war, Italy's war weariness, and the prospects of Austria's leaving the war. Furthermore, they would have had to announce their war aims publicly. Villa Urutia, the Spanish ambassador to the Vatican, started a rumor about a new peace note early in November.[41] Sonnino and Rodd believed that it was going to happen, but Salis did not think it possible.[42] Phillips noted that there was an ominous feeling in Rome that the pope might issue a new peace decree. This would, in his opinion, have had an "unfortunate effect owing to the weariness of the people in the war."[43] Spring-Rice believed that if the pope issued a further peace message, "the effect on the American sentiment is likely to be very great. If it is in the interest of the Central Powers and used as a weapon against the American government, there will be a very serious outburst of anti-Catholic feeling in large sections of the population." Two days later, he added that "it is feared that the new papal message will be taken up by a party in this country in opposition to the President's policy, and the Catholic priesthood will follow the Papal lead and agitate against the war."[44]

Nor did the Central Powers welcome a new papal initiative. The military and political situation seemed very promising, especially to Germany. With Russia out of the war, with Italy shaken and hardly able to hold its own, and with the U.S. divisions arriving slowly on the battlefields, papal action was hardly desirable. The Vatican was frankly told this. Hertling, the new German chancellor, advised Pacelli that it would not be *"convenient for the Holy See to make a new bid for peace."* He also remarked that he was not against correction of the frontiers of Alsace-Lorraine and the return of French ethnic groups to France. To Pacelli's astonishment, however, Hertling made clear that it would also be *"inconvenient for the Holy See to enter into the merits of the question."*[45] The German government, through its Catholic chancellor, crushed anew the pope's ambitions to mediate and forced the Vatican to abandon its efforts. Benedict XV was repudiated by the power he had mollified all along.

The Allies and Americans soon found out, to their great relief, that no peace note from the Vatican was forthcoming. On November 26, 1917, *L'Osservatore Romano* officially announced that the Holy See did not intend to make a direct "appeal for peace to both or either group of belligerents." The same day Salis was received by Gasparri and Cerretti and was told that under "existing circumstances issuance of a further note is quite out of question." This Salis considered "incredible."[46] Eager to dispel any remaining suspicion, Gasparri cabled Marchetti that the "Holy See does not intend to make a new step for peace, unless this is demanded by both belligerent sides."[47] Page also confirmed that the pope would not make a further appeal because the "present state of feeling here and possibly in America is such as to make an utterance on his part not only not acceptable to the public but possibly injurious to the Vatican."[48]

Hertling's suggestions to Pacelli were obviously interpreted by the Vatican as a veto to any general peace initiative on its part. Without further notice from Germany, there was no chance that a move of any importance would be forthcoming from the Vatican; German and French warnings persuaded Benedict XV and Gasparri that they had to get the approval of both sides before they could act. This sapped the remaining vigor and will of the Vatican, moderated its temporal ambitions, and made its actions more congenial and responsive to the pretensions of both sets of belligerents. The restrictions imposed upon the Vatican by Article XV of the Pact of London also helped to temper its initial zeal. Its remaining energy and freedom of action were to be used in promoting less ambitious proposals and schemes, primarily those intended to solve peripheral questions or to fight off restrictions the Curia considered dishonorable and spurious.

On December 4, 1917, the U.S. Congress declared war on the Habsburg Monarchy, a decision that had been expected for a long time. The U.S. declaration of war against Germany had ushered in a period of great uncertainty for Austria, since it only lukewarmly accepted and executed

Germany's military decisions and plans.[49] Relations between Washington and Vienna were becoming increasingly strained, however, and the Austrian government, manifesting its solidarity with Germany, had earlier severed its diplomatic relations with the United States. The declaration of war, therefore, was not a major step to take.

In his annual message, Wilson elaborated on his old theme: "the sinister masters of Germany," friendship for the German people, and the liberation of subject peoples from German military and commercial domination. As for Austria-Hungary, he insisted that "we do not wish in any way to impair or to rearrange the Austro-Hungarian Empire. It is no affair of ours what they do with their own life, either industrially or politically. We do not propose or desire to dictate to them in any way. We only desire to see that their affairs are left in their own hands, in all matters, great and small." The United States had had to declare war on Austria-Hungary, however, because Austria-Hungary was not for the time being "her own mistress but simply the vassal of the German government." The declaration of war was an "important matter" for the United States.[50] Czernin, for his part, termed Wilson's address "in many respects incomprehensible," but admitted that it took no effort on Wilson's part to become embroiled in the empire's internal affairs. The hopes of getting Austria-Hungary out of the war were crushed anew, although the U.S. government did not seem enthusiastic about waging an intensive war against the new enemy.

The U.S. declaration of war accentuated the internal problems of Austria-Hungary. U.S. political activities in this region were a potential threat that roused the Vatican's concern.[51] The Habsburg Monarchy was, after all, the Vatican's "dearest child," its last, most determined, and most loyal defender. However, the reaction from the Vatican was guarded. After the publication of Wilson's speech, Gasparri gave interviews to the Reuter's and Associated Press correspondents in Rome. With the former, Gasparri seemed to disparage Wilson's naiveté. With the latter, he was primarily concerned to allay the impression he had made in the first interview—he insisted that his statements had not been correctly reported. He had discovered that Page was reporting regularly to Washington about the Vatican, but believed that Page's information was hostile to the Vatican and its policies.[52]

Early in December, it was again rumored that the Vatican was ready to move for peace and was looking for encouragement from both sides and that the United States and Britain approved of the pope's desire for mediation (these rumors were particularly strong in Uruguay, Argentine, and Brazil). Lansing tried to stop such speculation, since it seemed to excite Catholics and encourage the Vatican. He instructed Ambassador Stimson to make public denials in the press and to inform the Brazilian government unofficially that the rumors had "no foundation in fact."[53] Several days later, Sonnino informed Page and Rodd that the pope was planning to make new peace proposals in collaboration with the Central Powers.[54] John Carrol, who was secretary of the U.S. embassy in Rome and who had been received by the pope, believed that it was possible, since the pope expected the Central Powers to ask his services in order to pass on their proposals to Wilson.[55] All this was untrue, however; the pope did not intend to start any peace initiative unless both sides asked him to do so.[56] The German warning still held the Vatican back.

The last several months of 1917 held bitter trials and disappointments for the Vatican in general and the pope in particular. All the Vatican's initiatives were either rejected or ignored. The only ray of hope and consolation came with the crumbling of the Russian Empire. The destiny of Catholics in Eastern Europe (Poland, the Ukraine), the Balkans, and Constantinople seemed assured and opened up the possibility of unifying the Eastern and Western churches and gaining control of Palestine as well. Ultimately, this suggested a possible change in the Vatican stand and made possible closer cooperation with the Allies and United States. Political observers in Rome did not fail to notice this change and report it to their respective governments.

On December 24 the pope greeted the cardinals on the occasion of the Christmas festivities. He advised them that he was "grieved particularly that the invitation addressed by Us to the chiefs of the belligerent peoples had gone unheeded." He could not understand why his peace proposal had been rejected: "We simply called the attention of the heads of the belligerent states to the principal bases of agreement announced by authoritative tribunes with the sole purpose of hastening the hour of fulfillment of the sacred desire in the hearts of all of us; but we found we were either deemed not worthy of a hearing or were not above suspicion or calumny." He promised to continue his pacifist efforts. The Americans in Rome did not think much of the pope's statement. Speranza found it to be a "labored, unspontaneous and defensively framed document." The speech was, in fact, a thinly veiled criticism of both the Allies and the Central Powers.[57]

The speeches of Lloyd George on January 5, 1918, and Wilson on January 8, 1918, were more congenial to the Vatican. It was believed in the Curia that the war aims announced by the British and U.S.

governments contained elements similar, if not identical, to those expressed by the pope on August 1, 1917. Most attractive for the Vatican was the fact that Lloyd George and Wilson did not advocate the dissolution of the Central Powers but did support the limitation of armaments, the creation of an international organization, and the solution of territorial problems (Poland, Alsace-Lorraine, Italian *irredenta*) in a way acceptable to the Holy See.[58]

Lloyd George's speech was received with high praise and benevolent comments. *L'Osservatore* lauded it for its clarity, open-mindedness, and precision and used the opportunity to tell the Allies that their program did not differ much from the pope's.[59] Gasparri told Salis about the "great satisfaction with which he had read the Prime Minister's recent speech respecting the war aims" and ventured to say that it was now for the other side to speak out.[60] On January 8, the Catholic *Giornale d'Italia* published an editorial exploring the analogies between the pope's and Lloyd George's programs. Lloyd George's insistence upon the restoration of Belgium and Serbia and the territories occupied in France, Italy, and Rumania and upon the independence of Poland coincided with the pope's proposals. The sanctity of treaties, the rights of peoples to decide their own destiny, and the creation of an international organization to limit the burden of armaments and to lessen the possibilities of war—all had been included in one form or another, it was emphasized, in the pope's various pronouncements.

On the heels of the prime minister's speech came Wilson's address in Congress. The Vatican press greeted Wilson's address in much the same way it had that of Lloyd George. It published the integral text and found "evident" analogies with the pope's program. It considered Wilson's program to be clear on the "internal questions and the organization of the states," especially on the Habsburg Monarchy and its internal problems.[61] Page informed Lansing that "only [the] clerical and socialist press praise the Note [Wilson's] without reservations," with *L'Osservatore* saying that it "should have appeared in August 1917, as it accords so well with the Pope's note."[62]

On January 11, Page received one of his regular visitors from the Vatican. He was told that Wilson's message was received in the Curia with great satisfaction, but Wilson was mildly reprimanded for making it too late, since the situation had since changed greatly. Wilson should have given his support to the papal note of August 1, 1917. As for renewed papal action, Page was told that the Pact of London made it impossible. The conversation ended, however, with the warning that the programs announced by Lloyd George and Wilson were not practical and realistic at the moment, since they could be "effectuated only if the Allies were on the road to Berlin or Vienna," that is, through victory on the battlefield. Obviously, the Vatican did not believe that the Allies were able to win such a victory. Three days later, Page was informed that Wilson's address was a step toward peace; that is, it "eliminated former statements interpreted to indicate interference in internal affairs of Germany or desire to dismember Austria."[63]

Wilson's address gave the Vatican its chance to move out of the corner it had found itself in since November 1917. A negotiated peace was preferable to the thunder of arms. The Curia was worried about the outcome of the war, especially about the preservation of the Dual Monarchy. It viewed with horror the struggle of the nationalities in the Habsburg Monarchy and throughout Central Europe for national freedom and independence. As the monarchy heartlessly carried on a hopeless war and as various national groups became active there and abroad, dissolution loomed large in Benedict XV's eyes. He was determined to avert dissolution and to prevent the failure of Vatican policy in that part of Europe.[64]

Once again, Vatican diplomacy was about to act. The stakes were definite, and the objectives were clear. On January 8, Gasparri instructed Pacelli to approach Hertling and suggest that the Central Powers, especially Germany, consider favorably the British peace proposals, especially in respect to Belgium. If the Central Powers made a reply to Lloyd George, the Vatican expected Hertling to include some reference to the pope's peace note; if Germany decided to make a counterproposal, it should be done through the Holy See and conveyed to the opposite side.[65] Gasparri advised Hertling that the entire world awaited his reply, which should not shut the door to final negotiations. Pacelli was to inform Hertling that in view of substantial gains in the east, it would be wise if Germany were to make a generous move with respect to Belgium, in the interest of the "entire world and her own."[66] The Vatican appeared to be very generously allowing Germany a free hand in Russia and the territories where the Orthodox church was predominant, but it pleaded for Catholic Belgium.

Hertling's speech was anxiously awaited in the Vatican. Meanwhile, on January 21, 1918, Gasparri granted another interview to Dr. Foa, provided its contents were transmitted to John Bass. In a lengthy monologue, he touched upon several problems. He expressed hope that Hertling's speech would open the way for peace discussions and insisted on the similarity of views held by the Vatican and the Allies. He also continued to press for the abolition of military conscription as the only effective way of limiting armaments. Such abolition, he felt, would make war improbable, if not completely impossible. Gasparri again expressed the Vatican's concern for the Habsburgs, saying that it was a mistake to believe that the Habsburg Empire could be dissolved.[67]

Page was informed of the contents of the interview on January 23. He was scornful and attacked what he considered the sinister dealings of the Vatican in respect to the United States. In a lengthy cable, he argued that the "Vatican is applying all efforts now to make America believe it is in accord with her, but really thinks that the Central Powers have won and that peace will be made within [the] year before America can effectively enter the war." He maintained that the principal idea behind this Vatican policy was to strengthen its position among the belligerents. Page found that the Vatican was patently insincere: "While apparently drawing closer to America and approaching in words the President's ideas about democracy, it [the Vatican] is sincerely in favor of authority, as represented by the Central Empires, and against democracy, American and other."[68] The State Department and the White House remained silent.

Hertling delivered his speech on January 24, 1918. He, like Czernin, discussed the general aspects of Wilson's address. He rejected any idea of returning Alsace-Lorraine to France and was ambiguous about the evacuation of Belgium and the occupied French territories. The question of Russia and Poland was reserved for the consideration of the Central Powers. Czernin, for his part, refused Wilson's suggestion of national self-determination and the possibility of making any concessions to Italy, and he declined to commit his empire to the evacuation of Rumania, Serbia, and Montenegro. He did agree that Poland should be independent.[69] Germany again thwarted the Vatican's hopes. Pacelli was told that the Holy See wrongly interpreted Hertling's speech, that he had actually intended to use "strong words," but not to shut the door to negotiations.[70] Gasparri said only that Hertling's speech did not "accord with the desire of the Holy Father" and expressed hope that the chancellor would be more conciliatory in the future. He encouraged Germany to demand the return of its colonies and repeated that the fragmentation of Russia would bring such political and economic advantages to Germany that it should gracefully make concessions on the other side (Belgium).[71]

The Habsburg Monarchy, however, showed substantial interest in the "American peace." Intellectual and Catholic circles, led by Joseph

Redlich, Heinrich Lammasch, and Ignaz Seipel, became enthusiastic supporters. Both Czernin and Wilson were eager to continue the dialogue, and although papal assistance was not considered, it was suggested to Wilson that the Vatican be used to let Germany know that no communications on peace were forthcoming.[72]

On February 1, 1918, Marchetti approached Hugh Wilson and suggested that the president make some answer to Czernin's speech. A statement by the president would lessen the differences. The pope was ready to help by asking Hertling to change Germany's attitude so that peace could be achieved.[73] The Pope did so, but Hertling did not prove amenable to the proposal. The Allies displayed no less interest and eagerness in beginning negotiations with Austria. Since none of the Allies were intent on the dissolution of the monarchy, it was natural that the Vatican whole-heartedly supported their advances made to Vienna.

On February 3 and 4, 1918, Dr. George Herron, an American professor well acquainted with the problems of Austria-Hungary, met Professor Heinrich Lammasch in a chateau near Bern.[74] Lammasch came to Switzerland with the approval of Emperor Charles in order to establish contacts with Herron. The emperor, Lammasch told Herron, was ready to work for a general peace and, internally, for the reorganization of the monarchy. Although Charles did not mention territorial questions, the proposal was attractive to Wilson, since it coincided with his program of January 8, 1918. Lammasch also asked Herron that Wilson reply to Czernin's speech and admit openly that Austria had announced its readiness to consider peace proposals. After Wilson's statement, Charles would send a letter to the pope describing "without entering into detail" his plan for internal reforms and the basis for a general peace.

Herron believed that Austria-Hungary was not playing Germany's game but felt sure that it was playing the Vatican's game—as he learned that the emperor, encouraged by the pope, was intent on restoring in modernized form the Holy Roman Empire. Lammasch inquired whether the pope might not assume the initiative instead of the emperor. Herron refused, saying that it would create a "lot more complications and difficulties" in predominantly Protestant America.[75] The proposal avoided giving any explicit promise of autonomy to the nationalities of the monarchy, since the emperor was to make this promise to the pope, and even this in principle only. Hugh Wilson had doubts about the feasibility of the emperor's proposal because he did not believe that the emperor would abandon German influences.

The Vatican was indeed behind the emperor's move. On February 4, Gaisford informed the Foreign Office that it would not be "displeasing to him [the Pope] if the British and American governments were to take action with a view of detaching Austria . . . . They might indeed receive some support from him [the Pope] ."[76] On February 11, Wilson addressed Congress again. He praised Czernin and encouraged him to proceed with detaching the Dual Monarchy from Germany. At the same time, Wilson insisted that "self-determination is not a mere phase, but an imperative principle of action," which no statesman should ignore. He also outlined "four principles" for the future peace settlement.[77]

The Vatican's anxiety over the ultimate outcome of the dialogue between Vienna and Washington made Gasparri commit another blunder. On February 9, Page cabled Lansing that he had been visited by his informant, most likely Dr. Foa, who had handed to him a precis of the conversation he had recently had with Gasparri. Page thought the document demonstrated "extraordinary ignorance of America and contains under fine phrases a veiled threat against the President and his policy." Gasparri insisted that

> Peace or war is now in the hands of President Wilson. It depends upon him whether he will cause war to continue until chaos . . . [ensues] . . . in Europe or [will] impose peace on reasonable terms. The Allies could not have resisted through this winter without [the] efficient cooperation of the US, not only from [a] military point of view but, more important from the commercial and economic. I have confidence in Wilson, believe him a superior man, upright [and] honest, and that pressure of public will guide his actions. His attitude has already undergone important modifications since his peace without victory note. He no longer declares for forcible democratization of Germany or dismemberment of Austria-Hungary . . . . Cardinal Gibbons, Msgr. Ireland, [are] too old, and, like Msgrs. Farley and O'Connell [are] unable to detach themselves from [the] atmosphere which influences them. It is not, however, conceivable [that the] great majority in America are disposed to support sacrifices [and] enormous losses of life and property for the triumph of entirely abstract ideas such as the best form of government for Germany or autonomy for Austrian nationalities. [The] first enthusiasm [is] already beginning to wane. [The] election of [a] Catholic and pacifist Mayor of New York is [an] important indication. Catholics in the US are twenty percent of the whole population but sixty percent of the Army . . . . If coming elections of one-third of [the] Senators are favorable to pacifists, this would show [the] true sentiment of [the] population.
>
> Wilson is too honest and constitutional to desire to govern contrary to [the] will of [the] country, even though [the] majority

continues favorable to war. In fact, [the] solution of European problems may come from rectitude and largeness of the President's views, which contrast favorably with the views of men like Sonnino. [The] clause of [the] secret treaty [XV] is an unjust, spiteful policy.[78]

Gasparri obviously held Wilson responsible for the continuation of the war, since the United States was supporting the Allies militarily, economically, and financially. He did not care much for Wilson's principles and "abstract ideas" and their practical application, and decided that the United States' initial enthusiasm for war was waning. A veiled threat lay in Gasparri's remark that Catholics account for sixty percent of the U.S. military forces. If the United States had stayed out of the war, it would have been ended by a negotiated peace; should the war continue, the Vatican predicted the crumbling of Europe's political, economic, and social order and the triumph of those elements that were against everything the Vatican stood for. Wilson and Lansing were dismayed to realize the extent of the Vatican's prejudice and lack of restraint.[79]

Despite Gasparri's unbalanced and erratic views, the Vatican fully supported the idea of detaching Austria from Germany. This revealed the Vatican's hidden feud with Germany for its sinister influence on Austria and its opposition to the pontiff's peace initiatives. After Wilson's speech on February 11, Cerretti assured Gaisford that "Wilson's last speech contained the germ of [an] invitation to Austria to separate from Germany." In replying to Gaisford's inquiry about possible support from the Vatican, Cerretti indicated that it was possible "perhaps indirectly," since the Vatican was aware that Austria would not be "averse to being helped to detach herself from Germany."[80] Father Fay conveyed the same notion to Cardinal Gibbons. "If the President follows what seems to be his policy now of separating Austria from Germany," wrote Fay "the Holy Father will lend whatever aid or assistance he can, though perhaps indirectly." In a letter to Polk, Fay insisted that the "Pope's attitude toward us, especially America, is one of great benevolence."[81] In fact, Fay suggested that the Allies and the United States pay more attention to the pope, as the Germans had done all along.

The campaign to induce the U.S. government to work to detach Austria-Hungary from Germany was carried out by Cardinal Gibbons. The old prelate accepted the task eagerly. On February 24, 1918, he met Lord Reading and discussed with him the position and role of the Vatican in this action. Lord Reading later told House of an "interesting conversation" he had had with Cardinal Gibbons. Pledging House to secrecy,

Reading told him that the "Pope wishes to sit at the peace conference." When Reading suggested that the reason for it was to regain temporal power, Gibbons denied it. When Reading proposed that it was to help Austria, "Gibbons only half-denied this."[82] House and Reading probably did not mention this conversation to Wilson. It was useless, since Wilson did intend to pursue this action and the pope's recommendation would not materially help his decision. Instead, it could have been interpreted as an indication of his cooperation with the Central Powers and the Vatican.

Despite his readiness to help, the pope was not asked to do the job assigned him by Lammasch. Charles's message of February 19, 1918, forwarded to Wilson through the king of Spain, suggested that a general peace on the basis of the status quo be concluded. It dropped the idea of a separate peace and said nothing of satisfying the political aspirations of the nationalities in Austria-Hungary. It hardly touched on territorial problems, except that Italy's claims to Habsburg lands were emphatically rejected. Gasparri did not consider this rejection justified or practical, since the Vatican was supporting irredentist claims.[83] Charles's message was intercepted by British intelligence and two days later was handed to Page, who transmitted it to Washington.[84]

In Washington, discussion of Wilson's next step started immediately. It was agreed to consult the British, who approved of Wilson's sending a reply to the Habsburg Emperor.[85] Wilson reacted promptly, since he seemed sure that his policy of detaching Austria from Germany was succeeding. The Spanish ambassador, Juan Riano, delivered the message at the White House on February 26. Two days later Wilson summoned Riano and handed him the reply to the emperor. The president declined to enter into secret negotiations with Austria-Hungary, since it was the emperor's responsibility to announce the terms. Instead, he raised numerous questions about the attitude of Austria-Hungary toward the Balkans, the national aspirations of the Slavs in the Empire, the Adriatic question, and other matters.[86] The Austrian reply, which was never officially delivered, refused to entertain Wilson's suggestion, and the German government was informed of the exchange of messages as well. Rumors about Austria's peace initiatives continued to reach the State Department until early in April, but Lansing did not seem ready to lend them credence.[87] By then, the difficulties confronting the Vatican were very delicate and substantial; indeed, the Dual Monarchy was collapsing from within.

Late in March, before the Allies launched their long-planned offensive in the west, the pope decided to call for an Easter truce. He hoped that this would lead to the beginning of negotiations for peace. Germany refused, demanding that the Allies act first; the British opposed it as well. On March 19, Lord Reading approached Wilson about the proposal. "The President," wrote Reading, "treated the suggestion as quite out of question before I have even stated your reasons for rejection." The Vatican was informed accordingly. Gasparri did not hide his disappointment with this "new failure of the Holy See," but pointed out that he could not understand the Allies' refusal in view of the situation on the battlefields. He also told the Spanish ambassador that the Allies were more afraid of the "consequences of the peace than of the continuation of the war."[88] In fact, as this episode indicated, the Vatican's and Wilson's efforts to detach Austria from Germany had failed. The pope was ignored in Vienna. This must have been most shocking to the Curia.

The final blow to the policy of separating Austria-Hungary from Germany came with the Czernin-Clemenceau imbroglio in April 1918. On April 2, in an address to the Vienna Municipal Council Czernin pointed out that Clemenceau, before the beginning of the Western offensive, "inquired of me whether, and upon which basis I was ready to negotiate." Since France would not abandon Alsace-Lorraine, negotiations were not possible, concluded Czernin.[89] This statement was not welcomed by Clemenceau, who on April 11 published a letter Emperor Charles had addressed to Raymond Poincaré through Prince Sixtus de Bourbon early in 1917. In it Charles promised to use his influence to exact Germany's consent to return Alsace-Lorraine to France. The net result of this imbroglio was that Czernin resigned, and Emperor Charles promised the Kaiser to fight for Alsace-Lorraine as if it were his own.[90]

The publication of the "Sixtus" letter coincided with the Congress of the Oppressed Nationalities of Austria-Hungary in Rome. The resolutions the congress voted demonstrated the substantial solidarity of the nationalities in their struggle for independence. They were also an open invitation to Wilson and the Allies to work for the dissolution of the empire. This caused great uneasiness and preoccupation at the Vatican. Gasparri very much regretted the publication of what he termed "alleged communications" between the French and Austrian governments. In this he perceived only one problem—imminent danger for Austria-Hungary—and insisted that Austria-Hungary had to be strong as a counterweight to Germany and its penetration toward the south. Naturally "no union of small, weak states would be of any use," since they would all come under the domination of Germany.[91] According to Gasparri, Germany would be a threat to England's interests in the Mediterranean if Austria-

Hungary disappeared as a strong, centralized state. The German threat was used as an argument against the federalization of the empire as well, since the Vatican appeared to have no concern for states such as Czechoslovakia, Yugoslavia, or Hungary. At this point, the Vatican's and Allies' solutions for Austria-Hungary were about to disappear; federalization of the Empire and ultimately its dissolution soon became the goal.

From October 1917 to April 1918, the Vatican approach to peace changed substantially. Most significantly the Curia stopped seeking the approval of only the Central Powers. It began to solicit opinions from the Allies as well. Yet the pope and Gasparri continued to nourish grandiose schemes; they fought tirelessly to secure for the Vatican the right to act for peace, invite the belligerents to negotiate, use its good offices, and make its own proposals. Both belligerent groups worked to prevent the Vatican from accomplishing its goals. They kept for themselves the right to practice the "old diplomacy," and denied that right to the Vatican. Germany forced the pope to withdraw from acting for a general peace, and the Vatican abided by this arbitrary ruling and remained aloof. The Allies applied the same pressure and discouraged the pope more gently.

On several occasions, the Vatican expressed its views and proposals on disarmament, insisting on the abolition of compulsory military service and permanent armies. Both sides, however, were cool to this proposal—announced in the midst of the war.

Russia's withdrawal from the war brought about a long-expected shift of Vatican policy away from the Central Powers and toward the Allies and America, a shift that was encouraged by Germany's rude treatment of the Curia. The publication of the Pact of London suddenly interrupted the brief lull. This came as a shock to the Curia, but it was cleverly exploited to justify the Vatican's withdrawal from the stage.

The Vatican used this retreat to clear the ground for solving peripheral, yet important, international questions—such as the arrangement between Italy and Austria-Hungary, Belgium, and others. Germany's domination of the Central bloc made the Vatican realize that the Hohenzollern Empire had dug the grave for the Habsburg Monarchy. For this reason, the major task of Vatican diplomacy was to persuade Austria-Hungary to break away from Germany. The pope offered full support to the United States and Britain and was ready to play the role of intermediary between Vienna and Washington, but with no success. Opposition toward Germany had assumed such proportions that the Vatican came to plead for the preservation of Austria-Hungary as a bulwark against Germany's penetration to the south.

By the fall of 1917, the list of the Vatican's grievances against the Allies, especially Italy, had been completed. On November 15, 1917, the Soviet newpaper *Izvestiia* published what purported to be the text of the Pact of London. Article XV of the pact, as it appeared in *Izvestiia,* showed clearly that the Allies intended to limit the Holy See's diplomatic activities in behalf of peace and confirmed that the Allies were suspicious of the Vatican. The inaccurate and incomplete text of the article stirred up great controversy in the press and in public and political circles, and it exposed the Allies to criticism of their political designs and practices.

From the beginning of the war, the Vatican had shown great interest in securing a place at the peace congress. The Italian government, however, decided that the pope's ambition ran counter to its own plans; it feared that the Vatican would bring about a reexamination of the Roman question as it had been settled by the Law of Guarantees of 1871. Thus, Article XV barred the Holy See from the peace conference and from making peace proposals. It was inserted in the text of the pact, and the Allies accepted it without opposition. Sonnino's pronounced anti-clericalism was an important factor in opposing Vatican political movements.[1] There was also a growing fear that the Vatican might protect Austria-Hungary and thereby deprive Italy of the spoils of war. Such fears seemed plausible because the Vatican had kept the issue of its participation at the peace conference alive throughout the war. It had hoped to induce both belligerent groups to accede to its pretensions, and it was encouraged in this hope by the Central Powers.[2]

The Vatican's ambition of securing a seat at a peace conference reinforced for all concerned the idea that it was intent on reestablishing the temporal power of the pope. The Vatican protested the limitations imposed upon its activities after Italy entered the war, complaining that its spiritual duties and political interests were hampered and that the pope's prerogatives were curtailed. For this reason, it declared, the Vatican expected the European powers to ensure the normal performance of its duties. In order to effect this, Gasparri in August 1915 advised nuncios abroad that the Holy See expected Catholic and non-Catholic states to consider the "abnormal situation of the Holy See and provide for its independence, authority, and divine mission." He instructed them to work actively to keep public opinion abreast of events and the respective governments aware of the position of the papacy. In principle, Gasparri believed that the Vatican ought to enjoy territorial sovereignty, but rejected the idea of achieving these demands through military intervention.[3] The Central Powers, however, used the Roman question as an excuse to retaliate against the Italian government, thus making the pope's situation worse and Italy's resistance more determined.

Article XV of the London treaty read that *"France, Great Britain, and Russia shall support such opposition as Italy may make to any proposal in the direction of introducing a representative of the Holy See in any peace negotiations or negotiations for the settlement of questions raised by the present war."* As worded, the article completely shackled Vatican efforts to settle any question, whatsoever, regardless of its merits. By the fall of 1915, the Vatican was fairly certain that its presence at the peace conference was not desirable and that the Roman question would not be raised at such a conference. This greatly disturbed the Vatican hierarchy, but it could do nothing to change the situation, at least for the time being.[4] Relations between Italy and the Vatican were tense, and the Allies, troubled by the ultimate outcome of their commitment, were also aware of the Vatican's hostility toward them.

The Vatican had entertained great hopes that Wilson and the United States would alleviate its troubles. Wilson was not obligated by the secret treaty, and it was believed that he would help the Vatican shed its shackles. He seemed to be a natural ally in the struggle against the "old diplomacy," and the millions of Catholics in the United States would certainly have brought the Vatican's demands to his attention. The United States knew about the existence of Article XV before the secret treaty was published in Russia,[5] but its reaction was not marked. Early in January 1917, the State Department was informed that the Curia knew that Italy had "guarantees from England and France that the Vatican would not be represented in the peace negotiations."[6] Again, no reaction was forthcoming. After the United States entered the war, Wilson and Balfour discussed the secret treaties in general, and Wilson received a copy of the pact with Italy. Although he did not seem to have paid much attention to Article XV, he must have learned of the Allies' intention to bar the Holy See from participating in any peace effort as well as from the peace conference itself.[7] He probably approved of this article privately, since he could see no reason for the pope to be represented at the peace conference.

By the fall of 1917, the essential features of the Pact of London were publicly known in the United States.[8] The press campaign started late in November, but the general public seemed little concerned. The administration did not pay much attention to the pact either, assuming that it could not be blamed for something that had happened without its knowledge and approval. The Catholic press, however, was most vociferous. Spring-Rice, realizing that Catholic agitation might hurt British interests, scrutinized the Catholic newspapers carefully and found that the existence of the "agreement [Pact of London] has done the Allies a good deal of harm." He did not believe, however, that the pope's participation at a peace conference would be popular in the United States. Other religious denominations would feel aggrieved at the privilege granted to the Holy See. Most Americans would object to a public acknowledgment of a spiritual sovereign's political rights. In view of this, Spring-Rice did not expect public demands for the pope's participation and hoped that it "should not be mooted officially."[9] The U.S. government acted as Spring-Rice expected and chose not to make its views about the document public. The Vatican thereupon decided to concentrate its efforts, for the time being, in Europe and to induce the British government to exert pressure upon Sonnino to modify Article XV or drop it completely.

Page at first merely observed the clash between the Vatican and the Italian government, notably Sonnino. The information he kept sending to Washington was contradictory and frequently confusing, since it came from different sources. In December 1917, Page was advised that Sonnino was trying to secure some rapprochement with the Holy See in order to avoid a direct attack on the government and eventual political crisis. This, of course, was not true.[10] Early in January 1918, after Sonnino and Lord Cecil delivered contradictory statements in their parliaments about the nature of Article XV and after they were fiercely attacked in the Catholic press, Page reported that the Vatican was seeking help among the Central Powers. The Holy See allegedly was about to ask Germany and Austria-Hungary to place before the peace conference the question of the internationalization of the pope's relations with Italy.[11] It considered Article XV highly insulting to the Vatican, contrary to the mission of the Holy Father, and opposed to the provisions of the Law of Guarantees. The Vatican justifiably interpreted its peace efforts not as political, but as spiritual, activities.

However, Page was not to remain just an observer in the clash between the Vatican and Sonnino. By the middle of January 1918, the Holy See had decided to intensify its efforts in the United States and to demand that Wilson support its fight for the revision of Article XV. Gasparri and others in the Curia did everything to compromise the Allies and their war aims by making appeals to Wilson's lofty principles and idealism. On January 21, 1918, Gasparri explained to Dr. Foa that the Vatican knew of the secret pact of 1915 for the division of enemy territories not yet conquered. To him, this document proved that it was "impossible to draw a line of distinction between the war aims of the Entente and those of the Central Empires." Both groups, Gasparri maintained, exhibited the same ambitions and lust for conquest, the only difference being that the Allies masked their aims under a "program which made them appear that they were struggling in defense of liberty for the rights of oppressed peoples and democratic principles." Since the division of spoils was based on the fact that it related to territories still unconquered, he insisted that some of the signatory powers must have had an *arrière-pensée* by which such treaties were to be considered "scraps of paper."[12] Gasparri thus appealed for the reconsideration or complete abolishment of Article XV, but his plea fell on deaf ears and was left unanswered.

A few days later, Dr. Foa informed Speranza that the Vatican intended to publish the secret treaties and certain unpublished parliamentary debates "showing that some of the men at the government in such countries have not been above telling lies." It was considered giving helpful aid to the Central Powers and trying to discredit the British and the Italian governments. Gasparri obviously waged an all-out war against Sonnino in order to get him ousted from office. He asked Wilson's help in this respect, since he was aware of the president's lack of sympathy for secret arrangements. If successful, the Vatican, together with Wilson, would appear before the rest of the world as a defender of justice and the "new diplomacy."

Gasparri succeeded to some extent.[13] Sonnino was much embarrassed by the publication of the Pact of London. When approached, he even refused to discuss it. He told Page that Article XV was not correct and had been substantially changed, but he would not specify what had been changed.[14] Several days later, Gasparri conveyed to Page his belief that the "clause of the secret treaty [Article XV] is an unjust, spiteful policy," further embarrassing Sonnino. The Italian minister held out against these attacks and accusations. He received a kind of support even from the Americans. Wilson and Lansing, despite all invitations to act against the secret treaty, refused to commit themselves and announce openly their position in respect to the Vatican's protests.

By the end of January 1918, the Vatican had stepped up its efforts. On January 22, Gasparri received Father Fay and inquired about the reaction of U.S. Catholics to Article XV. He told Fay that the Holy See wanted the article dropped and that it also wanted to be represented at the peace conference. He also suggested that Catholics in the Allied countries, including the United States, might work for that goal. The Vatican evidently expected Cardinal Gibbons's assistance in this drive, since Gasparri asked whether the cardinal might induce Wilson to advise the British government that it should drop the clause. Gasparri believed that this could be done if Gibbons and Cardinal Mercier of Malines would protest the exclusion of the pope from the peace conference as the war was approaching its end. Fay pointed out that U.S. Catholics were much annoyed with Article XV but commented that it would be difficult for Gibbons to approach Wilson; he suggested that the U.S. government should not be asked to demand abolition of the article. Instead, he proposed that this be done through the Foreign Office.[15] On February 11, Fay was received by the pope, encountering much the same questions he had discussed with Gasparri earlier. The pope expressed his belief that Gibbons and Mercier would secure the Holy See a place at the peace table, provided they lodge a protest with the British government. He asked Fay to go to London as soon as his work for the Red Cross was finished.[16]

The British were very unhappy with this turn of affairs. They did not want to take the brunt of responsibility for Article XV in the United States. They were willing to see the article dropped but would not insist on the rejection of the secret treaty in order to get Italy to let the clause pass into desuetude. The British government, for that matter, was against papal representation at the peace conference. Before the Foreign Office had time to react to this new situation, however, Gibbons approached Ambassador Reading in Washington on February 24 with regard to the problem. He submitted a lengthy memorandum explaining why Article XV should be dropped.[17] After listening to Gibbons's arguments, Reading declared that rescinding Article XV was not the right way to handle the question, although he did state that some action was necessary in order to avoid such a policy concerning the pope in the future. He added that there was concern that the pope, during a peace conference, would favor the Central Powers because of his regard for Austria-Hungary and would work for the restoration of his temporal power. He promised to send Gibbons's demands to London for consideration.[18]

Early in March 1918, Balfour informed Reading that Cecil had explained in the House of Commons on February 14 that the British government was not bound to any policy that would disregard any efforts the pope might make in the future. It was added that the Vatican had raised this question as well.[19] Gibbons was informed about this, and Reading was advised that nothing could be done about Article XV, since it established that only the belligerent states be allowed to attend the peace conference. On March 11, Balfour advised Reading about the origin of the article, adding that it was not fair that Great Britain should be blamed for it in the United States. The article, as such, was not justified, as it was "worded with singular infelicity, and which I should gladly see eliminated or profoundly modified." According to Balfour, however, the initiative for modification had to come from the Italian government, and Gibbons and Lansing should be so informed. At the end of his message, Balfour warned that any open protest on the part of the U.S. bishops or any action on the part of the U.S. government would have undesirable consequences. The next day Reading told Polk in detail about his interview with Gibbons and showed him Balfour's message. Polk noted only that "we discussed the treaty between Italy and other powers," but refrained from defining U.S. opinion concerning it.[20] Balfour's views seemed to be in accord with those of the State Department, and Polk quickly acquiesced in Reading's stand.

In the meantime, Sonnino declared in the Italian Chamber on February 16, 1918, that the Italian government honored its obligations and the Law of Guarantees with the Holy See but refused any suggestion for the internationalization of its position. He came close to Cecil in saying that Article XV meant that Italy had the right to consider whether any non-belligerent state, including the Vatican, could participate at the peace conference. In private, however, Sonnino accused the Holy See of playing the United States off against the Allies in this question. He found that it was, in reality, a "part of the game which was being played," a game the Holy See would continue in the belief that with the United States there was a "better prospect of arriving at a compromise, and possibly this attitude was the result of an understanding with Germany."[21] Sonnino was extremely sensitive about U.S. reactions to the Vatican's demand, since he was sensitive to everything relative to the secret treaty. His fears, however, were groundless: the U.S. government showed little interest in the question.

By this time, the Vatican knew that the Allies were suspicious about its real motives for participation at the peace conference. Gasparri hastened to explain the Vatican position and to define its ambitions. He denied that the Holy See was striving hard to be represented at the peace conference, although he did admit that, if invited, it would send a delegate. But papal representative's instructions would be limited; the Vatican would try only to bring about a peace that would preclude the possibility of another war. "The Roman question," declared Gasparri, "being foreign to the causes and events of the present conflict would not be raised by him."[22] Gasparri did not explain, except in very general terms, why the Holy See should be represented at the conference. The Vatican had obviously decided that in order to secure access to the conference, it was best to keep to generalities. There is no way of knowing whether such a lofty pretension might have helped the Holy See to get a seat at the conference or how sincere Gasparri's statement had been.

Cardinal Gibbons realized that the British government did not intend to help the Vatican's representative get admitted to the peace congress. He informed Gasparri of this, at the same time promising to continue his activities in the United States in order to further the Vatican's wishes in this respect. Numerous letters exchanged among the Curia, Gibbons, and the British government during March and April 1918 confirm this. Since the Italian government insisted that the text of Article XV should not be published, the Vatican decided to change its tactics.

On March 16, 1918, in London, the Italian and British prime ministers and their associates debated the question of Article XV. The U.S. embassy in Paris was informed about it, but no changes in the Italian attitude were evident.[23] Several days later, State Department officials discussed the necessity of defining the attitude of the U.S. government toward secret treaties and the public debate about them. In a letter to Representative J.T. Hefflin, Polk insisted that the U.S. government had not officially been informed by the Allies of secret treaties concluded before the United States' entrance into the war and therefore did not care to discuss their merits. He admitted that the department knew of their existence, but insisted that it was not concerned with their provisions.[24] At the same time, Wilson and Lansing agreed that sensitive political negotiations and treaty making ought to be carried out in secret, provided that final agreements were not concealed from the public.[25] This was somewhat peculiar support for secret diplomacy, even though Wilson was officially opposed to the "old diplomacy."

On March 28, 1918, the Foreign Office instructed Rodd to approach Sonnino and explain to him that Article XV was creating numerous difficulties in the United States and Ireland and was being used as a means of propaganda against Great Britain. Rodd was to tell Sonnino that the article as such was "invidious and unnecessary" and should be eliminated. But Sonnino absolutely refused to alter his stand. He admitted that the Vatican had used Article XV in political propaganda against the Allies but maintained that the article was really very innocuous. However, if the article were dropped, he argued, it would open the Vatican's way to the peace conference and allow it to make other, more specific demands.[26] The British government could do nothing to change Sonnino's stand on this question.

During the spring of 1918, the Vatican worked hard to have its position vis-à-vis Italy modified and the Law of Guarantees internationalized. On April 19, Rumbold informed the Foreign Office that the nuncio in Switzerland, Luigi Maglione, had told the French minister that the Vatican had its "war aims." These amounted to the restoration of the pope's temporal power and the acquisition of sovereignty over a district in Rome or a territory the size of San Marino; the Holy See, it was believed, should be completely independent from the Italian kingdom.[27] The next day, Gasparri cabled to Monsignor Ogno, secretary of the nunciature in Brussels, a part of the letter received from Cardinal Bourne to be transmitted to Cardinal Mercier. Bourne informed Gasparri that he had been received by King George V, on which occasion they had discussed the problem of the "independence of the Pope." King George allegedly promised to talk about it with the Italian king, Victor Emmanuel III, and expressed his desire to work for some sort of settlement.[28] Suggestions of this sort, however, were not very attractive to the Allies. At the same time, they made the Vatican vulnerable to charges of plotting with the Central Powers in order to restore its temporal authority.

Early in February 1918, Gasparri suggested to Cardinal Gibbons that a collective protest of the U.S. Catholic hierarchy against Article XV would be helpful. The idea was not congenial to Gibbons; he feared that such a protest would lead to counterprotests and would bring about a clash of opinions, which would be most undesirable during a war. In April, Gasparri toyed with this idea again, despite Gibbons's opposition. He seized on this point in Gibbons's letter to Balfour on March 6 and demanded of the British government that Article XV be abolished. In a letter to Salis, Gasparri alluded to the possibility of joint action with the U.S. bishops but claimed that Gibbons and other prelates were acting in this matter on their "own responsibility." He also defined Article XV as an "insult public and grave." Since it insults the "Father it also offends the children," and the bishops of all countries, Gasparri insisted, had a duty to protect the dignity of the Holy Father.[29] This was a sort of veiled threat in case the Allies decided not to heed the Vatican's demands. When Maria L. Storer approached Bishop Shahan of Catholic University and proposed that the U.S. hierarchy appeal collectively to Wilson to help the pope get his representative into the peace conference, Gibbons reacted energetically. He refused the suggestion as most impolitic and damaging to the Catholic church.[30] Obviously, he disagreed with the tactics used, and the pressure exerted, by Gasparri. He was not impressed with the worldly, political ambitions of the Curia, since he was most concerned with the effects of such a policy in the United States.

Gibbons's refusal to act in accord with Vatican desires did not deter the Vatican from using the church hierarchy in other countries. Late in May 1918, Cardinal Mercier was coordinating with the pope and Gasparri his action with the British government. Actually, early in May Mercier had forwarded to the pope a draft of his letter to be sent to Balfour. Three weeks later, Gasparri instructed Achille Locatelli, nuncio in Brussels, to inform Mercier that the "Holy Father was satisifed with the contents of the letter which should be forwarded to Balfour at once."[31] In his letter of June 2, Mercier informed Balfour that "Article XV made Catholics rebel against it." The provision barring the Holy See from the peace conference was an insult to the moral prestige of the pope and the piety of millions of Catholics fighting for the Allied cause. Since he was now sure that Article XV indeed existed, Mercier demanded that Balfour clear the matter up and exert pressure on the Allies, actually Italy, to change it. He also warned that new protests were forthcoming.[32]

The British were disturbed. The Foreign Office asked Rodd to approach Sonnino again, but it was to no avail. The Italian minister refused to consider altering Article XV and accused the Vatican of using Mercier to act as its cat's-paw. Late in June, Balfour replied to Mercier. He denied that the British government was responsible for Article XV and informed the cardinal that it could not alter it unilaterally. Finally, he warned the Belgian prelate that any public protest by the Catholic hierarchy would "militate seriously against the attainment of this object" and would create bad impressions among the Allies.[33]

Balfour's warning came too late to be effective, however. Early in June, protests from the heads of the Catholic hierarchy all over the British Empire began to pour in. The archbishops of Sidney (Kelly), Canada (Bequin), and New Zealand (Redwood) protested on behalf of their dioceses against Article XV and demanded its abrogation. Foreign Office personnel rightly believed that the Vatican stood behind this campaign.[34]

Gibbons was conspicuously absent from the protest to the British. Obviously, Gasparri was waiting to see the effect of the protests coming from Australia, Canada, and New Zealand before asking Gibbons to act. After the Curia realized that these protests would not produce any results, Gasparri demanded that Gibbons act. On June 18, he advised Gibbons that Cardinals Mercier and Dubois of Rouen had already forwarded their protests to the Allied governments. He proposed to Gibbons that the U.S. hierarchy do likewise. He also suggested that Gibbons see Wilson and tell him how insulting the Article XV was to the Holy See, to the Catholic hierarchy, and to Catholics in general. It was believed in the Curia that Article XV would be abrogated or modified only if Wilson asked Sonnino to do so. "Only the President of the United States," wrote Gasparri, "can say a friendly and at the same time efficacious word to the Italian government."[35] Gibbons, caught in the middle, felt uneasy. He promised to do it but pointed out several reasons why it should not be done. He especially insisted upon the impropriety of Wilson's dabbling in Italian internal affairs.

Despite these setbacks, the Vatican persisted. Early in July, Gasparri demanded that the Belgian government work with the British government to correct this anomalous situation. On July 20, he demanded revision of Article XV in such a way that no neutral state could participate at the peace conference except with the written consent of the powers. That is, he actually agreed upon the formula provided by the British. The Belgian government accepted the suggestion and on July 24 instructed its ambassador in London to act to that effect. The British were receptive. Sonnino was informed about the Vatican's proposal. On July 30, Gasparri cabled Bonzano about the proposed action and asked him to tell Gibbons that a word from Wilson to the Italian government would accomplish the purpose. Gibbons was asked to approach Wilson. But the cardinal from Baltimore defied the Vatican again; he did not see Wilson and advised Gasparri that for internal and external reasons the president would not be able to follow the Vatican's suggestion.[36]

The Italian government watched the Vatican's action with Belgium carefully. Sonnino was informed that Gasparri sought, through Gibbons, to secure Wilson's approval for his proposal. On August 2, Sonnino instructed Di Cellere to prevent any such proposal from being accepted, while pretending to be unaware of the Vatican's efforts.[37] Di Cellere used this opportunity to clear up the matter with the State Department. On August 7 he talked with Polk about whether the Vatican should be represented at the peace conference. He asked Polk, in view of Article XV and the recent action of the Vatican, what the U.S. attitude would be. "I told him I could not express the attitude of the government," wrote Polk, "but personally I felt the only parties represented at the peace conference would be the actual belligerents and not neutrals."[38] A week later Lansing confirmed Polk's statement, adding that he could not see any justification for the Vatican's participation at the conference and that it was hard for him to believe that the Vatican was working to gain a seat at the conference. He assumed, however, that the Vatican wanted to restore the temporal power of the pope and preserve the Habsburg Monarchy.[39]

In the summer of 1918, the Vatican made other moves to enhance its international standing and its chances of being accepted at the peace conference. In May 1918, the Austrian and German governments demanded that the Holy See prevent their subjects living in China from being deported to Australia. Gasparri eagerly accepted this task and instructed Bonzano to ask the U.S. government to do something about the situation.[40] At the same time, the Vatican established diplomatic relations with Portugal and decided to send a nuncio to China. The Allies' reactions to these moves were sweepingly hostile. They pressed the Chinese government to withdraw the agreement given to the Vatican, since it was believed to be directed against France, which was considered the protector of Catholics in China, and also to be a breach of the treaty between the two states. Since Nuncio Petrelli was suspected of having connections with Germany, Bonzano was instructed to inquire whether he would be acceptable to the U.S. government.[41] Di Cellere told Breckinridge Long, the third assistant secretary of state, that it was one of the numerous moves the Holy See had made in order to gain a place at the peace conference. "The Vatican could not expect any help at the peace conference," warned Di Cellere, "because the objects of the Allies were the direct antithesis of the autocratic ambitions of the Central Powers and the Vatican."[42] The U.S. government persuaded the Chinese government to change its decision about establishing diplomatic relations with the Vatican during the war. It thwarted the Holy See's designs in the same way as the Allies did.

U.S. cooperation in this particular question induced Di Cellere to try to work out a formal commitment, one that would bind the U.S. government to support a policy of excluding the Vatican from the peace conference. Di Cellere, though expressing his understanding for the delicate position of the U.S. government with regard to the large U.S. Catholic population, offered to reveal information about the relations between the Vatican and Germany.[43] The State Department seemed interested in the offer. On August 17, Long asked Di Cellere to present evidence of the Vatican's inclination to aid Germany and Austria-Hungary and of the Vatican's activities in league with these powers. These had to be imparted confidentially and informally, however. In order to capitalize on this opportunity, Di Cellere inquired whether the U.S. government might *"consider joining in a secret expression with Italy as regards their respective attitudes toward the Vatican's peace table and postwar ambitions."* But Long refused to commit the State Department to anything specific. Instead, he explained, he was ready to receive "as a war measure" any facts that the Italian government might come to impart. "There was no thought of entering into an agreement with Italy in regard to our attitudes to the Vatican; we do not even care to consider or to receive any such proposal," insisted Long. He told Di Cellere that the attitude of the U.S. government toward the representation of the Vatican at the peace conference had not been defined. He confirmed Polk's view, however, that there would seem no reason to warrant the belief that any but national interests should be represented there. Finally, Long insisted that in regard to postwar ambitions of the Holy See, there was "no desire on the part of this government to limit the spiritual power of the Vatican or to interfere with its authority."[44]

Long clearly defined the U.S. stand about the secret treaty in general and Article XV in particular. The pope's representative was not welcome at the conference, since only the belligerents were to attend. However, the Vatican was free to perform its spiritual duties, but not to get involved in temporal affairs. The State Department wanted to gain information about the Vatican's cooperation with the Central Powers in order to combat any influence exerted in their behalf. In fact, this solution was satisfactory for the Italian ambassador, since he must have been aware that the Americans were not willing to go further. Di Cellere jubilantly cabled Sonnino that the Vatican's efforts in the United States to secure a seat at the peace conference had come to nothing: "We do not need to be worried in this regard, since the convictions, attitudes, and program of this [U.S.] government are and will be in a complete discord with the aspirations and tendencies of the Vatican."[45] For all practical purposes, the question was solved in a manner contrary to the Vatican's desires and expectations.

Several weeks before the war came to an end, the Vatican made yet another effort to change its position vis-à-vis Italy. In October 1918, Cardinal Bourne suggested that the Law of Guarantees be internationalized. Gibbons was not enthusiastic and delayed taking a stand until the war was over. On November 9, Page was approached by one U.S. monsignor from the Curia suggesting the same action. He told Page that the pope no longer thought of the restoration of his temporal power, but indicated that "internationalization of the Holy See is naturally desired." Since Archbishop Cerretti was about to leave for the United States to represent the pope at the celebration of the fiftieth anniversary of Gibbons's promotion to bishop, Page believed that Cerretti would work toward this while in the United States.[46] Rodd had the same information, including the proposal that the Holy See should have sovereignty over the Vatican and the immediate neighborhood, together with a strip of territory connecting it with the sea.[47] But nobody seemed to pay any attention to the Vatican's proposals. The jubilant victors refused to be bothered with the Vatican's pretensions and presumed grievances. As the war ended, the Vatican's chances of being present at the peace conference remained slim, indeed.

The efforts made by the Holy See during 1918 to induce the Allies and the United States to revise Article XV of the Pact of London of 1915 had much broader implications than was generally assumed. The Vatican desired not only the abrogation of Article XV, letting it fall into desuetude or altering its contents. Although it claimed that Article XV prevented it from working for peace, this was not so. It was active in this respect throughout the war, and no Allied Power could or would stop it. In this respect, certainly, Article XV was not enforced by the Allies, including Italy—as the Vatican was well aware. The Vatican aspired to something different. Its ambition was to participate in a peace conference and directly influence the postwar settlement in Europe. But the belligerents, especially the victors, were not yet ready to acknowledge this pretension. Despite all its efforts, the Curia proved to be politically weak and unable to exert sufficient pressure upon the Allies and the United States to get them to accept its ideas and proposals. This very fact, as well as its isolation and disfavor with the victors, determined the policy of the Holy See and its rapprochement with France and Italy during the 1920s.

The end of the war found the Holy See politically disoriented at the same time as its basic principles and political views were being seriously questioned. Its conservatism and adherence to the concept of the universality and supranationality of Catholic dogma were in sharp contrast with triumphant nationalism. The Vatican oligarchy realized this and looked for ways and means to get rid of this stigma. Insistence upon the restoration of the temporal power was thought to be a solution; an effort to alter the Law of Guarantees was deemed to be another possibility. The Vatican sensed the danger inherent in its isolation and lack of adequate protection. Its old protector, Austria-Hungary, was cracking under internal and external pressures. All these thoughts and preoccupations would have not been necessary had the old European political system remained intact.

The Allies, including the United States, refused to respond favorably to the Vatican's demands. They agreed that the pope should have nothing to do in the domain of temporal affairs and politics. They believed that the pontiff was a spiritual leader of Catholics all over the world whose duties should not be interfered with. The Americans particularly insisted upon this. They thought that the pope's activities for peace were only a part of his broader spiritual duties and humanitarian concern and they used this argument to defend their stringent views on changing the Italian-Vatican relationship. To many people, this may have seemed a false and conservative position—in view of the radical changes that resulted from the world war.

If this was the normal reaction among the European states, the Vatican had hoped that Wilson and the United States, posing as fighters for the new international order, would be more cooperative. It believed that the United States was its natural ally in the struggle against the secret treaty. Wilson, however, did not meet the Vatican's expectations. He refused to condemn Allied secret diplomacy openly or to allign himself with the Holy See. The Vatican, obviously, would have leaned heavily toward his side in this fight. Strangely enough, Wilson enjoyed, in this respect, the full support of Cardinal Gibbons. The old prelate, contrary to Vatican expectations and promptings, did not want to politicize the Catholic masses in the United States in order to help the pope realize his temporal ambitions. The Vatican was not able to induce the U.S. Catholic hierarchy, as he had done in Europe, to petition the administration in regard to Article XV.

CHAPTER 9
THE AMERICAN REPRESENTATION
TO THE HOLY SEE

The need to reestablish diplomatic relations between the United States and the Vatican was voiced frequently during the war. It almost regularly came to the surface in times of crisis, when it was assumed that the Vatican might be able to stop an undesirable turn of events, ease the pressure, and help solve certain sensitive problems in the United States and Great Britain. The British government supported the proposal expecting, through the pope's cooperation, to make the Irish and Catholics in general in the United States and elsewhere less restive about certain war measures or to induce them to cooperate in carrying out war efforts. The Vatican also helped present this action as necessary for all concerned. The Vatican hierarchy wanted to make the Allies and the United States more amenable to its proposals and less insistent on a radical settlement of national problems in the Habsburg Monarchy; it also wanted to assure itself a seat at the peace conference. The internationalization of the Law of Guarantees loomed large behind this effort, since the reestablishment of diplomatic relations with the United States would be a significant step in this direction.

In official circles in the United States, the idea of having an ordinary diplomatic representative at the Holy See received little attention, even though Catholics gave it almost unanimous approval. Instead, the State Department and the liberal Catholic hierarchy around Cardinal Gibbons preferred to have merely an unofficial observer in the Vatican. The State Department expected the Vatican to make radical Catholics less critical and more restrained in their attacks on the administration. Cardinal Gibbons, for his part, wanted his voice to be heard in the Curia. He believed that certain actions of the Holy See demonstrated an ignorance of the situation in the United States and gave support to those Catholic groups that did not support administration policies. Since hopes and ambitions ran high, it was no wonder that the idea of reestablishing diplomatic relations was revived on several occasions and, indeed, was pushed to the very end.

The appointment of an official U.S. mission to the Vatican did not stand a chance from the beginning. Diplomatic relations between the United States and the Holy See had been broken in 1868, when Congress refused to vote the appropriations necessary to maintain the legation in the Vatican. The U.S. government and public opinion objected to the pontiff's pretensions to temporal power and supported the limitation of his prerogatives to the spiritual sphere. By supporting the movement for Italian unification, Americans gradually came to believe that papal authority ought to be limited to Rome and its immediate vicinity. They tended to feel that the temporal power of the pope was not in accord with modern times, was causing international tensions and disputes, was slowing down Italy's unification, and was responsible for the backwardness—political, social, and economic—of those parts of the Apennine peninsula controlled by papal administrators. The pope's *Syllabus* of 1864 and the doctrine of papal infallibility in 1870 made Americans even more suspicious of the Vatican. Finally, there was a widespread belief that a democratic republic such as the United States should have nothing to do with the Vatican, whose basic tenets were considered to be contrary to all the ideals the United States was supporting.[1]

Until the beginning of the world war, no change of policy or belief concerning the Vatican became apparent in the United States. Notions about the need to reestablish diplomatic relations between the Vatican and the United States did not change either. Those who eventually entertained the idea saw it as a practical necessity created by the war. The administration was fully aware of the potential dangers. The State Department and the White House reacted reluctantly and seemed much embarrassed when the pope, inadvertently or otherwise, appealed to them directly with proposals and demanded action. Wilson's upbringing and attitudes only strengthened his belief that contact with the Vatican should be avoided whenever possible. Members of his cabinet largely shared this opinion. Besides, Wilson was incensed at the Vatican because of his clashes with the Catholic hierarchy over the administration's Mexican policy.

During the early months of the war, the idea of sending a U.S. mission to the Vatican came to the fore. It was assumed in Europe and the United States that the pope and Wilson should join forces and exert their influence in order to get the belligerents to consider the idea of a negotiated peace. The Italian as well as the Vatican press published news and editorials to that effect. For more successful cooperation in carrying out efforts at mediation, it was argued, the dispatch of an envoy extraordinary and minister plenipotentiary was to be expected. Another pretext for sending a U.S. representative to the Vatican was to congratulate Benedict XV on his accession to the throne of St. Peter's.

But the various obstacles and objections were substantial. Ambassador Page was quite agitated and did everything he could to forestall any U.S.

mission to the Vatican. Early in January 1915, he warned Wilson and Secretary Bryan against it because the whole problem was fraught with potential dangers and risks. Page's arguments to dissuade the U.S. government from considering this proposal varied. First of all, he warned that it was well known that the Vatican desired to be "represented independently in an international congress . . . which will close up the present war, and it will lead to the internationalization of its concordat with the Quirinal." This Page saw as an exceedingly delicate and complicated problem—on account of Italy's firm opposition to the internationalization of the Roman question. If the proposal were accepted and the United States decided to appoint a minister to the Holy See, it would be considered a victory for the Vatican and a step toward the internationalization of its position in regard to Italy. Although the Italian government could not oppose the appointment of a U.S. minister to the Vatican, Page warned that it "will oppose determinedly any step looking to internationalization referred to."[2]

At this time, the British did not seem to be interested in the matter. The British mission, headed by Sir Henry Howard, arrived in Rome at the end of December 1914. The British government, aware of the opposition of the Italian government, did not want to press the matter, in view of pending negotiations for Italy's entrance into the war. British support for the sending of a U.S. envoy to the Vatican would have been detrimental to further negotiations with the Italians. Since the Italian government insisted upon the exclusion of the pope from a future peace conference, the British attitude was correct. Confronted with Page's telegrams, the U.S. government stayed back and fully supported Italy's contention about limiting the Vatican's activities in international affairs. Thus, Wilson and Bryan declared their opposition to the internationalization of the Roman question and to the pope's participation in the future peace congress. Bryan passed Page's telegram on to Wilson, who composed the reply that was to be sent back to Rome. "If it should become necessary," he stated, "to speak of the matter in official circles, you are authorized to say confidentially that the President would not think of acting upon such suggestions as are indicated unless and until he had ascertained whether such an action would be acceptable to the Italian government."[3] Thus, the pope's initial move failed because Italy, Great Britain, and the United States were either hostile or reluctant to respond favorably to the suggestion.

The Vatican by no means abandoned the proposal. Nor did agitation subside in the press. When in January 1915 Wilson decided that House should go to Europe and press for peace, Page wanted to resolve this problem with the "Colonel" once and for all. On February 6, 1915, House arrived in London, where he received Page's letter containing new arguments as to why the United States should not be represented at the Vatican. Page believed that such an appointment would cause great commotion in the United States itself and would stimulate attacks against the administration. It would also strengthen the Vatican's strategy aimed against liberal forces in Italy. In addition, Page informed House about the activities of Bellamy Storer at the Vatican. Storer, former U.S. ambassador in Vienna (1902-1906), was closely associated with the Holy See during the winter of 1914-1915, when he organized a bureau of inquiry for missing soldiers.[4] Page found Storer to "have some sort of billet now with the Vatican Foreign Office" and was suspicious about the real nature of his activities, "besides the foregoing and hunting up through ecclesiastical functions persons who have disappeared."[5]

Early in March 1915, the pope received Storer and his wife in private audience and talked mostly, it seems, about Archbishop Ireland.[6] The press in Italy, however, took this visit as a signal that the U.S. government was about to appoint Storer as its representative to the Holy See. Even the *Corriere della Sera* entertained this as a possibility. Page was annoyed, and his suspicions were confirmed by an ecclesiastic from the Curia, who told the ambassador that Storer was diligently working with this goal in mind. Once again, Page insisted that this would seem unnecessary, since there would be no reason to "have in Rome an additional representative to one accredited to the Quirinal."[7]

After Italy entered the war against Austria-Hungary, Vatican authorities approached Page early in May through the rector of the American College in Rome and asked him to hold for safekeeping in the embassy four trunks containing Vatican archives; there was fear of disturbances, with possible damage to Vatican property. Both the White House and the State Department promptly agreed to help the Vatican in this matter, with Wilson concurring that it was the "right way to handle this matter."[8] But the administration was suspicious about the real motives and the implications of such demands, which, at the same time, could obviously not be rejected.

For over a year, there was no mention of the proposal for a U.S. representative at the Vatican. Both the Vatican and the United States were involved with problems of greater urgency, such as submarine warfare, embargo, blockade, or neutral efforts at mediation. The Vatican seemed satisfied to convey its views and proposals occasionally through different channels and persons to Page or directly to Wilson and the State Department. By the summer of 1916, however, the British government concluded that its mission to the Vatican had not met its expectations and that its influence at the Vatican was waning. The troubles in the United States generated by the suppression of the Easter rebellion and the subsequent execution of Sir Roger Casement were additional reasons for London's preoccupation. Irish agitation in the United States against Great Britain and its policies was causing serious concern in the Foreign Office and, indeed, forced the U.S. government to reconsider its attitude carefully in a year of presidential elections. There was, thus, a valid reason for both the United States and Britain to find a better way to deal with the Vatican.

Although little was accomplished during 1916, the British government seemed to have found a troubleshooter, a man they recruited to work with the Vatican. It was hoped that he could induce the Holy See to advise U.S. Catholics to assume a less aggressive attitude toward the Allies and thus aid Wilson's reelection. The man was Count Jean Marie de Horodyski, a Pole from Galicia. He was a strange blend: a Catholic, a noble in exile, an adventurer, a man with excellent connections and of obvious intelligence. At the moment, his services seemed indispensable to the British government. Even though the intelligence services of several countries believed that Horodyski was a double agent and even though his activities generated heated debate in Allied capitals, the British seemed to have complete confidence in him. The Foreign Office helped Horodyski make his way wherever it was necessary, sometimes despite evident opposition, notably in Italy. In introducing Horodyski to Rodd, Drummond insisted that the Pole had an excellent relationship with the pope and the Vatican hierarchy. For this reason, he was to try to "influence the Vatican with regard to the Polish vote in the United States," which was very strong. Rodd was also informed that Horodyski proposed to go to the United States before the elections, and for that reason "encouragement from the Pope would be of the greatest value to him."[9] However, Horodyski's initial assignment did not come through, for the trip was postponed until the following year, when the Polish question began to attract attention in Europe and the United States

In January 1917, in the midst of negotiations with Germany and the excitement created by the "peace without victory" speech, the pope sent a personal letter to Wilson. He pleaded with him to intervene with the Mexican government to secure the release from prison of Archbishop Orozco of Guadalajara and Bishop Michele de la Mora of Zacatecas, who were accused of plotting against Carranza. The pope proposed that the prelates not stand trial in Mexico, but instead be brought before the impartial court of the Holy See.[10] On January 27, after consultations with

Alwin Adee and Lester Woolsey, Lansing drafted a reply. He drew Tumulty's attention to the fact that "we have no diplomatic relations with the Vatican and therefore no direct communication between the Papal See and this government has ever taken place." He thought that the Italian government might object to a direct reply to the pope. "You perceive that the telegram has caused an embarrassing situation," he added, suggesting that Tumulty, as secretary to the president, write to Bonzano or to one of the U.S. cardinals and inform them that one of the prelates was in hiding and the other was in jail. Money was being collected for their defense, and the U.S. government was doing all it possibly could in seeking the release of the jailed prelate. A letter to this effect was sent to Bonzano on the same day.[11] The State Department did not approve of direct action on the part of the pope and did not seem ready to encourage similar moves in the future. The pope's letter could have been a Vatican probe to ascertain the U.S. reaction.

Early in February 1917, the Foreign Office was awakened to the immediate danger of completely losing its influence with the Vatican. In a letter forwarded to Balfour, Rodd warned that the Vatican was very eager to enlist U.S. support for its future policy. Another threat was evident as well. In a memorandum submitted to Balfour by the Intelligence Department, it was pointed out that the Vatican hierarchy sympathized with the Central Powers as the representatives of all those goals and values dear to the Vatican. The Irish in Rome as well as in the United States greatly typified this attitude: "The Irish, as well as the American College, are the nest of conspiracy against England, and, consequently against the Allies and in favour of the Central Empires."[12] Drummond was much concerned with such a turn of affairs. With the prospect that the United States would soon declare war on Germany and increase its own political standing, there was good reason for such concern. Drummond himself admitted that British influence was declining at the Vatican, especially with respect to the United States and Spain. This demanded, it was believed, immediate and efficient action on the part of Britain.

After the United States entered the war, the British War Cabinet decided to act in order to make the U.S. Catholic hierarchy more sympathetic toward Britain and its policies. While in the United States as a member of the British War Mission, Drummond had a long discussion with Cardinal Gibbons in the hope of enlisting his support for British policies. Horodyski was also in the United States, staying on even after the British mission returned to England. On June 1, with Drummond's letter of introduction, he visited the State Department, where he told

Phillips that it would be necessary to raise a Polish army in America. He also emphasized that the United States "must be properly represented at Berne, since Minister Stovall was hopeless." As this suggestion indicated, Horodyski wished to make Switzerland the place where contacts between the Americans and the Vatican should be made. However, the Vatican was not explicitly mentioned.[13] Three weeks later, Horodyski told Phillips that the Polish revolution in Austria "did not signify much."[14] He also saw Lansing and talked "on [a] Polish army and [the] best method of proclaiming Poland's independence."[15] He traveled around the United States and visited Polish organizations. Early in November he was back in London, where he had consultations with Wiseman and Somerset Maugham about the Russian situation.[16] Horodyski did not discuss the Vatican problem with U.S. officials, in order to avoid making them suspicious. The reason for his actions was, however, apparent from the beginning. The talk of a Polish army was a way of enlisting the support of Polish Catholics in the United States. The lure of the creation of an independent Polish state after the war would be irresistible to Polish-Americans, who would gladly side with the Allies. It was in full accord with Drummond's instructions from July 1916.

It may be safely assumed, therefore, that Horodyski's activities in the United States did not touch only upon the political aspects of the Polish question. Ambassador Spring-Rice's letters indicate the concern growing in the administration and among supporters of the Entente over the increasing tension and clashes with the more radical elements of the U.S. Catholic church. Cardinal Gibbons, as the leader of a moderate group and as a supporter of the administration, shared this concern. Spring-Rice believed that the Irish clergy was controlled by the Sinn Fein and that Bonzano was completely helpless in this confrontation. This gave credence to the belief that the U.S. Catholic church was "hostile to France, England, and Russia and is actively working against the cause of the Allies." This problem, as far as the United States was concerned, raised sensitive questions about political opposition to the administration. Spring-Rice firmly believed that the responsible members of the administration were aware of this hostility.[17] Obviously, something had to be done to avoid open conflict between the church and the administration. Through his frequent contacts and conversations with the moderate members of the Catholic hierarchy, Spring-Rice paved the way for action on the part of Cardinal Gibbons and his followers.

Although Spring-Rice did not enjoy the complete confidence of the British War Cabinet and was not popular in Washington, he was indispensable in carrying out this action, for he had the confidence of the major leaders of the U.S. Catholic hierarchy. In much the same way, he was trusted by the leaders of the Republican party, Theodore Roosevelt, Taft, and Henry Cabot Lodge. Cardinal Gibbons wanted to use his services in order to get British approval for his forthcoming action. Early in September 1917, Spring-Rice reported to Balfour that prominent Catholics in America were evidently apprehensive about the "divergence that appeared to exist between the policy of the official directors of the Vatican and the Government of the United States." After Wilson's reply to the pope's peace note, the agitation in the press—Catholic and secular— reached its highest pitch. There existed a potential danger that U.S. public opinion might conclude from the polemics that "Catholics as a whole are devoted not to the cause of the United States, but to the cause of a foreign though spiritual sovereign." For this reason, wrote the ambassador, "Cardinal Gibbons. . .is anxious to represent this danger to the Vatican whose ear appears to be possessed by persons holding very different views."[18] Gibbons asked the War Cabinet to appoint somebody in Rome who would be able to communicate confidentially his views and suggestions to the Vatican. He proposed that Robert Wilberforce, an employee in the British Consulate General in New York and a man well acquainted with Catholic affairs in the United States, be sent to Rome; he would be in constant touch with Father Cyril Fay, who was officially attached to the American Red Cross mission to Italy. The cardinal wanted to make the Curia aware that he had some influence in the United States and in the administration as well.[19]

The Foreign Office eagerly seized upon this opportunity. Count Salis, consulted as to the feasibility of the Gibbons's proposal, agreed to it. Drummond thought that the proposal was very convenient for protecting British interests in the United States and suggested that Gibbons should be helped out. Wilberforce was given permission to go to Rome, but Spring-Rice was warned to consider with the cardinal the possible "outcry that might arise in the United States if [the] scheme became known." Spring-Rice was instructed to obtain approval from the State Department and inform the Allied ambassadors in Washington.[20]

Spring-Rice approached the State Department and the Italian ambassador immediately. Although the State Department was willing to aid Cardinal Gibbons in his efforts, Spring-Rice was advised that the whole problem would be considered more carefully. Di Cellere was receptive to the suggestion. On September 26, Spring-Rice advised Balfour that Lansing was leaning in favor of the plan but was wary of putting the government in an embarrassing situation should the proposal become known. It was decided that Gibbons should submit the application for Fay's passport. Lansing would promise the cardinal all facilities and assistance for Fay's trip. Both the French and Russian ambassadors supported this arrangement. Polk was more explicit about why the State Department was taking this step. He told Spring-Rice that the State Department "could have no objection—quite the contrary—to your [Balfour's] taking measures to keep your representative at the Vatican informed as to the United States affairs." Spring-Rice elaborated on this, saying that "the United States Government is keenly alive to the danger of American Catholics taking any line as a body which would disrupt American political life on religious grounds and is afraid that the Vatican is not aware of this danger."[21] The State Department and Cardinal Gibbons seemed to have almost identical aims in pushing this proposal forward.

This cautious attitude was confirmed several weeks later. Perhaps unaware of the proposal made to Spring-Rice as to the passport application procedure, Fay approached Lansing and requested a letter of introduction to Cardinal Gasparri. Lansing refused and insisted on writing only a letter to Cardinal Gibbons. Spring-Rice explained that the U.S. government could not do this, "as it would be interpreted as a move towards peace as an impression here is . . . that the Vatican is cooperating with the Central powers."[22] Although friendly toward Cardinal Gibbons, the State Department did not seem willing to take any steps that could be interpreted as a new departure in its policy toward the Vatican. On November 13, Polk handed Lansing's letter for Cardinal Gibbons to Fay, who was instructed to visit Balfour and Drummond on his way to Rome.[23] The success of the mission was by no means assured: in Spring-Rice's words, "Gasparri was not in good odour with this government because of his unfriendly interview relative to the President's message which, although some people say is not genuine, has never been denied."[24] By this time new elements were brought to bear upon Vatican policy toward the United States; the necessity for change was apparent. For this reason, Fay's conversations and interviews at the Vatican were not limited to the situation of the U.S. Catholic church.[25]

In the early months of 1918, with Fay in Europe, Horodyski and the Foreign Office continued to push more vigorously the idea of getting the U.S. government to send an official representative or mission to the Vatican. Early in January, Horodyski traveled to Switzerland in order to carry out his plan. While there, he met numerous politicians and diplomats, some of whom were in contact with papal representatives. He had also seen Hugh Wilson, the U.S. chargé d'affaires in Berne, and told him that he knew Nuncio Pacelli very well. Horodyski impressed upon Wilson the need for an American who enjoyed the complete confidence of the administration to be sent to Rome unofficially in order to influence Vatican efforts to make Hertling receptive to Wilson's suggestions and proposals. For his part, Horodyski was ready to go to Rome and see that the American was quickly introduced to the Vatican.[26] The State Department ignored this suggestion, although it seemed that certain U.S. diplomats in Europe were ready to entertain the idea of having a representative at the Vatican.

The U.S. press, in one way or another, learned about alleged "contacts" between Wilson and the Vatican. As a result, letters of inquiry and protest began to come into the White House and the State Department. Senator Knut Nelson of Minnesota forwarded to Wilson a letter he received from a certain W.A. Thompson, who wrote that he heard of the administration's intention of appointing a diplomatic representative to the Vatican. In a covering letter, Senator Nelson expressed his hope that it was not true. Wilson, realizing he could not keep silent on the matter, reacted immediately in order to prevent any agitation in the press or in Congress. In thanking Nelson for sending him the letter, Wilson commented, "I cannot imagine where Mr. Thompson got the idea that I was intending to send a representative to the Vatican. I, of course, have no authority to do anything of the kind and had never entertained the thought as you rightly divined."[27] But Wilson's letter did not silence the press campaign. In March, Congressman Arthur Overmyer of Ohio forwarded to Lansing a petition of the Patriotic Association of Steubenville, Ohio, protesting the pressure put on the president to appoint a minister to the Holy See. Members of the association, though claiming that this view did not come to them as a complete surprise, warned that "every loyal, patriotic, liberty-loving American citizen . . . will resent such a proposal with an earnestness that will make itself felt through coming generations."[28] The administration now moved swiftly to eliminate any possibility of action of this sort, and Horodyski's proposal thus lost even the slightest chance of gaining its approval.

The British, unaware of Wilson's firm commitment against the appointment of a representative to the Vatican, persisted in their efforts. Early in March, the pope asked Pacelli to come to Rome in order to discuss the Vatican's pending action. Horodyski wanted to proceed to Rome, via Paris, in order to talk to Pacelli.[29] But the meeting could not be arranged and was thus postponed until Pacelli consulted with the pope, Gasparri, and other officials in the Curia. The meeting between Horodyski and Pacelli, in the presence of Baron von Ritter, the Bavarian minister to the Vatican, was held only after the nuncio's return to Munich early in April. On that occasion, Pacelli told Horodyski that the pope did not intend to make any peace initiatives at that time in view of the German military offensive. The pope was, however, desirous of establishing closer "relations between the Entente and the Vatican and strongly advocated creation of an American mission to the Holy See." The Curia did not believe, Pacelli told Horodyski, that U.S. military assistance would be very effective, and he advised Horodyski to keep in touch with von Ritter in order to supply him with information in "regard to the reality of America's menace." The contents of the discussion were sent to the Foreign Office.[30] Through Pacelli, both the British and the Germans intended to use Horodyski's services to further their respective policies and interests. This, of course, caused a good deal of concern at the State Department.

After meeting with Pacelli, Horodyski proceeded to Rome early in May in order to get a definite sanction for his efforts toward a U.S.-Vatican rapprochement. By this time, the Curia realized that the war was moving contrary to its earlier plans and expectations. On May 11, 1918, Benedict XV received Horodyski in the Vatican. He told Horodyski about his readiness to act to make Irish opposition against conscription less vociferous and adamant. However, he indicated that if Wilson were willing to cooperate, there would be a better chance of success. In order to carry this out, he suggested that the U.S. government send a confidential agent to the Vatican to discuss how this cooperation could be effected. The pope's proposal made Horodyski believe that the Vatican's attitude toward the Allies was changing.[31] The British were encouraged to find out that their efforts were not all in vain. The Foreign Office decided to exploit this newly created situation and to give full support to the pope's suggestion that Wilson dispatch a confidential agent to the Vatican.

Before leaving Rome for Paris and London, Horodyski worked out a detailed scheme as to how the pope's proposal should come to full realization. His plan offered the president considerable flexibility as to the form of the mission. Horodyski himself clearly formulated the motives behind this action. He, and for that matter the Foreign Office, believed that this proposal, if carried out, would serve "not only her own [U.S.] interests, but the interests of the Allied cause." He suggested three ways it could be made: (1) to send soon an accredited mission to the Vatican; (2) to send a special and temporary mission to the Vatican;

(3) to send a confidential representative to the Vatican. For his part, Horodyski recommended the second alternative, which would have a better chance of success in view of conditions in the United States. He saw other advantages in a special mission: "It would consolidate Catholics of the Entente powers and have a helpful influence in Ireland, Canada and Australia and would have a good effect on the Catholic party in Italy; it would also deprive the Catholic powers of [the] pretext for saying that they are the only united council showing due reverence and respect for the Church." Furthermore, a special mission could exert a powerful influence in drawing the Poles, Czechs, Yugoslavs, and others in that part of Europe closer to the Allies and the Americans. The advantages for the United States were obvious: it would be in an especially good position to deal with the Vatican since it was not party to the Pact of London and had nothing to do with Article XV of that pact. As to the man to be sent to the Vatican, Horodyski insisted that a proper choice was vitally important. "He should not be a Catholic, as this would work against him at home. He should be a man of distinction and not a professional politician, boss; he should speak either French or Italian and he should have a first class secretary, who should be a Catholic." As candidates for the job, Horodyski suggested someone like President Wilbur of Stanford University or Dr. Vernon Kellogg. Finally, it was stressed that the decision ought to be made quickly and that House and the State Department should be informed about it.[32] House received Wiseman's cable on May 18, as it was intended for his private information. It was not possible to ascertain what action, if any, he had taken. In all probability, he discussed the contents of the cable with Lord Reading two days later.[33]

The proposal coming from Horodyski's conference with the pope was elaborate and precise. It gave the U.S. mission a status similar to that of the British mission, and the whole action was presented as an emergency measure arising from the demands of the war. As a temporary mission, it could be withdrawn as soon as the war was over without any obligation on either side. As such, it was believed to be acceptable to Wilson. Moreover, persons for the post were agreed upon. Besides Vernon Kellogg and President Wilbur, Horodyski considered that Herbert Hoover might well undertake the mission because he was already "persona grata at the Vatican . . . on account of his qualities." Ambassador Sharp and Hugh Frazier, secretary of the embassy in Paris, looked favorably on the proposal and expressed their trust in Horodyski.[34] The ultimate success or failure of the proposal thus depended upon the decision made at the White House.

The odds against the pope's proposal were heavy, and the chances of its being entertained in Washington were very slim, indeed. Lansing was not enthusiastic at all. The Secret Service opened an investigation of Horodyski and his previous activities. Although nothing was discovered against him, Lansing believed that Horodyski was "somewhat visionary and the Department has never taken him very seriously." He advised Stovall that "while information should be discreetly secured from him [Horodyski], care should be taken not to give him information of a confidential character."[35] Page was outraged at the British support for Horodyski. He considered Horodyski not only a British agent, but also an "adventurer who returned to his work to aid the Vatican employing as one means his faculty for insinuating himself into acquaintance of persons of consequence." Horodyski's trip to the United States was his "first step in this intrigue," which was a "devious way to inveigle the United States into departing from their time honored policy and becoming mixed up in matters the end of which no one knows." Page held the British responsible for this intrigue because their temporary mission to the Vatican had not accomplished much; "on the contrary," insisted Page, "it was deemed as a great triumph on the part of the Vatican and clericals." Instead of bringing the pope closer to the Allies, "it has had its part in stimulating the hope for the return to the Pope of his temporal powers and has had no part in settling the Irish or other question." Summing up his arguments, Page added, "I earnestly advise the President not to permit himself to be misled in this important matter. The immediate result would be to strengthen the Vatican fight against Sonnino. Another would probably be its attempt or intervention in our internal affairs against the President, unless he yielded fully to the Vatican ideas."[36]

Page complained to the British ambassador about Horodyski's action. After repeating his impressions of Horodyski and his proposal, Page told Rodd that he strongly opposed it; Rodd himself seemed doubtful whether any good would come out of it, since he was surprised to find out that Page was thoroughly informed about the British role in the game. He assumed that the Vatican was using Horodyski in order to secure representation and diplomatic recognition and was aware of the fact that the Holy See would go to great lengths to obtain a U.S. mission.[37]

Three days after his conversation with Rodd, Page wrote a lengthy letter to Wilson, summarizing his views and arguments about the whole affair. After repeating his assertions about Horodyski and British interference, Page went on to say that the "Polish adventurer" had led the Vatican to "believe that he could help get an American mission accredited to it." "It is absolute impertinence," he added, "for this man to be mixing up with our public policies and extraordinary that the British should be taken in by such a man." He underscored his opposition to the proposal: "If I had the least idea of favoring such a thing it would have been dissipated by what I have seen of Vatican policies since I have come to Rome . . . . I cannot imagine a greater mistake than it would be for us to send a mission to the Vatican and I never felt more certain in my life than I do of my position on this subject." Page believed that there were a good many people in England who would "like to see us in the same fix with themselves," thus alluding to the failure of the British mission. The U.S. government should not abandon its traditional policy, since it would inject the religious question into political life and create a Catholic party like the one in Italy. He apologized for the strong words he used, for "if I have spoken strongly it is because I feel strongly. Such a step would be an incredible error."[38] Page's letter reached Washington on June 11, 1918, and was passed on to Wilson. In returning it to Lansing, Wilson wrote, "Mr. Page need not concern himself about Horodyski. We are not likely to trust him in any way." This was the ultimate verdict, since Wilson, by that time, had cleared this question with Ambassador Reading as well.

On May 23, 1918, under instructions from Drummond of May 18, Lord Reading called on Wilson at the White House. In a lengthy conversation, Reading suggested to Wilson that the U.S. government should send a confidential agent to the Holy See. Wilson's response was what Reading expected. Wilson, in fact, told Reading politely that "the state of opinion in the United States would not permit him to accede to the proposal. It would be impossible for . . . [him] to send a confidential agent for it would be bound to be known that he had sent some representative to the Vatican." Wilson was quite candid in saying this to Reading. He further insisted that his knowledge of the situation in the United States had convinced him that "in the end the proposed course would be disadvantageous both to . . . [England] and to the United States. In addition, the powerful body of Irish opinion would particularly resent such action." Reading thought it wise not to press the matter, since it was clear that "Wilson obviously had not any intention of accepting the suggestion."[39] Immediately after that, the British government abandoned the proposal entirely, and it was never mentioned again during the war. Strangely enough, it seems that the whole idea was dear only to Drummond, who, as a Catholic, pursued the matter to its end.[40]

The whole incident seems almost unreal. The British government, intent upon using the Vatican to eliminate opposition to its policies and wanting to exploit the U.S. government's difficulties with Catholics, used highly unusual and unconventional methods. The U.S. government, for its part, gave unofficial support to Cardinal Gibbons in his efforts to make his voice heard at the Vatican; it did not want to commit itself further. The British also believed, after accepting the pope's proposal, that the appointment of a special U.S. mission to the Holy See would help bring the Vatican firmly to the side of the Allies. The entire demarche did not stand any chance, since the U.S. government believed that the pope was supporting the Central Powers. Although it may seem strange that the British pressed the matter to the end despite all odds, it was in fact not so unusual. The pope exploited the British troubles in Ireland and promised to use his authority over the Irish bishops as a lever to extract support for his rapprochement with the United States. The British government accepted, for their part, the pope's promise on the basis of quid pro quo and endeavored to carry the bargain out.

The British, in pressing the pope's plan, seemed to be interfering with U.S. internal affairs. Page denounced this, and the go-between Horodyski was not taken seriously. Strangely enough, the British Foreign Office completely ignored Italy and its opposition to bringing the Vatican into the political game. This may indicate that the British expected to accomplish a great deal through the pope's cooperation. The Americans tended to believe the opposite and rejected any idea of acting in league with the Vatican. Wilson, Lansing, and Page were unmistakably against the proposal. House, although familiar with the proposal, did not think much of it and tended to remain aloof. His lack of support probably further decreased British chances to win acceptance for the proposal.

Pietro Gasparri, Cardinal Secretary of State

CHAPTER 10

THE UNITED STATES, THE VATICAN,
AND THE DISSOLUTION OF THE HABSBURG MONARCHY

Throughout the war, the principal object of Vatican diplomacy was clearly to assure the survival of the Habsburg Monarchy. However, this policy was long obscure—as obscure as Wilson's policies and attitudes toward the Vatican were during this period. Furthermore, there have been strange, though justified, contradictions among historians regarding the Vatican's efforts to induce the United States and the Allies to keep the Habsburg Monarchy from falling apart. Information has been fragmentary or inaccessible. Very little or nothing can be said about concrete steps, proposals, and plans, and hardly more can be said about the aspirations or motives that prompted the Curia to act as it did. It is a curious situation. On one hand, there is a widespread belief that the Vatican did everything to save the monarchy; on the other hand, it is difficult to see just exactly what its efforts amounted to. This very fact makes the problem intriguing, interesting, and attractive. There are also a substantial number of minor questions that have not been answered adequately. Controversial interpretations of the Vatican's activities account, at least in part, for the fact that the problem has not been treated satisfactorily.

The Vatican's efforts to preserve Austria-Hungary have been the subject of numerous works; they have been treated in a variety of ways and with different degrees of success.[1] To a great extent, these writings reflect the political, social, and religious preferences and attitudes of their authors. Certain authors have discussed the Vatican's policies toward the monarchy in more general terms, stressing the pope's charitable efforts, his work with prisoners of war, his intervention with belligerents, his impartiality and neutrality, and the dilemmas he confronted with Catholics divided between the two camps. These authors tend to be more moderate and favorably disposed toward the Vatican and the pope.[2] Other authors have taken a more critical position: they have argued that the Vatican worked actively and sympathetically for the Central Powers. Yet they do not discuss in detail those problems of immediate concern to the Vatican.[3]

Most authors argue that the Vatican overtly supported the Habsburgs and the Hohenzollerns. Their arguments for such a claim are numerous, ranging from the Vatican's approval of the Austro-Hungarian attack on

Serbia in July 1914 to the last efforts on behalf of the monarchy in the fall of 1918.[4] Some historians go a step further and claim that the Vatican's efforts on behalf of Austria-Hungary and its other initiatives were doomed precisely because of its pronounced sympathies for the Habsburgs.[5]

The Vatican's fear for the future of Catholicism in East-Central Europe was apparently the single most significant factor influencing Vatican policies toward Austria-Hungary. Gasparri and many others expressed this fear, which is reflected in the existing literature. There is no uniformity of opinion on this, however. Some authors insist that the Curia worried about the spreading of Orthodoxy; still others argue that it feared primarily the proliferation of Lutheranism. In fact, the Vatican feared both. In the eyes of the pope and the cardinals, both Orthodoxy and Lutheranism menaced Catholicism, Italianity, and even Latinity. Indeed, Benedict XV was not only the leader of international Catholicism, but also an Italian patriot.[6]

Contrary to all of this, another group of historians argues that the Holy See was not much concerned with the political future of Central Europe in general and Austria-Hungary in particular. One author insists that the Vatican undertook no diplomatic or political action of significance from the end of 1917 to the end of the war. It waited the end of the war, he argues, before taking any initiative.[7] Several authors insist that the Vatican gained freedom of action only with the dissolution of the Habsburg Monarchy, thus implying that the Holy See was indifferent toward Austria-Hungary and its destiny. It should be added, however, that this latter view has not won many adherents; in fact, the implication of this view may well be totally irrelevant.[8]

No historian, except Goyau and Ori, seems inclined to discard the Vatican's concern for the preservation of Austria-Hungary. Benedict XV obviously was not and could not be disinterested in the outcome of the war, since the Vatican had too much of a stake in it. Actually, the aforementioned works point out the difficulties and certainty of historians and reflect, above everything else, the methods and style of Vatican diplomacy. Indeed, the Vatican's moves and actions permit the drawing of contradictory and unfounded conclusions about its actual policies and innermost desires. After its initial efforts to separate Austria-Hungary from Germany, early in 1918, had failed, the Vatican applied different methods and intensified pressure in its drive to save the Dual Monarchy from extinction.

Despite its failure to detach Vienna from Berlin, the Vatican did not cease its activity on behalf of the Dual Monarchy. It also continued to work diligently to secure representation at the peace conference: this was believed to be another way of helping the Habsburg Monarchy. Throughout 1918 the pontiff and his diplomats endeavored to keep the monarchy intact—through internal reorganization and territorial cession if necessary— and to pose as the defenders of European civilization against anarchy and bolshevism. They also used the threat posed by German expansion and the lack of a barrier to prevent it.

However, these basic elements of Vatican policy did not necessarily eliminate other arrangements and solutions. One was the possibility of getting Austria-Hungary and Italy to work out their frontier problem through negotiation—after all, Italy was war-weary after Caporetto and a long winter, its finances were depleted, and the morale of its army and population was low. The Austrian government was disposed to negotiate and conveyed its views to the Vatican. During February and March 1918, proposals and letters were exchanged between Gasparri and Francesco S. Nitti, the minister of the treasury, concerning the territorial concessions Austria-Hungary might make.[9] However, the positions of the Vatican, Italy, and the Dual Monarchy proved irreconcilable. Emperor Charles's insistence upon the territorial integrity of the monarchy, in fact, shut the door to negotiation. For its part, the Italian government demanded Trentino, Trieste, and several islands in the Korčula archipelago. In return, it was ready to make concessions to the monarchy in Somalia and Benadir. The Vatican stood in between: it wanted to see the monarchy preserved, but at the same time it believed that certain corrections on the Italian-Austrian frontier were needed.[10] Negotiations came to a standstill, and when Germany's March offensive began, Orlando ordered the cessation of all contacts with the Vatican.

The Vatican decision makers proved to be more farsighted than the monarchy's statesmen and politicians. Failure to reach any accord between Italy and Austria-Hungary increased the Vatican's concern for the latter. The Curia clearly realized the threat to its own standing and policies in Central Europe and tended to ascribe this to the monarchy's lack of flexibility and growing dependence upon Germany's military victories. It was particularly concerned over Poland and its Catholic population, which clamored for national independence. There, as well as in other parts of Central Europe, the Vatican hierarchy was afraid of suffering defeat in the spiritual sphere and of losing the allegiance of the population. Still, the Curia considered Emperor Charles's reliance on Germany temporary. Charles was an ardent Catholic and a protector of Catholicism in his realm, and it was believed that the Dual Monarchy would ultimately turn to the pontiff for help. In Jaszi's words, "the more the national decomposition of the Monarchy progressed, the more the sentiments of the dynasty became intense towards its Church."[11] As the war progressed and the military defeat of the monarchy became certain, this prophecy proved to be only too accurate.

The Vatican's preoccupations were genuine. In order to learn more about political realities in the Habsburg realm, the Curia dispatched Monsignor Achile Ratti, the prefect of the Vatican Library, to Poland. His task was to counteract the extreme agitation of the nationalists there and thus help the authorities cope with the situation. He found Poland totally committed to independence from the Habsburgs. However, the Vatican decided that most Poles were sufficiently pacifistic and tractable and that they presented no danger to the Empire. By further assuming that Catholics in the South Slav parts of the monarchy were indifferent or even loyal to the crown, the Curia thus singled out the Czechs as the troublemakers. It did so in order to drive a wedge among the nationalities and ease the pressure on the Vienna government. It indulged in activities similar to this until the end of the war.[12] The Vatican's preoccupation with the monarchy and its destiny was natural. The bonds that united the political interests of the monarchy and the spiritual concerns of the Holy See were strong. Both acted in harmony and accord in the same geographical regions; both wished to preserve the status quo ante bellum, except in cases where limited changes were advisable; and both dreaded social and political upheavals.

The Vatican also took new steps to intensify the peace campaign in the Allied countries. On May 1, 1918, the London *Daily Chronicle* published an article in which it claimed that the pope was ready to mediate for peace. The Vatican decided to deny it. However, the rumors persisted. In May the pope urged prayers for peace and justice, and on June 29 he directed all priests to celebrate a mass for peace and justice. On May 18, Cardinal Amette, archbishop of Paris, informed French President Poincaré about the pacifistic activities of Nuncio Pacelli in Switzerland.[13] In June Brand Whitlock, the U.S. minister to Belgium, informed Lansing that Nuncio Pacelli had written to the pope, which indicated that in "connection with the present offensive the Pope will renew his efforts for peace."[14] Nothing came of these moves and rumors, except that it became evident to a good many people that the Vatican was trying to neutralize recent Allied actions.

Since all the efforts made by Wilson and the Allies to drive a wedge between Germany and Austria-Hungary had failed, a new policy had to be defined. Recent developments in Central Europe clarified the situation and made the need for a new approach to Austria-Hungary even more obvious. Internal as well as external factors account for the change in U.S. policy. Externally, there was the Clemenceau-Czernin imbroglio, which tied Austria-Hungary to Germany more firmly than before. And the changes that occurred in Romania in April 1918, when the Germanophile Prime Minister Marghiloman assumed power, launched that country on a new course. Early in May Romania signed the Treaty of Bucharest with the Central Powers, which forced it to withdraw from the war.

Internally, the new policy seemed even more promising. The effects of the Rome conference of the "oppressed nationalities" began to be felt as the clashes between the imperial government and the nationalities became more pronounced and hostile. Adjournment of the Austrian parliament was an open admission that the government was not able to control national groups or carry through promised constitutional reforms. Food shortages in Austria became more critical than ever before. The situation in Central Europe had changed completely, and any delay in effecting the transformation of Allied and U.S. policy toward Austria-Hungary appeared dangerous. Besides the disappointment that such a delay could have had on the nationalities, it was obvious that the Central Powers were about to search for an immediate solution of the Polish problem in their own interest. After the conclusion of the Romanian and Polish peace, they would undoubtedly endeavor to settle the problem of Serbia, forcing a solution that would thwart Yugoslav ambitions.

The United States and Great Britain decided almost simultaneously, although independently of each other, that a policy of detaching Austria-Hungary from Germany would not help them and should therefore be abandoned. On May 9, 1918, Albert Putney, head of the Near East Division in the State Department, submitted to Lansing a long memorandum on "the Slavs of Austria-Hungary." Lansing, after reading the document, informed Wilson that a change in policy toward the monarchy was necessary. The next day Wilson approved Lansing's proposal to break up the monarchy by supporting and encouraging the rights of its peoples. The new policy received substantial support in Congress, and subsequent events confirmed the validity of Putney's and Lansing's recommendations.[15]

The British, for their part, were kept well informed of the intentions of the U.S. Catholic hierarchy. On May 14, Lord Reading was informed by Shane Leslie that Cardinal O'Connell, whose sympathies for Austria-Hungary were well known, would send a letter to the pope, recommending that he make "effective the President's policy of detaching Austria from

Germany."[16] Balfour was not enthusiastic about this action and informed Lord Reading that the British should not get mixed up in this move, the "utility of which in present circumstances is, in my opinion, most doubtful." Since the Catholic hierarchy insisted, Drummond, with Cecil's approval, informed Lord Reading that British policy was about to change. "We think," he wrote, the "best plan is to give all possible support to the oppressed nationalities of Austria in their struggle against Austro-Hungarian domination. Austria thus may be reduced to a reasonable frame of mind." Any U.S. advances to Austria-Hungary in existing circumstances "will only afford encouragement to the Central Powers and may give rise to misconceptions and misunderstandings between the Allies." The ambassador was asked to transmit this decision to House, which he did through Gordon Auchincloss.[17] The British ambassador felt that the "best policy to pursue was only our encouragement for the oppressed nations, such as the Czechoslavaks and the Jugo-Slavs."[18] The net result of this change in attitude was Lansing's statement of May 29, 1918, declaring that "the proceedings of the Congress of the Oppressed Nationalities...have been followed with great interest by the government of the United States and that the nationalistic aspirations of the Czecho-Slovaks and Jugoslavs for freedom have the earnest sympathy of this government."

In the spring of 1918, the Vatican also launched an energetic press campaign against the forces—primarily nationalist groups—that were working for the dissolution of the Dual Monarchy. The Jesuit *La Civilta Cattolica,* the official *L'Osservatore Romano,* the semiofficial *Corriere d'Italia,* and other periodicals and dailies produced a flood of articles and comments on the current situation. On the whole, they demonstrated the fluidity of the Vatican's thinking and preoccupations, showing that the Curia found itself irresistibly confronted with ideas of self-determination and national emancipation. Some articles openly criticized Italy's "excessive" pretensions toward Italian-populated areas of the monarchy, but at the same time they did not mention the Italians living in Malta, Corsica, Savoy, Nice, and elsewhere. The Vatican press also attacked all of Vienna's proposals about working for constitutional reforms on the basis of self-determination of the nationalities.[19] All of these articles were inspired or written by Gasparri himself.

The changed attitude in Washington and London could not have gone unnoticed by the Vatican, although Lansing's statement of May 29 was only the first and a very vague sign of the U.S. commitment to the policy of dissolution of the Habsburg Monarchy. The Curia replied by expounding its own program for settling the national problems of the Dual Monarchy. Its views on the rights of the subject peoples and how to attain their aspirations were set forth in a lengthy article entitled "Le giuste aspirazioni dei popoli," which came out on the day the Austro-Hungarian offensive on the Piava River was to begin. The article stressed numerous points and insisted, above all, that the aspirations of these subject peoples should be restrained; it condemned and proclaimed as illegal any rebellion against legally established authority; instead, the legitimate desire for independence, it suggested, was to be expressed by "carrying out every duty and honoring all rights acquired."

Significantly, the author of the article seemed to deny that nationality justified changes; only aspirations beneficial to all peoples and nationalities in the state were legitimate. He went on to make clear why it was dangerous to put excessive stress on the ethnic concept of nationality. The ethnic factor narrows the horizons of people, and "the philosophy of excessive nationalism, it should be clear, inspires among the peoples the instincts of separation; it prompts them to break down their providential formations, thus threatening to create odious jealousies and push them one against the other." Since moral laws are immutable, he argued, they are the guardians of peoples' rights, and consequently education ought to be in the spirit of this morality. It would satisfy the real rights of peoples much better than empty phrases.

At the conclusion of the article, the philosophy of national freedom and the policies of the Holy See were summarized as follows:

1. The principle of nationality, as expounded by modern nationalists, is contrary to history.

2. Nationality as a point of unity, harmony, and moral force, however, represents the most valid element in the emergence of national states.

3. Politically autonomous peoples have the right to remain such; those subjugated can aspire to autonomy, justice, and other rights.

4. There are cases in which it is practical and necessary that peoples achieve their autonomy.

5. No state should keep other peoples in subjugation, much less oppress them. The subjugated peoples have the right to fight for their freedom.

6. Every form of oppression ought to be removed, as well as all pretexts for complaints and disputes. Politicians and newspapermen must not aggravate existing difficulties by inciting nationalistic hysteria and creating false pretensions. The Catholic church wished justice and the enforcement of laws and peace; it desired no oppression, it supported no special

interests but the interests of the faithful. Only this, concluded the article, "will discourage a rebellion against the legitimate authority."[20]

The Vatican obviously intended to reduce the effect of the recent proclamation made by the U.S. government—its preoccupation with and concern for the Habsburgs is unmistakable throughout the article. By attacking extreme nationalism and making it only one element among several that justify national freedom and independence, the Vatican also admitted that its position as a universal, moral, and political force was seriously threatened. For that reason, it branded extreme nationalistic pretensions as contrary to history and promoted the principle of welfare for all, not just individual nationalities. Its appeal for law and order should be seen in the light of the internal tensions, protests, demonstrations, and disregard for the authority of the government in various parts of the monarchy. Its insistence upon moral education was apparently intended to uproot nationalistic hysteria, which would eventually turn against law and order. However, the Vatican affirmed the political rights and the position of the dominant nations—the Germans and Hungarians. Other nations, such as the Poles, could receive autonomy only when necessary and practical. The idea of autonomy, however, was not new to the Vatican. Most important, however, was its intention to render the nationalists' aspirations ineffective and sterile by insisting upon a community of interests, law, moral education, and adjustment in relations between various nations living in the monarchy. As all these elements in fact indicated, the Vatican consented to the Habsburg realm's being transformed into a form of federation promoted by the Curia. Of course, the Habsburgs, as a supranational dynasty, had to stay at the head of such an organization.[21]

The Austro-Hungarian military defeat on the Piave marked a new phase in the monarchy's struggle for survival. Late in June, Wilson and House gave their full approval to the policy of the dismemberment of the monarchy as well.[22] Wilson's attitude was firm, since he let it be known that nothing could be done with respect to the Vatican's proposals. The shock produced in Vienna was followed by changes on the highest level in the government and the army. In July 1918 Baron Max von Hussarek was appointed Austrian prime minister. He had definite clerical leanings and no program, although he was aware that if it were to survive, the monarchy must be reorganized. Thus, Vienna's views on internal reform were becoming more compatible with the Vatican's. This was all in vain, however, since the relations between Vienna and its subject peoples were becoming more strained than ever before. Nationalities and their leaders were defiant, and the press was becoming even less restrained in its attacks upon the imperial bureaucracy. It openly voiced the idea of independence for the peoples of the monarchy and lavishly praised Wilsonian idealism.[23] The impending disaster made the bureaucracy, the court, and even the Catholic church more confused, their respective actions more uncoordinated, and their statements more contradictory. The Catholic church tried to rally the remaining forces for the last effort when, on August 4, the Viennese papers published the letter of the Austrian bishops, which pointed out that the "strength of Austria-Hungary lies in the unity of its peoples, while the strength of its peoples lies in their confidence in Catholicism."[24] This was to no avail: it was clear to all that the end was near. On August 10, Emperor Charles declared categorically that peace must be concluded during 1918 and that if no general peace were negotiated, he would have to conclude a separate peace.[25]

By now, the Vatican was becoming more concerned with the United States than with the other Allies, and by making constant inquiries about peace, it worked harder to slow down destructive diplomatic attacks on the monarchy. The Vatican decision makers were very resourceful in looking for a convenient moment to snatch the initiative from Wilson. Their policy toward the United States was described as "vacillating between friendliness and unfriendliness; this policy serves to assay and test public opinion and enables the Vatican to swim with the tide." Speranza also found that the "Italian clerical press, openly sceptical of President Wilson's plan for a League of Nations, is giving scant notice and scanter praise to his address."[26] There were good reasons for this. The Vatican's confidants in Switzerland, on Gasparri's demand, sought to arrange an interview with Dr. George Herron. They inquired whether the U.S. government wanted to enter into negotiations with the Vatican about the conditions of peace. They also suggested to Herron that the pope wanted to know how Wilson would react if Benedict XV proposed the establishment of a league of nations.

Herron was not encouraging. He informed Wilson that it would be one of the "greatest calamities of history if it should turn out that the Society of Nations were to receive its releasing impulse from the Pope." Later in August Gasparri found it expedient to stop further discussion of the subject.[27] At the same time, the U.S. press, especially the nationalist and superpatriotic newspapers, responded by hurling vicious attacks at the pontiff for urging a negotiated peace. These accusations further weakened the pope's influence and effectiveness as a mediator, left him discouraged and facing the prospect of ultimate failure.[28]

On August 14, Emperor Charles, Foreign Minister Burian, and Army Chief of Staff General Artz von Straussenberg arrived in Spa to confer with their German counterparts. There they proposed a plan for a joint peace action. The Germans hesitated to accept it, hoping to be able to stop the Allied offensive. But the Austrians did not want to wait. After the meeting in Spa and after Britain and the United States recognized the Czecho-Slovak National Council as a de facto government, Burian initiated a campaign for an exploratory conference of all belligerents, on neutral soil, to bring hostilities to an end. The Germans were shocked to learn that Vienna was prepared to deal unilaterally. The first Austrian note, issued on September 14, invited all belligerents to a confidential exchange of views, while operations on the fronts were to continue during the deliberations.[29] The U.S. reaction was altogether negative. Wilson, in rejecting the proposal, reminded Vienna of the principles he had earlier laid down as a basis for negotiations, and Lansing insisted that the United States could entertain no proposals in the matter. The U.S. reply to Vienna's invitation, transmitted through the Swedish minister in Washington on September 17, had the support of a group of influential senators and the press.[30] A few days later, the British, Italian, and French governments joined Wilson in rejecting the Austrian proposal.

The Vatican attentively watched this new rebuke to the Austrian government. Since Vienna was still hopeful, there was no reason for excessive alarm in the Curia. It refrained from making its views public but found ways to convey its impressions to all concerned. After scrutinizing the Catholic press in Italy, Speranza found that the clericals "cannot be expected to support a policy which would mean the end of the one imperial remnant left to the Vatican."[31] Peter Jay, chargé d'affaires of the U.S. embassy in Rome, wrote that the U.S. stand was supported enthusiastically. He did find that some Allied diplomats were nervous and afraid of hostile propaganda from the Vatican. Jay added that he hoped that the Vatican would keep out of the matter in view of the deliberate U.S. reply and the determined attitude of the Allies. The State Department was thus aware of the Curia's persistent interest in the outcome of the Austrian peace offensive.[32]

In fact, the Vatican had reason to be worried: events were turning rapidly against the Habsburgs. On September 20 Wilson again implied that the monarchy could not be maintained. On September 29 Bulgaria collapsed, and its armistice terms represented virtual surrender. The monarchy was by now exposed and vunerable from the south. The Vatican quickly realized this new danger. Maglione suggested that Wilson's reply to the Austrian note was made in order to prevent the pope from making new moves for peace. "It was obvious," he added, "that the Entente, by exploiting its military superiority, does not want to discuss the peace."[33] In order to secure Wilson's cooperation, the Curia played up the danger of anarchism and bolshevism, in both the Central Powers and the Allies. Wilson was described as the "greatest living force, standing between fighting Europe and Bolshevism." Nevertheless, Wilson was warned that if his intentions for securing peace did not come at the proper moment, "Europe will become chaotic, corrupting democracy and civilization and immeasurably pushing back true progress in tragic and terrifying ways."[34] This first appeal elicited no reaction.

After some hesitation, the Austrian government decided to make a new proposal. The Crown Council met on September 27 and decided, among other things, to send a second note to Washington. Early in October, Germany, confronted with Allied advances on the western front, proposed to Vienna to act jointly. The Austrian note was dispatched on October 4, asking for an armistice on the basis of the Fourteen Points, Four Principles, and Wilson's speech of September 27 in New York. On October 8 Hussarek read the text before the Reichsrat.[35]

The Vatican inner circles were now becoming uneasy, aware of the impending crisis. The Vatican also decided that the monarchy could survive only with a thorough reorganization of its internal structure. Gasparri expressed this view in a long conversation held on October 2 in the Vatican with Lieutenant-Colonel Charles A'Court Repington, the London *Times* correspondent on military affairs. Gasparri repeated the Curia's fear of collapse in Central Europe and attacked the political persecution of Polish Catholics by Russia. Like Durian, he believed that the best solution of the Polish question would be a kind of internal arrangement between the Poles and the Habsburgs.[36] His argument for the preservation of the monarchy in federal form reflected the Curia's fear of Germany and its hundred million inhabitants. If the monarchy were dissolved, he insisted, the small, weak, and noncohesive successor states would be easy prey for Germany. What power, except a confederation of the Habsburg countries, he asked, could contain a defeated and dissatisfied Germany? Poland, yes, because it had history and traditions; Yugoslavia, no, because it did not have natural frontiers, history, or traditions. Repington commented that the Allies did not agree. At the end, Gasparri insisted that the Vatican was concerned only with religious problems, not with political ones.[37] This reasoning was in accord with the view voiced in *La Civilta Cattolica* in June 1918; in approving the claims of Catholic Poland to an autonomous state, Gasparri could not but attack Yugoslav claims, since Orthodox Serbia did not enjoy the confidence of the Curia.

The Vatican's growing concern over the monarchy's ultimate destiny prompted it to frenzied activity with the aim of preventing the worst. It made appeals and interventions in several directions—with the U.S. representatives in Rome indirectly and through Cardinal Gibbons to Wilson directly. On October 4 Emperor Charles hastened to inform the Vatican about the contents of the new note to the U.S. government, the demand for an armistice, and the beginning of discussion about peace terms.[38] It was also evident by now that the Holy See would not be allowed to participate in the peace conference. There were rumors that Vienna had offered to make peace with Italy. All these factors prompted the pope and Gasparri to act at once.

On the same day that the Austro-Hungarian note was received in Washington, Monsignor Cerretti of the Congregation for Extraordinary Ecclesiastical Affairs approached John H. Hearley, the director of the Italian Section for Propaganda into Enemy Countries of the Committee on Public Information in Rome. Cerretti gave advance information on Vienna's decision to send a new note and revealed its contents—which confirmed how closely Vienna and the Vatican acted together in an emergency. After dwelling upon the conditions Austria-Hungary proposed as a basis for peace, Cerretti insisted that only Wilson was consistent and above personal egotism, and he promised, in Austria's behalf, its readiness to "democratize internally and adopt many popular and social-democratic measures." Cerretti also repeated the claim that Wilson's influence was strong among the peoples of Austria and Germany and, furthermore, that Wilson was the "real master of the situation in all belligerent countries." Hearley was warned, however, that Wilson should closely watch the Allies, individually and collectively.

The essence of this conversation was cabled at once to George Creel in Washington, who forwarded it to Wilson the next day. Wilson must have read it with interest and great concern. Apparently dismayed at the Vatican's renewed attempt to make him aware of his influence and standing with the Central Powers, he discerned in it an effort to make him responsible for the dissolution of the Habsburg Monarchy. In thanking Creel for sending him Hearley's report, Wilson complained that it "represents a very unexpected aspect of the attitude of the Vatican."[39] The Vatican's standing with Wilson dropped even lower with this implicit imputation of responsibility for events in Central Europe. Wilson decided to ignore the warning, since he believed that he could not be held responsible for the ultimate outcome of the war there.

In order to assure a favorable outcome for this action, Benedict XV decided to make a personal appeal to Wilson. On October 7 Bonzano was instructed to send the White House a message in which the pope asked the president to terminate "as soon as possible the ruthless scourge which for too long [a] time has been afflicting humanity." It asked Wilson to consider Austria-Hungary's request for an armistice and peace negotiations.[40] On the same day Bonzano was instructed, in a separate cable, to ask Cardinal Gibbons to see Wilson personally and ask him to "give consideration to the Austrian appeal for peace and thus have the glory of bringing a speedy end to the conflict." Gibbons agreed to do this but declined to visit the White House personally. Instead, on October 12, he forwarded a letter to Wilson in which he conveyed the pontiff's message. He excused himself for not presenting it personally in order to avoid public comments but offered his good services in communicating Wilson's reply to the Vatican. Bonzano had relayed the pope's message to Wilson a day before.[41]

Thus, the Austrian demand for an armistice could have not had more enthusiastic support in Washington. The pontiff timed his step with consummate skill, since it was believed that the U.S. government was about to consider a reply to the Austrian note. Interestingly, the pope's appeal did not mention Austria's demand for peace directly; it was left to Gibbons to dwell upon the real reason for the action. The pope did not consider it necessary to intercede in Germany's behalf. As this frantic communication with the White House indicated, the Vatican had concluded that the destiny of the Habsburg realm was in Wilson's hands.[42]

The second Austrian note was delivered to Lansing on October 7 through the Swedish minister. Wilson and Lansing already knew its contents. After receiving the note as well as the appeals in Austria's behalf, Wilson found himself compelled to compose a formal reply. Lansing favored a decisive rejection and insisted that the Austrian offer be considered only after the Austrian government proved its sincerity by withdrawing from all occupied territories and denouncing the treaties of Brest-Litovsk and Bucharest.[43] House, for his part, suggested that the reply be drafted along the lines of Wilson's speech of September 27, 1918, in New York.[44] Wilson again tended to follow Lansing's advice. On October 7, the day the note arrived in Washington, Wilson told Sir Eric Geddes, the first lord of the admiralty, that the breakup of the monarchy was imminent owing to the U.S. commitment to its nationalities.[45] He also insisted that the U.S. position had changed radically since January 8, 1918, but showed a certain uneasiness as to how to convey the news to Vienna.[46] His remarks clearly indicated what the ultimate fate of the pontiff's and Cardinal Gibbons's interventions on behalf of the monarchy was to be.

While composing and dispatching the appeals to Washington, the Curia in general and the pope in particular were discussing, and pressing Emperor Charles to effect, the internal reorganization of the Dual Monarchy. The idea of federation again came to the fore. It was the natural step to take in view of the Vatican's appeals to the Fourteen Points and the Four Principles. The Vatican obviously felt if Wilson adhered to the solutions suggested in these speeches, the dissolution of the monarchy would be forestalled. Emperor Charles seems to have entertained similar thoughts: various schemes for federalization were discussed on all levels of government, and diplomats journeyed abroad to relay these to Allied and U.S. diplomats. The final decision was made after the pope, in a personal letter to Charles on October 10, advised him to rush the reorganization of the empire: "The Emperor should, by solemn and public act, reorganize the Empire on the federal principle, granting large autonomy to the Czechs and the Yugoslavs." The pope also maintained that Germany should accept Wilson's reply and that the troops should be withdrawn from the occupied territories.[47] The pope thus assumed the commanding position in the Central Powers' drive for an armistice and peace. Charles decided, accordingly, to take the pope's advice, and on October 15 the Crown Council formally approved the imperial manifesto, transforming the Dual Monarchy into an aggregation of nationalities. Obviously, the imperial manifesto could not itself solve the national problems of the monarchy. Rather, it was an attempt to impress Wilson favorably before he answered the Austrian note and ultimately to prevent his intrusion into Austria's internal affairs. Since it formally satisfied Wilson's earlier demands, Vienna and the Vatican awaited the next move from the White House. However, the manifesto, published on October 16, came too late. Austria-Hungary was on the verge of dissolution, and there was no last-minute remedy for it.[48]

Meanwhile, Wilson replied to the appeals of the pope and Cardinal Gibbons. On October 17 in answering Benedict XV through Bonzano, Wilson was restrained, although he expressed appreciation for the spirit that prompted the pope's message. He insisted that "in common with the whole world the desire of the people of the United States is for peace, if peace can be founded with some prospect of permanence upon genuine and impartial justice. My every endeavor will be to pursue such a course as will bring the world the blessings of such peace."[49] Apparently, Wilson believed that genuine justice and a lasting peace could not be secured unless the Austro-Hungarian problem was solved radically. Bonzano immediately forwarded Wilson's reply to the Vatican, but it reached the pope only on October 26, 1918. The president affirmed this belief and expressed it more frankly a day later, on October 18, when he replied to Cardinal Gibbons. After excusing himself for having delayed the reply and after explaining that the dealings with the Habsburg Monarchy had become complicated by the change of circumstances after January 8, 1918, Wilson explained why he could not comply with the pope's suggestion. "Since then," wrote Wilson, "we have recognized the Czecho-Slovaks and the national aspiration of the Jugo-Slavs and have thereby created obligations of honor toward them." He believed, however, that Gibbons would be able to explain this to the pope.[50] Wilson's letter to Gibbons was a complete refusal of the Vatican's appeal for an armistice. The Curia was becoming more desperate than ever but held on tenaciously believing that the monarchy could still be saved.[51]

The U.S. reply to the second Austro-Hungarian note, a reply drafted by Wilson personally, reiterated the very arguments Wilson had expressed to his advisers and visitors and had also conveyed to Cardinal Gibbons. He added, however, that he was not "at liberty to accept the mere autonomy for the Czecho-Slovaks and Jugo-Slavs as the basis for a peace." The note was released to the press and sent to Vienna on October 19, where it was published on the following day. In the opinion of many, it was a death sentence for the old regime, history's final verdict against the Habsburg Monarchy.[52] As the note showed, Wilson did not regard himself as being bound by the Fourteen Points, which the Vatican and Vienna accepted as a basis for peace.

The first reaction was that no new note from Vienna would be sent. If one were sent, however, it would be said that Austria-Hungary had solved its national question "in accordance with Wilson's ideas." For that reason, an armistice ought not be connected with the solution of the national problem, which would take some time to do.[53] The Curia admitted that Wilson had abandoned his earlier program when Cerretti told Ambassador Page that the pope seemed now less puzzled about Wilson's attitude toward Austria-Hungary than before.[54]

In accord with the letter to Emperor Charles of October 10, the Vatican initiated its press campaign for the federalization of the Habsburg Monarchy. Unconfirmed rumors circulated that the Curia desired a

Danubian confederation, that the Italian, English, and American cardinals opposed such a proposal, and that the French and Spanish cardinals favored it. Page confirmed this impression after talking to Cerretti and ·suggested that "France either assured Austria through the Vatican or the Vatican through Austria about the plan and likelihood of a Danubian Confederation." The Vatican decided that it would not depend on the goodwill of the U.S. government alone and sought the support of France and England for its schemes. On several occasions Gasparri intervened with Page through Count Salis and submitted to both of them several memorandums outlining the Vatican's plans for a peace settlement. In these memorandums, he revived the idea that Austria-Hungary, as a counterpoise to Germany, should be completely reorganized and given a new constitution and that the emperor should be stripped of his authority. There were also rumors to the effect that Cardinal Gibbons had sent a memorandum to the Curia in which he argued for the dissolution of the Dual Monarchy.[55]

Many Frenchmen and Englishmen did everything they could to prevent the disintegration of the monarchy. As is known, Austria-Hungary requested intervention from Spain, Japan, and other powers. Even Clemenceau did not then have a clear vision of the future of Central Europe— as reported by Poincaré. British General Sir Henry Wilson and Winston Churchill were skeptical about breaking up Austria-Hungary into small states such "as made this war" and predicted that "if Europe was Balkanized there could be no peace."[56] This accounts for the Vatican's attempts to enlist their help and influence and thus stave off the worst. In fact, even before seeing Wilson's answer to the second Austrian note, several Austrian diplomats in Switzerland (Baron Vaux, Count Palffi, and Prince Schönburg) approached Nuncio Maglione and asked him to intervene with the pope in order to secure help from England, America, France, and even Italy.[57]

About October 20, 1918, the Italian army started massing its troops and equipment for the final attack against the Austrian positions. On October 23 Emperor Charles, in an effort to prevent military collapse, which would seal the fate of the monarchy, again appealed to Benedict XV. This time he demanded the pope act to save lives. On that very day, however, the long-expected Italian offensive began, and the emperor's appeal came to naught.[58] In desperation he decided to send a third note to Wilson. The note, forwarded from Vienna on October 27, was signed by Count Julius Andrassy, the last Austro-Hungarian foreign minister. It was sent with the Vatican's approval and concurrence, as the pope followed suit and made another appeal of his own. On October 29 Cardinal Gibbons was instructed to convey to Wilson the pope's joy over his attitude on the question of peace, and to plead that peace, in order to be permanent and stable, must not be punitive and that whatever they were, the terms of the armistice should constitute the basis for the ultimate peace settlement. This suggestion meant, in fact, that the Central Powers expected the pope to arrange that Wilson would become a guarantor of justice at the peace conference.[59] But when this message arrived in Washington, it was too late. Austria-Hungary was in its death throes, and the Allies and Americans were drafting the armistice terms at Paris.

Andrassy's note reached the White House on October 29. He informed Wilson that the Habsburg Monarchy had "accepted all conditions which the President had put upon entering into negotiations on the subject of armistice and peace." It invited the U.S. government to start negotiations as soon as possible but refrained from accepting Wilson's contention about the Czechoslovaks and the Yugoslavs. This angered Wilson, since he had instructed Lansing to tell the Swedish minister that he assumed that the Austrian government had not only accepted, as conditions of peace, his statements of January 8, July 4, and September 27, 1918, but had also consented to "deal with the now *definitely* constituted representatives of the Czechoslovakian and Jugoslavian peoples as with regularly constituted political authorities and for the purpose of making such arrangements of independence as will be satisfactory to those peoples."[60] This was, in fact, the sharpest rebuttal to Austria-Hungary and the Holy See, as Wilson indicated his intention to propose to the Allies that negotiations for peace be carried out on the basis of such an understanding.

On October 31, Page received a visit from the rector of the American Catholic College in Rome, Monsignor Charles A. O'Hern. O'Hern was under the complete influence of the Vatican and its views, Page found, since he argued with Page that the "Austrians would not be pushed too far as Italy would get more by other means." He also added that Austria was inclined to cede Trentino, Trieste, and other territories to Italy. The aim of O'Hern's visit was different, however, as he insisted that the pope was still prepared to use his powerful influence to seek solutions to various outstanding problems after the war was over.[61] Several days later, the Austro-Hungarian representatives signed the armistice in Villa Giusti, which brought the monarchy's war efforts to an end and opened a new era in the history of Central Europe.

Contrary to some opinions, the Vatican was sincerely concerned with the survival of the Dual Monarchy and did everything possible to prevent its dissolution. In doing so, it was motivated by the fear of political, social, economic, and religious convulsions and upheavals. The fear of socialism and radicalism of all sorts accounts for the Vatican's pronounced pacifism and its doubtful neutrality. It acted on behalf of Austria-Hungary, one of the pillars of European reaction and a bastion of Catholicism.

The pope himself, in this case, did not conceive of his apostolic duties too abstractly. He realized that the strength of the Vatican lay in the union of religion and politics; only thus could the interests of the Holy See and those of the universal Catholic church be protected. There was an apparent tendency to exploit the political situation for the interests of the Vatican. This dualistic approach was evident in the Vatican's desire to help Austria-Hungary survive the war, while at the same time toying, albeit unenthusiastically, with the idea of national emancipation and freedom for oppressed nationalities. The Vatican also made the dangers of the Lutheranism and Orthodoxy an excuse for intervening in behalf of the monarchy. Ironically, the end of the war shattered the myth that the Habsburg Monarchy was the sole defender of Catholicism against the two religions. Its dissolution and the emergence of national states indeed opened avenues for the penetration of Germany's political and economic influence and hegemony. In this respect, Gasparri's concern seems to have been justified. However, Germany's entrenchment in that part of Europe brought no substantial change in the religious configuration. Thus, the Vatican's motives for its support of the monarchy may well have been more political than religious.

Surprisingly, the fundamental postulates of Vatican policy toward the Habsburg Monarchy during 1918 did not differ much from those in 1915. During 1918 the Vatican worked actively in Vienna and in Rome to get Austria-Hungary to cede Trentino, Trieste, and possibly Albania to Italy. It did so because it believed that small territorial amputations would not irreparably damage the monarchy's structure or in any way menace its existence. Vienna's constant refusal to accede to the Vatican's demand forced the Curia to assume the role of mediator between Austria-Hungary and the Allies and United States. The same was the case with the idea of national emancipation, which in 1918 received its definite shape in the proposal for the Danubian federation.

The Vatican's efforts on behalf of Vienna were detrimental to its own interests. It seemed to ignore the political realities of the postwar Europe. At the end of the war, the Holy See was politically isolated and in open conflict with triumphant nationalism—so contrary to its concepts of universality and supranationality. It found itself at the mercy of Italy and

France and was forced to look for new perspectives and policies. The Vatican's position would have been different had it succeeded in preserving the monarchy in whatever form. But the monarchy's dissolution was indeed a disaster for the Holy See.

Wilson had little confidence in the Vatican's actions and initiatives: his own motives and policies ran contrary to the Vatican's expectations and suggestions. He was aware that the Holy See considered him responsible for events in Central Europe. The Vatican's subsequent appeals upon his morality and humanitarian feelings did not, therefore, elicit a favorable reaction. When urgent appeals from the Vatican began to arrive at the White House, he could pose as a friend of the Holy See in a search for peace. But Wilson was by then aware that no action could have forestalled the disintegration of the Dual Monarchy. His reply to the pope's personal appeal was thus the only one possible. Wilson's and America's commitments to the Czechoslovaks and Yugoslavs represented the end of the road for the multinational empire.

James Cardinal Gibbons, Archbishop of Baltimore

CONCLUSION

Papal diplomacy, regardless of its cumbersome methods and unconventional nature, had its place in the international milieu of the time. The church, after all, was universal; it had numerous political, ideological, religious, social, and economic interests and preoccupations around the world. Vatican diplomacy—ambitious, alert, and concerned with numerous questions in European, American, and Asian affairs—was instrumental in launching numerous initiatives or in making proposals to temporal authorities on several important matters.

The reasons for such activity were obvious. First, there was Benedict XV's ambition to play an instrumental role in bringing about peace. His basic desire was to return to the Vatican the influence and prestige it had lost after 1870. The Holy See undoubtedly wanted to regain the prerogatives of a temporal, sovereign state. Second, the Curia intended to alter its position in relation to Italy. Its efforts to assure itself a place at the peace conference were motivated by a desire to get more formal, even international, guarantees than those provided by the Law of Guarantees of 1871. Third, the Vatican greatly feared the social and political revolution that threatened Europe and the rest of the world. It condemned socialistic ideas as subversive, as an attack upon established dogma and the existing social order. Similarly, it feared that extreme nationalism and anticlericalism threatened the very existence of certain states. Although the Vatican's concern for Catholic Austria-Hungary was evident throughout the war, its efforts in France and Germany were directed toward improving the position of the church and settling outstanding disputes between the belligerent blocs.

The Vatican did not hold firm views, especially political or diplomatic ones. Its arguments were flexible and persuasive, although not always up to date or well argued. The Vatican's official diplomatic language and style during the war were solemn and unctuous, and in this respect they differed from those of the secular powers. In essence, however, they were entirely political and strictly European, motivated by political considerations that often betrayed the Vatican's real sympathies. The Curia aided or hindered the policies of various countries without openly pushing its own demands. Not infrequently, it deliberately tried to be mysterious—as was characteristic of its diplomacy—to "foster the idea that mightier events are taking place behind its bronze door than actually are," wrote a contemporary observer.

The claim that the war, involving as it did the whole world, was essentially immoral, contrary to civilization, and heedless of the basic elements of humanity represented a sincere and deep-seated belief of the Curia and the pontiff. Ironically, however, it was the dying pope who had helped to ignite the war and spread it over Europe when he sanctioned the Dual Monarchy's attack on Serbia. The Curia quickly realized this, and the new pope tried to get the belligerents to cease fighting. His efforts in this respect, however, were regarded as one-sided and politically motivated. Given the circumstances, Benedict XV's appeals to the United States to avoid either direct or indirect involvement by not supporting the Allies financially, materially, or diplomatically did have political implications. They betrayed the Vatican's inclination to recognize Germany's political and military preponderance in Europe and to sanction Germany's struggle to quash any other bid for supremacy. A German triumph in Europe would have drastically altered the world balance of power, but the Vatican's policies of neutrality ignored the dangers inherent in German domination. Very few historians seem to consider this view, and even fewer are ready to concede that it was indeed a possibility.

Both belligerent blocs, the United States excepted, tried throughout the war to draw the Vatican to their sides. The Curia was much aware of this and tried to use it to its best advantage. But neither the Central Powers nor the Allies were truly sincere in their overtures. Both wanted to use the Vatican to achieve their own aims while completely disregarding both the head of the church and church interests. For a variety of reasons, the Central Powers were more successful in competing for the Vatican's favor. Only in 1918, after Russia had left the war, did the Vatican's sympathies turn toward the Allies. Even then, however, the Allies' policies and goals did not accord well with those of the Vatican.

Vatican policy was not always motivated by religious or moral considerations. It was also guided by political ideas and expediency. The pope and his collaborators tended to believe that the Central Powers might be more successful than the Allies, a sentiment they did not try to hide. The governments in Vienna and Berlin were aware of this sentiment and, on occasion, were reminded of it by the Curia itself. Whenever the Vatican's sympathy was in accord with their interests and policies, the Central Powers acted to strengthen this belief and confirm the feelings of mutual concern.

The Vatican did not hesitate to use people in any position or of any nationality in pursuing its ideas and plans. This was the most important way for achieving its basic tenets, and the list of people involved was impressive and cosmopolitan. Its achievements, however, were meager and unimpressive. The Vatican's proposals and demands lacked originality and boldness. They were usually compromises, compromises that all concerned found impossible to accept, but they were occasionally one-sided and overtly partial.

Benedict XV's general appeals and interventions for peace and the cessation of war on behalf of humanity, equality, and justice can be understood only if compared with his own (and his close advisers') views, actions, and proposals. The pope and the Vatican hierarchy obviously believed that the war should not be waged to the ultimate detriment of one or the other side—a belief that, of course, was in accord with the established pattern of thought and the European balance of power. A victory by one side or the other would have entailed certain radical changes that the Curia opposed. It held a firm conviction that no such changes were necessary.

Throughout the war, therefore, the Vatican persistently supported the idea of minor territorial readjustments (Austria-Hungary, Italy, France.) Minor territorial changes did not threaten the existence of the states concerned, they were accepted diplomatic practice, and they could have been acceptable to all the belligerents. This sort of compromise would have been compatible with a negotiated peace and the preservation of the original European balance-of-power system. It could have opened the way, the Curia believed, for the Vatican's good offices in mediating and ending the war.

In the case of Austria-Hungary, the Curia proved more farsighted than the statesmen and politicians in Vienna. After it became clear that certain changes in the monarchy's constitutional structure were imminent, the Vatican supported the idea of a federalized polity with the Habsburgs at its head. There was nothing new in the idea of federation, but its desirability and practical value could be debated. The Vatican's suggestion might have also reflected its awareness that the United States lacked confidence in Germany's good intentions and sincerity, on the one hand, and the fact that the Allied Powers felt no strong animus or resentment against the monarchy, on the other hand.

The fundamental preoccupation of the Vatican decision makers during the war was the conclusion of a peace or the cessation of military operations. Since this goal appeared unattainable, the Vatican tried at least to prevent the expansion of the war and keep neutrals out of it. Its numerous proposals and hints of its willingness to mediate between the belligerents and to lessen tensions between belligerents and neutrals confirm this view. Some of the pope's moves in this direction were well hidden or barely discernible, others were made public, and generally they were shrewdly conceived and elaborately arranged. In order to achieve some of its goals, the Vatican followed events carefully and appeared to be familiar with virtually every initiative or movement for peace in the world. When it appeared most convenient, the Curia used these for its own purposes in the most effective way possible. The Vatican's efforts were especially directed toward the United States, which could have—and eventually did—upset the balance in the European war.

The Vatican did not interpret the United States' entry into the war as merely an extension of the war, as many people may have assumed. For the pope and the church hierarchy, Wilson's participation in determining the general principles as well as the details of the future peace settlement was more important. Obviously, many of the Vatican's views and proposals were not in accord with those of the U.S. president. It may be safely assumed, therefore, that the Curia would have preferred to deal with the Allies, whose views were in many ways more congenial than those of Wilson. This became clear in the Curia even before the United States entered the war. The Vatican's earlier attempt to solicit and secure Wilson's support for its policies had failed because their respective views diverged on so many questions. For instance, the Vatican's concept of neutrality and U.S. neutrality policies were not mutually compatible; U.S. neutrality, it seemed to the Vatican, favored the Allies and worked against the Central Powers. Their views also diverged on the peace program, Austria-Hungary, and other significant questions.

Finally, in evaluating Wilson's influence on Vatican policy during the war, it appears that Wilson figures prominently in its failures. He distrusted the Vatican and disapproved of its actions as well as its motives. He and his close advisers believed that the Vatican was pro-German and especially pro-Habsburg. Wilson was not pleased with the pressure Catholics in the United States brought to bear on him during the war. He resented the efforts of the Vatican and the church hierarchy to induce him to mediate jointly with the pope and their efforts to influence the administration's policy toward the belligerents. Formally, in public or in official statements, Wilson welcomed the Vatican's initiatives and proposals. He assumed the pose of a generous and anxious man who wanted to help. Yet, in reality, he refused to heed any suggestion from the Vatican and the pope. As the war progressed, this became more and more evident. Wilson seemed inimical toward the Vatican's peace note of August 1917 and toward other similar initiatives in the early months of 1918 because he reserved for himself the exclusive right to make proposals for peace. The pope could do nothing to alter Wilson's disposition in this respect.

The Holy See's confrontation with the belligerent blocs during the war, thus, ended in total defeat, disorientation, and temporary isolation. Thus, it fared little better than its real or assumed protectors. Besides, the Curia's pro-Habsburg stand until the end of the war earned it the substantial distrust and enmity of the newly emerged states, which tended to limit further its access to and position in the international councils of the time.

In this light it is necessary to reassess the policies and review the achievements of Benedict XV. A strong and persistent consensus insists that the pontiff was an excellent diplomat, that he was sincere in his neutrality, and that his activities during the war were successful. However, if his pretensions to historical greatness are measured by accomplishments, which is of course the only valid measure, then Benedict XV fares poorly. His political and diplomatic achievements were few indeed:

—he could not generate support or acceptance for the idea of a negotiated peace;

—he could not secure an agreement between Italy and Austria-Hungary in 1915, lack of which brought Italy into the war on the Allied side;

—he appeared reluctant to admonish Germany for its treatment of the population in occupied Belgium and northern France;

—although very active and persistent, he failed to induce the United States to stop sending financial and material aid to the Allies;

—his efforts to prevent submarine warfare and the blockade also failed;

—his strenuous efforts to keep the United States out of the war did not succeed;

—his peace note of August 1917 proved to be a complete failure, although the pope does not bear the sole responsibility for the failure;

—his efforts to detach Austria-Hungary from Germany and to mediate between Italy and Austria-Hungary early in 1918 came to nothing;

—he could not induce, despite all the pressure he exerted, the Allied Powers to drop or modify Article XV of the secret pact of 1915, which excluded any Vatican representative from the peace conference;

—his efforts to reestablish diplomatic relations with the United States did not succeed;

—the pope, finally, could not induce the United States and the Allies to help transform Austria-Hungary into a federation of peoples under the Habsburgs.

This was too much frustration for the pope. The belligerents were aware of the stakes involved and simply did not want to listen to him. His views on any question of political importance were disregarded. The pope's only successes were in humanitarian work and charities (sick and wounded soldiers, prisoners of war and their exchange).

These arguments seem to require a revision in historical interpretation. If Benedict XV and the Vatican initiated and carried out these and other actions and suffered only humiliation, as undoubtedly was the case, then any claims that the Curia was impartial and neutral ought to be abandoned or revised. Political defeats are not compatible with alleged neutrality and impartiality.

NOTES

CHAPTER 2

1. Jean Brugerette, *Le Prêtre Francais et la Société Contemporaine*, 3 vols. (Paris, 1937), 3:548; Edmond Paris, *Le Vatican contre l'Europe* (Paris, 1959), pp. 24-28; Giorgio Candeloro, *Il Movimento Cattolico in Italia* (Rome, 1953), pp. 370-374; Arthur May, *The Passing of the Hapsburg Monarchy, 1914-1918*, 2 vols. (Philadelphia, 1966), 2: 287, 297; Friedrich Engel-Janosi, "The Roman Question in the First Years of Benedict XV," *Catholic Historical Review* 40, no. 2 (1954): 270; for the pope's stand, see *Österreich-Ungarns Aussenpolitik von der Bosnischen Krise 1908 bis zum Kriegsausbruch 1914*, 9 vols. (Vienna, 1930), 8: 893-894.

2. The pope told Erzberger that "if the war continues for some time longer, we are bound to have a social revolution, such as the world has never seen before." Mathias Erzberger, *Souvenirs de guerre* (Paris, 1921), p. 62; Danilo Veneruso, "Ricerche e problemi relativi ai rapporti tra Cattolici e Socialisti durante la Prima Guerra Mondiale," *Critica Storica* 4, no. 2 (May 31, 1965): 129-154.

3. Luigi Salvatorelli, *La Politica della Santa Sede doppo la guerra* (Milan, 1937), pp. 8-11.

4. Erzberger, *Souvenirs de guerre*, p. 60.

5. Klaus Epstein, *Mathias Erzberger and the Dilemma of German Democracy* (Princeton, 1959), pp. 408-409.

6. When Cardinal Aidan Gasquet visited the new pope and asked him to make some general pronouncements on church principles, the pope replied that it would not be practical, since "any condemnation of practices would be construed into a condemnation of Germany." Shane Leslie, *Cardinal Gasquet: A Memoir* (London, 1953), p. 236.

7. Silvio Negro, *Vaticano Minore* (Milan, 1936), pp. 148, 219; Francesco Vistalli, *Benedetto XV* (Rome, 1928), Chapter 15.

8. *The Diary of Gino Speranza: Italy 1915-1919*, 2 vols. ed. Florence C. Speranza, (New York, 1941) 1: 128.

9. Gregory to Lord Cecil (secret), November 30, 1917, Foreign Office (hereafter FO), 371, vol. 3086, Public Record Office (Hereafter PRO), London.

10. Cambon to Lord Cecil, London, August 30, 1917, FO 371, vol. 3083, PRO.

11. *This Was Germany: An Observer at the Court of Berlin. Letters of Princess Marie Radziwill to General Mario di Robillant (1908-1915)*, ed. Cyril S. Fox (London, 1937), p. 304; Duncan Gregory, *On the Edge of Diplomacy: Rambles and Recollections (1902-1928)* (London, 1929), pp. 88-89; Catholics in both Vienna and Munich received the news of Della Chiesa's election very favorably. Engel-Janosi, "The Roman Question," p. 273.

12. Leslie, *Cardinal Gasquet*, pp. 213-214, 216, 218, 224-225, 231, 234-235.

13. Gaetano de Felice, *Il Cardinale Pietro Gasparri*, (Milan, n.d.), pp. 17-22. Francesco M. Taliani, *Vita del Cardinale Gasparri, Segretario di Stato e povero prete* (Milan, 1938); Charles Loiseau, "Ma Mission auprès du Vatican (1914-1918)," *Revue d'Histoire Diplomatique* 54, no. 2 (1960): 102-104.

14. Felice, *Il Cardinale Gasparri,* pp. 23-24, 26-30, 36, 39; Francesco Crispolti, *Corone e Porpore: Ricordi Personali* (Milan, 1936), pp. 233-240.

15. *Il Cardinale Gasparri e la questione Romana (con brani delle memorie inedite),* ed. Giovanni Spadolini. (Florence, 1972), pp. 156-57.

16. *Dictionaire Diplomatique,* vol. 5 (Paris, n.d.), p. 210; *La Civilta Cattolica,* May 20, 1933.

17. Charles C. Tansill, *America Goes to War* (Boston, 1938), p. 17; Dragan Živo-jinović, "Stav Američkog Javnog Mnenja i Vlade prema Dogadjajima na Balkanu, 28.VII-28.VII. 1914," in *Jugoslovenski narodi pred Prvi Svetski Rat,* ed. Vasa Čubrilović et al. (Belgrade, 1967), pp. 230-260.

18. *New York Times,* July 28, 1914.

19. Arthur S. Link, *Wilson: The Struggle for Neutrality, 1914-1915* (Princeton, 1960), p. 5.

20. Bryan to Page, August 1, 1914, Papers of Walter H. Page, Houghton Library, Harvard University, Cambridge, Massachusetts.

21. Page to Bryan, London, August 3, 1916, Page Papers. Arthur Walworth, *Woodrow Wilson: American Prophet,* (Boston, 1965), p. 403.

22. House to Wilson, Austin, Texas, August 1, 1914, Papers of Woodrow Wilson, series II, Manuscript Division, Library of Congress, Washington, D.C.

23. *Papers Relating to the Foreign Relations of the United States, 1914, Supplement, World War* (Washington, D.C., 1922), p. 37. Hereafter cited as *FR-US, 1914, Supp.* Writing to House, Wilson explained that "all I wanted to do was to let them [European Powers] know I was at their service." Wilson to House, Washington, August 1, 1914, Wilson Papers, series III.

24. Bryan to Wilson, August 3, 1914, and Wilson to Bryan, August 4, 1914, Papers of William Jennings Bryan, Manuscript Division, Library of Congress, Washington, D.C.

25. McCaffrey, Berkowitz, and Sutherland to Wilson, New York, September 9, 1914; H.J. Klemperer to Wilson, Minneapolis, September, 14, 1914, Wilson Papers, series IV.

26. John C. Cummins, *Missouri and the World War, 1914-1917* (Columbia, Mo., 1947), pp. 14-15.

27. Leslie, *Cardinal Gasquet,* pp. 218, 220-221.

28. Ray H. Abrams, *Preachers Present Arms: The Role of the American Churches and Clergy in World War I and II, with Some Observations on the War in Vietnam* (Scottdale, Pa., 1969), pp. 31-32; Dean R. Esslinger, "American German and Irish Attitudes toward Neutrality, 1914-1917: A Study of Catholic Minority," *Catholic Historical Review* 53, no. 1 (1967): 203.

29. Link, *Wilson: The Struggle for Neutrality,* p. 24, goes so far as to say that the Catholic Church "tended toward open partisanship."

30. Leslie, *Cardinal Gasquet,* pp. 220-221. The Curia discovered this fallacy only during 1917, but by then it was too late to change it.

31. Speranza to Ernest Abbot, Rome, December 2, 1916, Papers of Gino Speranza, Correspondence 1916-1918, New York Public Library, New York.

32. Esslinger, "American German and Irish Attitudes," pp. 194-216; Cuddy, "Pro-Germanism and American Catholicism," *Catholic Historical Review* 54, no. 3 (1968): pp. 427-454; Robert H. Lord, John E. Sexton, and Edward T. Harrington, *History of the Archdiocese of Boston in Various Stages of Its Development, 1604-1943,* 3 vols. (New York, 1944), 3: 585. For different Catholic views, see *Ave Maria,*

America, Catholic World, Sacred Heart Review, Fortnightly Review, Our Sunday Visitor, Cincinnati Catholic Telegraph, Catholic Citizen (Milwaukee), *New World* (Chicago), *Western Catholic* (Springfield, Illinois) and many others.

33. Arthur S. Link, ed., *The Papers of Woodrow Wilson,* 11 vols. (Princeton, 1968), 1: 643-646.

34. Woodrow Wilson, *A History of the American People,* 5 vols. (New York, 1902), 5: 212-213.

35. John M. Blum, *Woodrow Wilson and the Politics of Morality* (Boston, 1956), p. 48; idem, *Joe Tumulty and the Wilson Era* (Boston, 1951), p. 39. Tumulty denied energetically that Wilson was a "religious bigot" by citing the names of Irish and Italians appointed to offices.

36. John Higham, *Strangers in the Land: Patterns of American Nativism, 1860-1925* (New York, 1965), p. 190.

37. Ministerial Association of McKeesport, Pa., to Wilson, February 4, 1913; Des Moines Presbytery to Wilson, Indianola, Iowa, March 4, 1913. Similar warnings came from Portland, Oregon, and Montrose, Colorado. Wilson Papers, series VI. The citizens of Nevada County, Arkansas, to Bryan, June 10, 1913, expressed "a deep anxiety about conditions." Archives of the State Department, Diplomatic, Legal, Fiscal Branch, Record Group 59, National Archives, Washington, D.C.

38. "Rome on the Potomac: What the Papal Hierarchy is Doing at the American Capital," *The Outlook,* February 11, 1913, pp. 10-12.

39. Speranza, *Diary,* 1: 15.

40. Ibid., 2: 179.

41. House to Wilson, Paris, April 14, 1915, Wilson Papers, series II.

42. Page to Wilson, Rome, May 21, 1918, Wilson Papers, series II.

43. Page to Bryan, Rome, August 20, 1914; Bryan to Page, August 20, 1914; Page to Bryan, Rome, August 26, 1914, State Department Archives.

44. Page to Bryan, Rome, September 3, 1914; Benedict XV to Wilson, September 23, 1914; Wilson to Benedict XV, October 2, 1914, State Department Archives.

45. Horne to Wilson, Indiana, August 21, 1914; American Federation of Patriotic Societies to Wilson, Washington, August 27, 1914, Wilson Papers, series IV.

46. "Church and State," *Western Recorder* (Wichita, Kansas), September 3, 1914.

47. *New York Times,* August 19, 1914; Walworth, *Wilson,* p. 407.

48. Abrams, *Preachers Present Arms,* pp. 21-22; *L'Osservatore Romano,* August 20, 1914.

49. House Diary, August 30, 1914, Papers and Diary of Edward M. House, Sterling Memorial Library, Yale University, New Haven, Connecticut.

CHAPTER 3

1. Ernest R. May, *The World War and American Isolation, 1914-1917* (Cambridge, Mass, 1959), pp. 72-73; Arthur S. Link, *Woodrow Wilson and the Progressive Era, 1910-1917* (New York, 1954), pp. 115-140; Harley Notter, *The Origins of the Foreign Policy of Woodrow Wilson* (Baltimore, 1937), pp. 342-344; Karl E. Birnbaum, *Peace Moves and U-Boat Warfare: A Study of Imperial Germany's Policy toward the United States April 18, 1916-January 9, 1917.* (Stockholm, 1958), p. 94.

2. Paris, *Le Vatican contre l'Europe,* pp. 44-45; M.M. Sceinman, *Il Vaticano tra due guerre* (Rome, 1951), pp. 56-57.

3. Bryan was most active in carrying out this suggestion. He believed that "no one can afford to take the responsibility for continuing it [war] implacably" and that the belligerents might use it to explain to the rest of the world "their attitude, the reasons for continuing war and the terms upon which the peace is possible." Bryan to Walter Page, September 8, 1914, Bryan Papers; Ray S. Baker, *Woodrow Wilson: Life and Letters,* 8 vols. (New York, 1927-1939), 5: 278-280. Nothing came from it; the Kaiser refused to commit Germany to anything, insisting that it was "up to the United States to get our enemies to make peace proposals." *FR-US, 1914, Supp.,* p. 104.

4. Harry C. Koenig, ed., *Principles for Peace: Selections from Papal Documents Leo XIII to Pius XII* (Washington, D.C., 1943), pp. 128-129; Denis Gwynn, *The Vatican and War in Europe* (Dublin, 1941), pp. 18-19.

5. In his letter, however, Bryan came very close to the pope's stand on a variety of questions, notably armament and arbitration, as well as "the substitution of friendship for hatred," as he termed it. Baker, *Life and Letters,* 5: 284-285.

6. Bryan to Walter Page, October 7, 1914, Page Papers; Baker, *Life and Letters,* 5: 288-289; Notter, *Origins of the Foreign Policy,* p. 357.

7. Wilson to Bryan, October 8, 1914. Private and Confidential Correspondence between President Wilson and Secretary of State, William Jennings Bryan, 1913-1915. Diplomatic, Legal, Fiscal Branch, National Archives, Washington, D.C.; Baker, *Life and Letters,* 5: 291.

8. Page to Bryan, Rome, October 16, 1914, State Department Archives.

9. *L'Osservatore Romano,* November 17, 19, 1914; Koenig, *Principles for Peace,* pp. 131-139; Gwynn, *The Vatican and War,* pp. 24-26. Father H.P. Mender informed Wilson about his discussions with Cardinal Farley "as to the propriety of the clergy taking some action to promote peace among warring nations in Europe." He suggested that the clergy "open the door for such overtures to be made by the President." Mender to Wilson, New York, November 24, 1914, Wilson papers, series IV; Wilson to House, December 2, 1914; Wilson to Thomas N. Page, December 8, 1914, January 28, 1915; Bryan to Wilson, December 17, 1914, Wilson Papers, series II.

10. Bryan to Wilson, December 1, 1914, Wilson-Bryan Correspondence; Notter, *Origins of the Foreign Policy,* pp. 360, 369, on Wilson's Christianity.

11. House Diary, December 3, 1914; May, *The World War and American Isolation,* pp. 77-79. On December 4, House informed Walter Page about his trip and Wilson's decision to offer his services as mediator. The basis for mediation was indemnity for Belgium and a cessation of militarism. House to Page, December 3, 1914, Page Papers; Baker, *Life and Letters,* 5: 297.

12. Koenig, *Principles for Peace,* pp. 144-146, 146-147; Gwynn, *The Vatican and War,* pp. 26-28.

13. Page to Wilson, Rome, January 1, 5, 1915, Wilson Papers, series II; Page to Bryan, Rome, January 5, 12, 1915, State Department Archives. The British minister to the Holy See also noted that the pope might "make very decided advances to President Wilson to combine with him in a vigorous attempt at mediation." Sir Henry Howard to Lord Edward Grey, Rome, January 11, 1915, Cabinet Papers, 37/123/41, Public Record Office, London.

14. Bryan to Page, January 7, 1915, State Department Archives. In replying to Page, Wilson insisted: "I am looking for the right opportunity to influence, if I may,

the course of events towards peace." Wilson to Page, January 28, 1915, Wilson Papers, series II.

15. Page to Bryan, Rome, February 5, 1915, House Papers. Page again warned that "the matter is such a delicate one that it is difficult for me to write about." He also hinted that "the Vatican is strongly pro-German and Austrian." Page also wrote that the *Corriere della Sera* reported that Belamy Storer, former ambassador in Vienna, was interested in mediation, to be "arranged between the Pope and Wilson in favor of a treaty of peace whenever events shall enable such a step to be taken." Page to Bryan, Rome, March 17, 1915, *Papers Relating to the Foreign Relations of the United States: The Lansing Papers, 1914-1920,* 2 vols. (Washington, D.C., 1939-1940), 1: 721-722.

16. Koenig, *Principles for Peace,* pp. 150-151; Grand Master to Wilson, Pittsburgh, February 24, 1915, Wilson Papers, series IV; Cuddy, "Pro-Germanism and American Catholicism," p. 428.

17. Emphasis added. House to Wilson, Paris, April 14, 1915, House Papers. In conversation with Willard, House was told that King Alfonso XIII desired to figure in peace overtures but was willing to "allow the President to take the lead and will cooperate with him in a secondary capacity." House did not see the possibility of accepting this, unless "the belligerents become dissatisfied and embittered with our neutral policy." House Diary, April 8, 1915. Wilson sounded pleased with the information. Wilson to House, April 19, 1915, House Papers.

18. House Diary, April 19, 1915; House to Wilson, Paris, April 20, 1915, Wilson Papers, series II.

19. Memorandum on the conversation with Gibson Fahnestock, March 29, 1915, Wilson Papers, series II. Lansing's desk diary for March 29, 1915, notes that Fahnestock discussed Italy's situation, "particularly German sympathy of the Vatican." Papers and Diaries of Robert Lansing, Manuscript Division, Library of Congress, Washington, D.C. Cardinal Felix von Hartman, archbishop of Cologne, told Admiral Georg Alexander von Muller, chief of the Kaiser's naval cabinet, that the "Pope is frankly Germanophile." Walter Görlitz, ed., *The Kaiser and His Court: The Diaries, Note Books and Letters of Admiral Georg Alexander von Muller, Chief of the Naval Cabinet, 1914-1918,* (London, 1961), p. 79.

20. Notter, *Origins of the Foreign Policy,* p. 373; May, *The World War and American Isolation,* p. 85.

21. Willard to House, Madrid, May 2, 1915, House Papers. This was a hint that the pope was disappointed as well. In fact, the Kaiser was fully aware that Alfonso XIII was "strongly pro-German." Görlitz, *The Kaiser and His Court,* p. 223.

22. Page to Bryan, Rome, May 3, 1915, State Department Archives; *Messagero* (Rome), May 3, 1915.

23. Page to Bryan, Rome, May 23, 1915, Papers of Lester Woolsey, Manuscript Division, Library of Congress, Washington, D.C.

24. Jane Addams, *Peace and Bread in Time of War* (New York, 1945), pp. 12-19; Jane Addams, Emily Balch, and Alice Hamilton, *Women at The Hague: The International Congress of Women and Its Results* (New York, 1915), p. 46.

25. Page to Bryan, Rome, June 8, 1915, State Department Archives; Page to House, Rome, June 24, 1915, House Papers.

26. House to Wilson, July 17, 19, 1915, Wilson Papers, series II; Lansing's Desk Diary, July 12, 1915.

27. *La Liberté* (Paris), June 22, 1915.

28. Page to Lansing, Rome, June 25, 30, 1915, State Department Archives.

29. Wilson to Lansing, July 27, 1915, Archives.

30. *L'Osservatore Romano,* July 30, 1915; Koenig, *Principles for Peace,* pp. 179-182; Gwynn, *The Vatican and War,* pp. 39-40; Christine Alix, *Le Saint-Siège et les Nationalismes en Europe, 1870-1960* (Paris, 1962), pp. 114-115.

31. *Papers Relating to the Foreign Relations of the United States, 1915, Supplement, The World War* (Washington, 1928), pp. 52-53. Hereafter cited as *FR-US, 1915, Supp.* In a letter to the bishops of Lombardy, he purported to continue to work for peace. Koenig, *Principles for Peace,* p. 183. In a conversation with Sir Henry Howard, the pope insisted that his proclamation was only "an open letter" made on the anniversary of the war. Howard to Grey, Rome, August 17, 1915. FO 371, vol. 3505, PRO.

32. Spring-Rice to Grey, Washington, September 2, 5, 14, December 9, 1915; John Wilson to Grey, Rome, September 4, 5, 1915, FO 371, vols. 2380, 2591-A, 3505, PRO; *L'Osservatore Romano,* September 5, 1915; *Temps* (Paris), September 5, 1915.

33. Ernesto Vercesi, *Il Vaticano, l'Italia e la guerra* (Milan, 1925), p. 74, argues that it was a message to the Americans to act for peace. Gwynn, *The Vatican and the War,* pp. 41-42, claims that Gibbons transmitted an invitation to Wilson to act for peace, which he refused to do. Several weeks later, the Vatican press published news that Bryan was received at the White House before he departed for Europe in a special mission. *L'Osservatore Romano,* September 24, 1915.

34. May, *The World War and American Isolation,* pp. 347-352.

35. Gwynn, *The Vatican and the War,* p. 41. The contents of the pope's plan were confirmed in a conversation between the British and French ambassadors, Arthur Hardinge and Geoffray, in Madrid, in November 1915. The pope believed that France should accept the plan because Germany was, by all measures, the winner of the war. The pope believed that Great Britain was the major obstacle to peace on the basis of the status quo ante bellum. Hardinge to Grey, Madrid, November 11, 1915, Cabinet Papers, 37/137/27, PRO.

36. Notter, *Origins of the Foreign Policy,* pp. 446-448.

37. Lansing's Desk Diary, November 5, 1915.

38. Stovall to Lansing, Bern, November 10, 1915, State Department Archives. The Reichstag pressed the government to act for peace after discreetly securing the support of the pope. Leo Valiani, *La Dissoluzione del Austria-Ungheria* (Milan, 1967), p. 250.

39. Page to Wilson, Rome, November 27, 1915, Wilson Papers, series II; *Memoires du Chancelier Prince de Bülow (1897-1919),* 3 vols. (Paris, 1931), 3: 240-241.

40. Grant-Duff to Grey, Bern, November 29, 1915, FO 371, vol. 3505, PRO. Grant-Duff ascribed this statement to von Bülow's visit.

41. The pope also complained about the inconveniences imposed upon the Vatican by Italy's entrance into the war. Koenig, *The Principles for Peace,* pp. 190-192; Leslie, *Cardinal Gasquet,* p. 214. *L'Osservatore Romano,* December 8, 9, 10, 16, 1915, published numerous editorials about the pope and the peace, repeating the parts of the allocution and urging the salvation of Europe.

42. Notter, *Origins of the Foreign Policy,* p. 468; Speranza, *Diary,* 1: 121.

43. Emphasis added. House Diary, January 14, 1916; House to Wilson, London, January 15, 1916, Wilson Papers, series II; Notter, *Origins of the Foreign Policy* pp. 470-471; Arthur S. Link, *Wilson: Confusions and Crisis 1915-1916* (Princeton, 1964), pp. 117-118.

44. House to Wilson, Paris, February 7, 1916, Wilson Papers, series II.

45. Link, *Wilson: Confusions and Crisis,* pp. 134-136; idem, "Woodrow Wilson and Peace Moves," *The Listener* (London) 75, no. 9 (June 6, 1966): 869. For more information about the attitude of the British War Committee in regard to the House-Grey Memorandum, see John M. Cooper, Jr., "The British Response to the House-Grey Memorandum: The New Evidence and New Questions," *Journal of American History* 59, no. 4 (March, 1973): 958-971.

46. Link, *Wilson: Confusions and Crisis,* pp. 222-279.

47. "La politique du Benoit XV, " *La Revue de Paris* 25, nos 20-21 (October 15, November 1, 1918): 210; *New York Times,* April 24, 25, 1916; *Messagero* (Rome), May 6, 1916; Ferdinando Martini, *Diaro, 1914-1918,* ed. Gabriele Di Rosa (Milan, 1968), p. 692. The Vatican papers denied it officially.

48. Lansing's Desk Diary, May 6, 1916. There were numerous stories in the Catholic press that Wilson refused to receive the papal legate, Bonzano, who wanted to hand him the pope's message. On August 15, 1916, Tumulty explained to Wilson that Bonzano did not want to see the president "as he feared that it might result in sensational newspaper publicity." Tumulty to Wilson, Wilson Papers, series IV.

49. Wilson to House, May 8, 1916, Ray Stannard Baker papers, Wilsoniana, Manuscript Division, Library of Congress, Washington, D.C. Arthur S. Link, *Wilson: Campaigns for Progressivism and Peace, 1916-1917* (Princeton, 1965), pp. 16-19.

50. Bernstorff to House, Washington, May 8, 1916, Wilson Papers, series II; House Diary, May 14, 22, 1916. On May 22, Bernstorff told House that the German government had asked him to find out what "answer the President had sent in reply to the Pope's plea for continued peaceful relations between Germany and the United States."

51. May 18, 1916, Papers and Diary of Frank L. Polk, Sterling Memorial Library, Yale University, New Haven, Connecticut; Spring-Rice to Grey, Washington, May 18, 19, 1916, FO 371, vol. 2794; Cabinet Papers, 37/148/37, PRO.

52. Polk to Wilson, May 22, 1916, Polk Papers; Polk to Wilson, June 6, 1916, Wilson Papers, series II. Polk was reporting on his conversations with Jusserand.

53. Willard to Wilson (confidential), Madrid, May 11, 1916, Wilson Papers, series II; *Papers Relating to the Foreign Relations of the United States, 1916, Supplement, The World War* (Washington, 1929), pp. 28-29. Hereafter cited as *FR-US, 1916, Supp.*

54. Penfield to House, Vienna, June 6, 1916, House Papers.

55. Lansing's Desk Diary, August 21, 1916, *FR-US, 1916,* Supp., pp. 46-47.

56. Koenig, *Principles for Peace,* pp. 213-214; Gwynn, *The Vatican and War,* p. 43.

CHAPTER 4

1. *Il Cardinale Gasparri e la questione Romana,* p. 178, writes about "la disgraziata ed immorale guerra sottomarina."

2. Jean Leflon, "L'Action diplomatico-religieuse de Benoit XV en faveur de la paix durant la première guerre mondiale," in *Benedetto XV, i Cattolici e la Prima Guerra Mondiale: Atti del Convegno di Studio Tenuto a Spoleto 1-5 settembre 1961,* ed. Giuseppe Rossi (Rome, 1962), p. 68.

3. Gasparri wrote in his memoirs that "the American intervention, caused by the submarine warfare, was of the greatest assistance to the Allied victory; this made possible enormous loans, helped make needs of the war met, at the time when the

energies of the Allies were at *bout de force." Il Cardinale Gasparri e la questione Romana,* pp. 179-181.

4. Marion C. Siney, *The Allied Blockade of Germany, 1914-1916* (Ann Arbor, Mich., 1957), pp. 21-23, 26-29.

5. *New York Times,* October 13, 21, 26, November 12, 24, 26, 28, 1914; *Literary Digest,* October 3, 10, 1914.

6. Birnbaum, *Peace Moves and U-Boat Warfare,* p. 23.

7. May, *The World War and American Isolation,* pp. 47-49.

8. Clifton J. Child, *The German-Americans in Politics, 1914-1917* (Madison, Wisc., 1939), pp. 4, 6.

9. There were numerous attacks upon Great Britain for its alleged "economic motives" in the war, its responsibility for the destiny of Belgium, and its attempts to influence U.S. policy with false propaganda. Cedric Cummins, *Indiana Public Opinion and the World War (1914-1917)* (Indianapolis, 1945), p. 65; Jerry Del Gimarc, "Illinois Catholic Editorial Opinions," *Historical Records and Studies* 48 (1960): 167-184.

10. Esslinger, "American German and Irish Attitudes," pp. 202, 204, 205.

11. Koenig, *Principles for Peace,* pp. 131-139.

12. *Church Union and Times,* December 17, 1914; *Catholic Citizen,* January 30, 1915; Esslinger, "American German and Irish Attitudes," pp. 200-201; Cuddy, "Pro-Germanism and American Catholicism," p. 432.

13. *Indiana Catholic,* December 4, 1914; *Freeman's Journal and Catholic Register,* January 5, 1915; *Echo,* February 4, 1915; Gimarc, "Illinois Catholic Editorials," pp. 178-179.

14. *Indiana Catholic,* January 22, 1915; Cuddy, "Pro-Germanism and American Catholicism," p. 433.

15. Esslinger, "American German and Irish Attitudes," p. 205; Gimarc, "Illinois Catholic Editorials," p. 180.

16. *New York Sun,* December 23, 1914; May, *The World War and American Isolation;* pp. 115-116; Görlitz, *The Kaiser and His Court,* pp. 50-51, relates that the chancellor was "very pessimistic and full of justifiable scorn for Tirpitz whose Wiegand interview was merely one of a series of blunders." Alfred von Tirpitz, *Erinnerungen* (Leipzig, 1919), p. 340, claims that he wanted to "sound out American public opinion on submarine warfare."

17. Clifton Child, "German-American Attempts to Prevent the Exportation of Munitions of War, 1914-1916," *Mississippi Valley Historical Review* 25, no. 3 (December 1938): 351. A similar move was made in the Senate early in December by Senator Gilbert Hitchcock of Nebraska.

18. Crighton, *Missouri and the World War, 1914-1917,* pp. 90-91.

19. Armin Rappaport, *The British Press and the Wilsonian Neutrality, 1914-1917* (Stanford, Calif., 1951), pp. 17-20.

20. *L'Osservatore Romano,* January 6, 1915.

21. "La Politique de Benoit XV," *La Revue de Paris* 25, no. 20 (October 15, 1918): 890, claims that the pope believed–in demanding that the United States stop selling munitions and arms–that the Allied plans and ambitions were more dangerous than Germany's.

22. Birnbaum, *Peace Moves and U-Boat Warfare,* p. 24.

23. *L'Osservatore Romano,* February 3, 1915. During subsequent weeks, it published the notes exchanged between the U.S., British, and German governments

concerning the U-boat campaign. Ibid., February 13, 14, 15, 16, 19, 1915. Soon after, the British were advised that according to an opinion given by Cardinal Gasparri, German submarine warfare was justifiable in international law. Count John Salis to Lord Curzon, London, October 25, 1922, FO 371, vol. 7671, PRO.

24. Emphasis added. Bernstorff to Foreign Office, Washington, February 27, 1915, in Link, *Wilson: The Struggle for Neutrality,* p. 24.

25. Stephen Gwynn, ed., *The Letters and Friendships of Sir Cecil Spring-Rice: A Record,* 2 vols. (Boston and New York, 1929) 2: 259-261. The Jesuit *America* encouraged its readers to accept the justice of Germany's cause and disregard neutral rights. *America* 12 (April 1915): 634. The pro-Allied *Catholic World,* published by the Paulist Fathers of New York, took a strong stand against German U-boat warfare. Esslinger, "American German and Irish Attitudes," pp. 198-199.

26. Epstein, *Erzberger,* pp. 126-127; Erzberger, *Souvenirs de Guerre,* pp. 62-63, while denying that he arranged the audience, admits that he knew von Wiegand.

27. *New York World,* April 11, 1915. Lansing was advised about the pending publication of the interview. Lansing's Desk Diary, April 10, 1915.

28. *FR-US, 1915, Supp.,* pp. 157-158; Tansill, *America Goes to War,* pp. 56-57, 60-61. On April 21, Bryan refused the demand, arguing that it would not be in accord with strict neutrality.

29. The text was authentic, since the pope composed it in Italian and gave it to von Wiegand. Howard to Grey, Rome, April 13, 1915, FO 371, vol. 2561, PRO.

30. *L'Osservatore Romano,* April 15, 1915, published an editorial that endeavored to minimize the significance of the pope's interview. Howard to Drummond, Rome, April 14, 1915. FO 800, vol. 67, PRO.

31. Leslie, *Cardinal Gasquet,* p. 242. The pope told Gasquet that he believed that such trade was contrary to the law of nations.

32. House Diary, April 13, 1915; House to Wilson, cable, April 14, 1915. House repeated his statement to Delcassé, adding that Germany used von Wiegand and the pope for the purpose of "not only stirring up resentment, but to bring pressure upon you through the Catholic world," House to Wilson, Paris, April 14, 1915, Wilson Papers, series II.

33. Wilson to House, April 15, 1915, House Papers; Stelio Marchese, *Francia e il Problema dei Rapporti con la Santa Sede (1914-1924)* (Naples, 1969), pp. 92-93.

34. Epstein, *Erzberger,* pp. 102-103, 122-123; Erzberger, *Souvenirs de Guerre,* pp. 43-52, 233-234.

35. Link, *Wilson: The Struggle for Neutrality,* pp. 368-409; Thomas A. Bailey, "The Sinking of the Lusitania," *American Historical Review* 41, no. 1 (October 1935): 54-73, shows that the liner carried 4,200 cases of cartridges as well as 1,250 empty shrapnel cases.

36. Benedict XV to Cardinal Gasquet, May 12, 1915, in Leslie, *Cardinal Gasquet,* pp. 241-242. *L'Osservatore Romano,* May 9, 1915, published news about the sinking of the Lusitania. It expressed only "regrets" for it, which implied that the Allies should be blamed as well.

37. *New York Times,* May 11, 1915.

38. *Catholic Telegraph,* May 20, 1915.

39. Cardinal O'Connell to Wilson, Boston, May 11, 1915, Wilson Papers, series II.

40. Esslinger, "American German and Irish Attitudes," p. 201; Gimarc, "Illinois Catholic Editorials," p. 176. In the city of Milwaukee not a single minister mentioned

the disaster. Abrams, *Preachers Present Arms,* p. 29. The *Josephinum Weekly* (Columbus, Ohio) wrote in May 1915 that Germany acted in accord with accepted rights and insisted upon the "vicious" food blockade. The *Catholic Columbian Record* (Columbus, Ohio), June 18, 1915, rejected Wilson's policy of atonement and insisted that peace be continued without too many questions. Other Catholic publications took more moderate attitudes: *Sacred Heart Review* 13 (May 1915): 324, 341; *Extension Magazine* 10 (June 1915): 5; Crighton, *Missouri and the World War,* p. 87.

41. Koenig, *Principles for Peace,* pp. 170-171; *Italia* (Rome), May 25, 1915; Humphrey Johnson, *The Papacy and the Kingdom of Italy* (London, 1926), pp. 104-105.

42. *La Liberté* (Paris), June 22, 1915; Howard to Grey, Rome, June 24, 26, 28, 1915, FO 371, vol. 2378, PRO; *L'Osservatore Romano,* June 28, 1915; Leslie, *Cardinal Gasquet,* p. 244.

43. Tansill, *America Goes to War,* pp. 103-104; Child, *German-Americans in Politics,* pp. 57, 59-66, 82-83; idem, "German-American Attempts", pp. 364-365; *Kansas City Catholic Register,* September 23, 1915; *Western Watchman,* September 30, 1915; *L'Osservatore Romano,* October 1, 4, December 1, 1915.

44. Link, *Wilson: The Struggle for Neutrality,* pp. 582-585. Several days later, Gerard was informed that the pope was "responsible for the change of German submarine policy; in return he is to work for peace which a friend says Germany now desires." Gerard to Lansing, Berlin, September 5, 1915, *FR-US, 1915, Supp.,* p. 534; Görlitz, *The Kaiser and His Court,* p. 102, does not mention that the pope's message was discussed at the Imperial conference at Pless Castle on August 26, 1915.

45. John Tracy Ellis, *The Life of James Cardinal Gibbons, Archbishop of Baltimore, 1834-1921,* 2 vols (Milwaukee, 1952) 2: 231; Lansing's Desk Diary, September 2, 1915; Vercesi, *Il Vaticano, l'Italia e la guerra,* pp. 208-209; Gwynn, *The Vatican and the War in Europe,* p. 41.

46. Fritz Fisher, *Germany's Aims in the First World War* (New York, 1967), p. 283. *L'Osservatore Romano,* September 12, 1915, comments on Germany's *Arabic* pledge.

47. Birnbaum, *Peace Moves and U-Boat Warfare,* pp. 46, 50-51, 53. The Kaiser approved the decision that unrestricted U-boat warfare begin from March 1, 1916. For his part, the chancellor was toying with the idea of cautiously inviting Britain to discuss peace.

48. Koenig, *Principles for Peace,* pp. 193-196.

49. Howard to Grey (private), Rome, January 10, 1916, FO 800, vol. 67, PRO.

50. *Fortnightly Review* 23 (January 15, 1916): 20-21; Cuddy, "Pro-Germanism and American Catholicism," p. 437; Gimarc, "Illinois Catholic Editorial Opinions," pp. 180-181; Ellis, *Gibbons,* 2: 236-237.

51. *L'Osservatore Romano,* January 30, 1916, published the substance of Wilson's address before the Railway Business Association on January 27, 1916. Link, *Wilson: Confusions and Crisis,* pp. 45-46.

52. Cuddy, "Pro-Germanism and American Catholicism," pp. 433, 435-436. *Die Amerika,* April 23, 1916, accused Wilson of becoming "the lackey of the King of England." *Chicago Daily News,* May 16, 1916; *America* 15 (August 26, 1916): 475.

53. *FR-US, 1916, Supp.,* pp. 208-209, 224.

54. *Western Watchman,* March 2, 1916; Crighton, *Missouri and the World War,* p. 105; the British had acquired confidential information that the pope, in the summer of 1916, used "a language hostile to the Entente, and blaming them for the continuance of the war." Salis to Curzon, London, October 25, 1922, FO 371, vol. 7671, PRO.

55. Rappaport, *The British Press and Wilsonian Neutrality,* p. 89; Birnbaum, *Peace Moves and U-Boat Warfare,* pp. 75-92.

56. Adee to Lester Woolsey, May 15, 1916, State Department Archives. Adee's text was dispatched to Rome over Wilson's signature. Wilson to Benedict XV, May 15, 1916, Wilson Papers, series IV; Ellis, *Gibbons,* 2: 234-235.

57. Wilson's reply to Jeremiah A. O'Leary, president of the German-financed Truth Society, became a noted piece of history itself. To O'Leary's telegram predicting his defeat, Wilson replied, on September 29, 1916, that "I would feel deeply mortified to have you or anybody like you vote for me. Since you have access to many disloyal Americans and I have not, I shall ask you to convey this message to them." Link, *Wilson: Campaigns for Progressivism and Peace,* pp. 104-105; Blum, *Tumulty and the Wilson Era,* p. 106.

58. Blum, *Tumulty and the Wilson Era,* pp. 105-106.

59. Child, *German-Americans in Politics,* pp. 122-126.

60. For an analysis of much of the Catholic vote, see William M. Leary, Jr., "Woodrow Wilson, Irish Americans and the Election of 1916," *Journal of American History* 54, no. 1 (June 1967): 57-72; Link, *Wilson: Campaigns for Progressivism and Peace,* p. 161.

61. *L'Osservatore Romano,* November 13, 1916.

CHAPTER 5

1. Link, *Wilson: Campaigns for Progressivism and Peace,* pp. 165-175, 187-206; May, *The World War and the American Isolation,* pp. 360-365.

2. "Note from a reliable source," September 9, 1916, The Papers of David Lloyd George, Beaverbrook Library, London. F. Engel-Janosi, "The Church and Nationalities in the Habsburg Monarchy," *Austrian History Yearbook* 3, no. 3 (1967). 81.

3. Gaisford to Drummond, Rome, September 9, 1916, FO 800, vol. 67, PRO.

4. Link, *Wilson: Campaigns for Progressivism and Peace,* p. 176; Rappaport, *The British Press and Wilsonian Neutrality,* p. 115. Early in November the pope complained to Cardinal Gasquet that he was "put up" by Lloyd George's statement. He admitted that he "does not intend to make any attempt to bring about peace unless both sides approach him." Gaisford to Drummond, Rome, November 4, 1916, FO 800, vol. 67, PRO.

5. *Official German Documents Relating to the World War,* 2 vols., (New York, 1923) 2: 989. Bernstorff insisted that no action on Wilson's part ought to be expected before the elections, "nor that he will put himself in communication with the pope and the King of Spain, since up to this time every proposal for joint action was met with invincible opposition here." Ibid., p. 990, Bernstorff, *My Three Years in America,* pp. 293-294.

6. Rodd to Lord Hardinge, Rome, October 20, 1916, Lloyd George Papers.

7. Lansing's Desk Diary, November 15, 1916. There was talk about House's new trip to Europe.

8. Baker, *Life and Letters,* 6: 381-386; Link, *Wilson and the Progressive Era,* pp. 257-258.

9. Angelo Martini, "La 'Nota' di Benedetto XV per la pace (1 agosto 1917)," *La Civilta Cattolica* 4 (1962): 4-5. The Russian minister to the Vatican claimed that the pope had known earlier about Germany's action for peace. M.M. Sheinman, *Vatikan i Katolitsizm v kontse XIX-nachale XX v.* [The Vatican and Catholicism at the end of the nineteenth century and beginning of the twentieth] (Moscow, 1958), p. 409.

10. Gasparri to Bonzo, nuncio in Vienna, Rome, December 12, 1916, Papers of Sidney Sonnino, Vatican file on microfilm, reel 48. Sonnino's papers are deposited in Montespertoli, Italy. Reinhold Lorenz, *Kaiser Karl und der Untergang der Donau Monarchie* (Graz, 1959), p. 244. Friedrich Engel-Janosi, *Österreich und der Vatikan, 1846-1918,* 2 vols. (Vienna-Graz-Koln, 1960) 2: 291, claims that the pope took a restrained attitude toward this demand.

11. *FR-US, 1916, Supp.,* pp. 85-86; *New York Times,* December 13, 1916. The *Washington Post,* December 13, 1916, reported that the neutrals and the pope were informed of the proposal. On December 14, *L'Osservatore Romano* printed the same news.

12. Link, *Wilson and the Progressive Era,* p. 261; on December 15, the *Chicago Tribune* expressed hope that the European powers might accept "an offer of the good offices of the United States."

13. Lansing's Desk Diary, December 14, 1916.

14. Gasparri to Bonzo, Rome, Sonnino Papers, 48.

15. Salis to Balfour, Rome, December 16, 1916, War Cabinet Papers, I, 23, Public Record Office, London. On December 18, the War Cabinet decided to refuse the German proposal.

16. For a discussion of Germany's war aims, see Fischer, *Germany's Aims,* pp. 310-322; Hans W. Gatzke, *Germany's Drive to the West* (Baltimore, 1950), pp. 139-144. For British views on the Vatican, its moves and sympathies for Austria-Hungary, see David Lloyd George, *War Memoirs,* 2 vols., (London, 1938), 2: 658.

17. Gasparri to Bonzo, Rome, Sonnino Papers, 48; Martini, *La Civilta Cattolica,* 4:5.

18. "La nota degli Stati Uniti ai governi belligerenti e ai neutri per affretare la fine della guerra," *L'Osservatore Romano,* December 24, 1916, January 2, 1917.

19. *FR-US, 1916, Supp.,* p. 144.

20. Page to Wilson (confidential), Rome, December 29, 1916, Wilson Papers, series II.

21. Salis wrote, "President Wilson was distrusted at the Vatican because he was not understood. The Pope himself told me that the moment did not appear to him suitable for making suggestions to the belligerents, a conclusion which may well have been confirmed by the cold reception given to President Wilson's intervention into the discussion." Salis to Curzon, London, October 25, 1922, FO, 371, vol. 7671, PRO; Erzberger, *Souvenirs de guerre,* p. 316, claimed, however, that Wilson's note enjoyed support from the Holy See.

22. Cardinal Farley to Lansing, New York, Lansing Papers. Cardinal Farley also endeavored to reach Colonel House. House, however, was not impressed. House Diary, November 18, 1916.

23. Spring-Rice to Balfour, Washington, December 29, 1916, Papers of Arthur J. Balfour, First Earl of Balfour, vol. 49740, Division of Manuscripts, The British Museum, London.

24. Spring-Rice to Balfour, Washington, January 12, 1917, FO 371, vol. 3076, PRO; Maurice Pernot, *Le Saint Siège, l'Eglise Catholique et la Politique Mondiale* (Paris, 1924), p. 129, claims that the Vatican exerted influence upon the Catholic clergy in order to prevent U.S. intervention in the war.

25. Willard to Lansing (confidential), Madrid, December 12, 1916, Woolsey Papers. Strong pressure was exerted by the Holy See on the Spanish government to intervene. Sidney Sonnino, *Diario,* 1916-1922, vol. 3, ed. P. Pastorelli (Bari, 1972), p. 89.

26. *FR-US, 1916, Supp.,* p. 118; Lansing's Desk Diary, December 27, 1916. Page wrote that many had drawn the inference that the Vatican was working with Spain to be, if possible, selected as the arbiter for the peace conference to be held in the future. *FR-US, The Lansing Papers,* 1: 750-751.

27. *FR-US, 1916, Supp.,* pp. 117-118; *Papers Relating to the Foreign Relations of the United States, 1917, Supplement I, the World War* (Washington, 1931), pp. 6-7, 17-21; May, *The World War and American Isolation,* pp. 368-369; *L'Osservatore Romano,* January 13, 14, 1917.

28. Page to Lansing, Rome, January 21, 1917, *FR-US, 1917, Supp.* 1: 22; *FR-US, The Lansing Papers,* 1: 750-751. This letter was forwarded to Wilson but was returned without any comment. Wilson to Lansing, February 14, 1917, State Department Archives. The Vatican fear of Russian domination, on the other hand, was expressed very strongly. In the instructions sent to Nuncio Aversa in Munich, to be handed to the German chancellor, Gasparri insisted that guarantees should be made to exclude any possibility of imperialistic designs in Europe. "This," wrote the cardinal, "ought to be especially designed against Russia, which, if she realizes all that was promised to her, would have absolute domination in Europe and the Orient." Gasparri to Aversa, Rome, January 17, 1917, Martini, *La Civilta Cattolica,* p. 7; Sheinman, *Vatikan i katolitsizm,* p. 410.

29. Wedel to Bethmann-Hollweg, Vienna, December 27, 1916; Jacques Grunevald and Andre Scherer, eds., *L'Allemagne et les problemes de la Paix pendant la Premiere guerre Mondiale, Documents extraits des archives de L'Office Allemand des Affaires Etrangères,* 2 vols. (Paris, 1962) 1: 643-644; Martini, *La Civilta Cattolica,* p. 5; Valiani, *La Dissoluzione del Austria-Ungheria,* pp. 254-255, 318.

30. *FR-US, The Lansing Papers,* 1: 744-745. Page's letter reached Washington on January 18, 1917; Sheinman, *Vatikan i katolitsizm,* p. 411.

31. House to Wilson, January 19, 1917, Wilson Papers, series II.

32. Spring-Rice to Balfour, Washington, January 5, 1917, FO 371, vol. 3070, PRO.

33. Horace Rumbold to Balfour, Bern, January 9, 1917, FO 371, vol. 3075, PRO. Marchetti was in constant contact with the German and Austro-Hungarian diplomats in Bern. He tried to present to them the need for making a definite reply to Wilson's note in an effort to deny accusations that Germany's peace offer was a bluff. With this in view, he asked the pope to make an appeal to the Kaiser. Martini, *La Civilta Cattolica,* p. 6.

34. Benedict XV to Emperor Wilhelm, Vatican, January 16, 1917, Grunevald and Scherer, *L'Allemagne et les problemes de la paix,* 1: 676-677. It took the Emperor more than a month to reply to the pope. When the reply was sent, on February 27, 1917, it completely failed to answer the pope's concrete proposals. The Kaiser explained that the Central Powers had to continue fighting because their very existence had been threatened by the Allies. All responsibility for the

continuation of hostilities was to fall upon "those who, pushed by their hatred and limitless ambitions, eliminate any chance to stop the hurricane they had helped unleash," Martini, *La Civilta Cattolica,* p. 7.

35. January 8, 1917, *Official German Documents,* 2: 1205.

36. Link, *Wilson: The Struggle for Progressivism and Peace,* pp. 253-289.

37. "Un nuovo messagio di Wilson per la pace," *L'Osservatore Romano,* January 23, 1917. Further comments appeared on January 25, 1917. On January 26, the *New York Times* published the pope's comment about it. The pope called the speech "the most courageous document which appeared since the beginning of the war. It contains many truths and revives the principles of Christian civilization."

38. Wilson did not have in mind the dissolution of the Habsburg Monarchy, as was charged indirectly by the Vatican. He told Ambassador Jusserand on March 7, 1917, that it would not be desirable. He only had in mind a broad autonomy for the empire's subject nationalities. Link, *Wilson: The Struggle for Progressivism and Peace,* p. 268, May, "Woodrow Wilson and Austria-Hungary to the end of 1917," pp. 220-221.

39. Page to Lansing, Rome, State Department Archives. Page privately relayed this information to Ambassador Rodd. He also remarked that "Wilson was not likely to be taking lessons as to the proper interpretation of neutrality from the Vatican." Rodd to Balfour (private), Rome, February 8, 1917, FO 800, vol. 202, PRO. Sir Rennell Rodd, *Social and Diplomatic Memoirs, 1902-1919 (Third Series)* (London, 1925), pp. 330-331.

40. Jones to Cecil (private and very confidential), Rome, February 26, 1917, Lloyd George Papers. In a covering letter, Jones informed Cecil that he was sending the reports from a person high in the Vatican's confidence. The information came directly from Gasparri and should not be published since "we will kill the goose which bears golden eggs."

41. *Official German Documents,* 1: 150; *FR-US, 1917, Supp,* 1: 100-102; Link, *Wilson: The Struggle for Progressivism and Peace,* pp. 284-289. The same day Zimmermann told Gerard that Germany should use the U-boats "no matter what the consequences are." Gerard remarked that "there is no doubt but that Germany believes that Americans are [a] fat, rich race without a sense of honor and ready to stand for everything in order to keep out of war." Gerard to Lansing, Berlin, January 31, 1917, State Department Archives.

42. Link, *Wilson: The Struggle for Progressivism and Peace,* pp. 290-301; Notter, *Origins of the Foreign Policy,* pp. 610-616.

43. *L'Osservatore Romano,* February 3, 5, 1917.

44. Rodd to Balfour (private), Rome, February 8, 1917, FO 800, vol. 202, PRO. Cecil remarked that the Vatican was more pro-German than Howard thought.

45. Jones to Cecil (confidential), February 26, 1917, Lloyd George Papers.

46. Page to Lansing (confidential), Rome, February 10, 1917, State Department Archives.

47. Page to Wilson (confidential), Rome, February 13, 1917, Wilson Papers, series II.

48. Jones to Lord Cecil, Rome, February 26, 1917, Lloyd George Papers. Cecil commented that the whole affair put the Vatican in an unflattering light. Balfour was more philosophical. He wrote that "the moral failure of the Papacy in this crisis is a blow to all forms of Christianity. Christianity has survived many bad Popes, and many Vatican intrigues. We must hope for the best."

49. Bonzo to Gasparri, Vienna, February 7, 1917, Sonnino Papers, 48; Czernin said the same to the U.S. ambassador in Vienna, Penfield, early in February 1917. *FR-US, 1917, Supp.*, 1: 113.

50. Gasparri to Bonzo, Vatican, February 10, 1917, Sonnino Papers, 48.

51. House to Wilson, New York, January 27, 1917, Wilson Papers, series II; House Diary, January 26, 1917.

52. Walter Page to Wilson and Lansing, London, February 20, 1917, Page Papers.

53. Lansing to Penfield, February 22, 1917. *FR-US, 1917, Supp.*, 1: 57-58.

54. Gasparri to Bonzo, Vatican, February 23, 1917, Sonnino Papers, 48.

55. Rodd to Balfour (private), Rome, January 31, 1917, FO 800, vol. 202, PRO. This information was transmitted by the Prussian minister to the Holy See. Aversa to Gasparri, Munich, February 2, 3, 4, 1917, Sonnino Papers, 48; Fischer, *Germany's Aims in the First World War,* p. 304.

56. Gasparri to Aversa, Vatican, February 7, 1917, Sonnino Papers, 48.

57. Rodd to Balfour (private), Rome, February 13, 1917, FO 800, vol. 202, PRO; Drummond to Salis, February 21, 1917, FO 800, vol. 383, PRO.

58. Link, *Wilson: The Struggle for Progressivism and Peace,* pp. 340-346.

59. Rodd to Balfour (private), Rome, February 26, 1917, FO 800, vol. 202, PRO.

60. Salis to Balfour (secret and confidential), Rome, February 28, 1917, FO 371, vol. 3081, PRO.

61. War Cabinet Papers, 23, 2, PRO. Lord Curzon wrote to Balfour insisting that the blockade and submarine warfare could not be compared; there were clear differences. Definite distinctions between the two ought to be made. He demanded that the German method should be described as a "novel crime contrary to both [the] law of nations and to humanity [sic]." Curzon to Balfour, London, March 2, 1917, Balfour Papers, vol. 49734.

62. Balfour to Salis, March 2, 1917, FO 371, vol. 3081, PRO. The text of the reply was composed by Cecil and Drummond. The Foreign Office did not inform the Allies about the proposal.

63. Page to Lansing, Rome, March 7, 1917, State Department Archives; Speranza to James Shotwell, Rome, January 13, 1919, Speranza Papers, Correspondence 1919-1925; for a detailed account, see Epstein, *Mathias Erzberger,* pp. 112-113, 149-150, 163.

64. Page to Lansing, Rome, March 14, 1917, State Department Archives.

65. Page to Lansing, March 20, 1917, *FR-US, 1917, The Lansing Papers,* 1: 760-761; Rodd to Balfour (private), Rome, March 25, 1917, FO 800, vol. 202, PRO.

66. *L'Osservatore Romano,* April 15, 1917. The Italian censor cut out much of the editorial. The reaction was natural in view of the fact that Gasparri claimed that the preservation of America's neutrality was one of the principal objectives of Vatican policy. *Il Cardinale Gasparri e la questione Romana,* pp. 180-181.

67. Gibbons to Wilson, April 18, 1917; Wilson to Gibbons, April 27, 1917, Wilson Papers, series III, Ellis, *Gibbons,* 2: 240; Abrams, *Preachers Present Arms,* pp. 73-74. The texts of numerous proclamations and prayers of Catholic churchmen are preserved in the Wilson papers. Gimarc, "Illinois Editorial Catholic Opinion," pp. 183-184.

CHAPTER 6

1. Angelo Tamborra, "L'idea di nazionalita e la guerra, 1914-1918", in *Atti del XLI Congresso per la Storia del Risorgimento Italiano* (Trento, October 9-13,

1963) (Rome, 1965), pp. 224-225.

2. Dragan R. Živojinović, "Robert Lansing's Comments on the Pontifical Peace Note of August 1, 1917," *Journal of American History* 56, no. 3 (December 1969): 558-559; Mario Bendiscioli, "La Santa Sede e la Guerra," in *Benedetto XV, i Cattolici,* pp. 37, 39-40, 42; Jean Leflon, "L'action diplomatico-religieuse de Benoit XV en faveur de la paix durant la première guerre mondiale," in ibid., p. 68; Pierre Renouvin, *La Crise Européenne et la Grande Guerre (1904-1918)* (Paris, 1934), pp. 461-468.

3. Otakar Czernin, *In the World War (New* York, 1920), p. 164; Friedrich Engel-Janosi, "Benedetto XV e l'Austria," in *Benedetto XV, i Cattolici,* p. 347.

4. Angelo Martini, "La nota di Benedetto XV alle potenze belligerenti nell' agosto 1917," in *Benedetto XV, i Cattolici,* (reprint), pp. 8-10. In the Czernin-Sixtus conversations in Vienna in March 1917, Czernin did not agree to yield any of the monarchy's territory to Italy. The same refusal was made in the Armand-Di Revertera talks. Robert A. Kann, *The Multinational Empire: Nationalism and National Reform in Habsburg Monarchy, 1848-1918,* 2 vols. (New York, 1950), 2: 268-269.

5. Gasparri to Bonzo, Vatican, Sonnino Papers, 48; Kann, *The Multinational Empire,* 2: 270-271, claims rightly that Austria-Hungary refused the demand to cede a part of Tyrol to Italy.

6. Pacelli to Gasparri, Cologne, Sonnino Papers, 48; Martini, "La nota di Benedetto XV.," in *Benedetto XV, i Cattolici,* pp. 13-14.

7. Viktor Naumann, *Dokumente und Argumente* (Berlin, 1928), pp. 234-276; Erzberger, *Souvenirs de guerre,* p. 316; Martini, *La Civilta Cattolica,* p. 8-9; V.H. Rothwell, *British War Aims and Diplomacy 1914-1918* (Oxford, 1971), pp. 102-104.

8. Pacelli to Gasparri, June 6, 1917, Sonnino Papers, 48; Gwynn, *The Vatican and the War,* p. 46.

9. Benedict XV to Emperor Wilhelm, June 13, 1917; Gasparri to Pacelli, June 13, 1917, Sonnino Papers, 48; Martini, "La nota di Benedetto XV.," in *Benedetto XV, i Cattolici,* pp. 12-13.

10. Engel-Janosi, "Benedetto XV e l'Austria," pp. 347-348. Engel-Janosi does not consider that the socialist threat was instrumental in getting the Vatican ready to act. However, the Austro-Hungarian ambassador to the Vatican, Count Schönburg, demanded the pope's action "in order to avoid that the Socialists get all credit for bringing about peace." Pacelli to Gasparri, May 30, 1917, Sonnino Papers, 48.

11. Pacelli to Gasparri, Cologne, Sonning Papers, 48; Bendiscioli, "La Santa Sede e la guerra," in *Benedetto XV, i Cattolici,* p. 42.

12. For a detailed analysis, see John M. Snell, "Benedict XV, Wilson, Michaelis, and German Socialism," *Catholic Historical Review* 38, no. 1 (June 1951): 152-156.

13. Pacelli to Gasparri, Cologne, June 30, 1917, Sonnino Papers, 48; Eugenio Pacelli, "A propos de l'offre de Paix du Saint Siège en 1917," *Revue d 'Histoire de la Guerre Mondiale* 4 (1926): 131-140.

14. Fulvio d'Amoja (in discussion), in *Benedetto XV, i Cattolici,* p. 284; Olindo Malagodi, *Conversazioni della guerra, 1914-1919,* ed. Brunello Viggezzi, 2 vols., (Milan and Naples, 1960), 2: 159-160.

15. Veneruso, "Ricerche e problemi," pp. 129-156.

16. Epstein, *Erzberger,* pp. 182-213.

17. William Phillips Diary, June 12, 1917, Papers of William Phillips, Houghton Library, Harvard University, Cambridge, Massachusetts; *Papers Relating to the*

Foreign Relations of the United States, 1917, Supplement 2, the World War, 2 vols. (Washington, 1932), 1:128.

18. *FR-US, 1917, Supp. 2,* 1: 130, 131; Gwynn, *The Vatican and the War in Europe,* p. 44.

19. Pacelli to Gasparri, June 27, 1917, Sonnino Papers, 48; Humphrey Johnson, *Vatican Diplomacy in the World War* (Oxford, 1933), pp. 24-25; Gwynn, *The Vatican and the War in Europe,* p. 46.

20. These were (1) the pope's preoccupations for peace; (2) appeal to the Kaiser to work for peace, even with sacrifices if necessary; (3) favorable impression to be made upon the Allies by declaration of Germany's readiness to discuss the problems of armament; (4) Belgium's independence; (5) problem of Alsace-Lorraine, (6) problem of a separate peace with Russia and the destiny of Poland. Martini, "La nota," p. 13.

21. Pacelli to Gasparri, June 30, 1917, Sonnino Papers, 48; Martini, "La nota," p.13; Fischer, *Germany's Aims,* pp. 394-395, insists that the Kaiser gave the nuncio plainly to understand that he was not interested in a peace move. Gwynn, *The Vatican and the War in Europe,* p. 46, claims erroneously that the Kaiser consented to what the chancellor had said. Görlitz, *The Kaiser and His Court,* p. 279, writes that the Kaiser told Pacelli that the Catholic church had given him no support in his peace feelers and that he would "continue the war until his enemies had bitten the dust."

22. Gasparri to Pacelli, Sonnino Papers, 48; Martini, "La nota" pp. 14-15.

23. On this occasion, Pacelli, on Gasparri's demand, inquired about the possibility of democratizing the political and constitutional system in Germany. Michaelis thought it was not possible to introduce the parliamentary system in Germany. Pacelli to Gasparri, July 30, 1917, Sonnino Papers, 48; Martini, "La nota," p. 16.

24. The discussion between Michaelis and Czernin followed after the reception of the nuncio. The two statesmen met on August 1, 1917, but the German government confirmed its intention to retain a free hand in Belgium. On August 9, Czernin's suggestion that Germany give up Alsace-Lorraine was coldly rebuffed. Fischer, *Germany's Aims,* pp. 412-415; Snell, "Benedict XV, Wilson, Michaelis and German Socialism," pp. 156-157.

25. James Brown Scott, ed., *Official Statement of War Aims and Peace Proposals, December 1916 to November 1918* (New York, 1925), pp. 129-131; *FR-US, 1917, Supp. 2, 1:* 162-164; Friedrich Ritter von Lama, *Die Friedensvermittlung Papst Benedikt XV und ihre Vereitlung durch den Deutschen Reichskanzler Michaelis (August-September, 1917); eine historisch-kritische Untersuchung* (Munich, 1932); Engel-Janosi, *Österreich und der Vatikan,* 2: 292-325.

26. Pacelli to Gasparri, Munich, August 12, 1917, Sonnino Papers, 48; Martini, "La nota" pp. 18-19.

27. On August 15, Gasparri instructed Pacelli to demand the German government to state its acceptance of the pope's proposal, leaving the discussion of the specific questions to the peace conference. Gasparri to Pacelli, Sonnino Papers, 48.

28. Salis to Balfour, Rome, August 9, 1917, FO 371, vol. 3083, PRO; Lansing's Desk Diary, August 11, 1917.

29. Ellis, *Gibbons,* 2: 244. The cardinal did as he was asked and published an interview in the *New York Times* on August 16, suggesting that more attention be given to the document. He also promised Bonzano to do everything in his power to "further the wishes of the Holy See in the matter."

30. Salis to Balfour, Rome, FO 371, vol. 3083, PRO. Balfour approved Salis's reply.

31. Wiseman to House, London, August 11, 1917, House Papers; House to Wilson, Magnolia, Mass., Wilson Papers, series II.

32. *FR-US, 1917, Supp. 2,* 1: 162-164; Jay to Lansing, Rome, August 14, 1917, State Department Archives; Spring-Rice reported that "the President is considerably put out by the proposal coming at the time when the United States government are doing their utmost to kindle the warlike spirit throughout the States and to combat the pacifists." Spring-Rice to Balfour, Washington, August 15, 1917, FO 371, vol. 3083, PRO; see the *New York Times, Philadelphia Inquirer, Washington Post, Chicago Tribune, Boston Evening Transcript,* August 17, as well as others.

33. Phillips Diary, August 16, 1917, "Brazilian Ambassador expressed his disapproval of the Pope's note." Lansing's Desk Diary, August 16, 1917, note on the attitude of "Brazilian amb. on Pope's appeal"; Justus, *V. Macchi di Cellere all'Ambasciata di Washington. Memorie e Testimonianze* (Florence, 1921), p. 80. Lansing told the Italian ambassador that the note provided for the status quo ante bellum and that to accept it would mean to have another war tomorrow. On August 18, Jusserand wrote to Lansing asking him to be consulted with respect to the reply to the pope; the same day Jay cabled from Rome that Sonnino maintained that no response was necessary, Sharp made a similar suggestion from Paris, insisting upon the need for consultation. State Department Archives.

34. Lansing's Desk Diary, August 17, 18, 1917. Frederick Dixon, editor of the *Christian Science Monitor* wrote to Lord Cecil that the "Note is sheer pro-Germanism and I have hammered that in, in our editorials." Several days later, he advised that "the Pope's note is a complete failure here." Dixon to Cecil, Boston, August 18, 23, 1917, Papers of Lord Robert Cecil, First Marquess of Chelwood, vol. 51092, Division of Manuscripts, British Museum, London.

35. House to Wilson, August 15, 1917, Wilson Papers, series II; Charles Seymour, ed., *The Intimate Papers of Colonel House,* 4 vols., (Boston, 1926-1928), 3: 153-154; Gordon Auchincloss, House's son-in-law and his eyes and ears in the State Department noted that the "Colonel" has written to Wilson on how to handle the pope's note. Auchincloss insisted that "peace is in the air but the difficulties in the way of it seem very great indeed." House's argument was more convincing in view of the fact that the king of Spain had informed Villard confidentially that the Germans intended to propose peace terms in January 1918. Papers of Godron Auchincloss, Diary, August 15, 1917, Sterling Memorial Library, Yale University, New Haven, Connecticut.

36. House Diary, August 15, 1917.

37. "I feel that this peace proposal is fraught with danger and that it should be given the gravest consideration before any answer is sent." House to Wiseman, Magnolia, Massachusetts, August 18, 1917, House Papers.

38. House to Wilson, August 17, 1917, Wilson Papers, series II. Part of it is in Seymour, *The Intimate Papers,* 3: 156; Wilton B. Fowler, *British-American Relations, 1917-1918: The Role of Sir William Wiseman* (Princeton, 1969), pp. 91-92.

39. Incidentally, House himself persuaded Wilson that it was not opportune to discuss the question officially. House to Wilson, April 22, 1917, House Papers; House Diary, April 27, 1917.

40. Wilson to House, August 16, 1917, Ray S. Baker Papers. On August 20, the contents of Wilson's letter to House were discussed by the British War Cabinet. It was decided that no immediate action should be taken to encourage Wilson to make a reply. War Cabinet Papers, 23, III, PRO.

41. Joe Tumulty, *Woodrow Wilson as I Know Him* (Garden City, N.Y., 1921), pp. 280-281.

42. Henry C. Lodge, *The Senate and the League of Nations* (New York and London, 1925), pp. 80-83; Baker, *Wilson, Life and Letters,* 7: 220-221.

43. Lansing's Desk Diary, August 17, 1917.

44. *FR-US, 1917, Supp. 2,* 1: 165; Baker, *Wilson, Life and Letters,* 7: 226; Phillips Diary, August 20, 1917.

45. Lane to Lansing, Beverly, Massachusetts, August 18, 1917, Lansing Papers.

46. House Diary, August 18, 1917. Walworth, *Wilson,* 2: 141, claims that the "Colonel" got his way with Wilson.

47. Phillips Diary, August 24, 1917.

48. Lansing's Desk Diary, August 20, 1917; a copy of the document is in the Woolsey Papers and Wilson Papers, series II.

49. Lansing's Desk Diary, August 21, 1917. For an extensive analysis of this document, Živojinović, "Robert Lansing's Comments," pp. 556-571.

50. Abbot Lowell to Wilson, August 18, 1917, Wilson Papers, series IV. Wilson thanked Lowell for his letter on August 21, 1917.

51. Thomas B. Neely to Lansing, Philadelphia, August 21, 1917, Lansing Papers.

52. Arthur Chapman to Wilson, New York, August 21, 1917, Wilson Papers, series IV.

53. Henry Demarest Lloyd to Wilson, Boston, August 21, 1917, Wilson Papers, series IV.

54. Sosnowski to Wilson, New York, August 21, 1917, Wilson Papers, series IV.

55. Bolton Hall to Wilson, August 22, 1917; Robert Kohn to Wilson, August 23, 1917, Wilson Papers, series IV.

56. Wilson to House, August 22, 1917, House Papers; Baker, *Wilson: Life and Letters,* 7: 231; N. Gordon Levine, Jr., *Woodrow Wilson and World Politics: America's Response to War and Revolution* (New York, 1968), p. 53.

57. House Diary, August 23, 1917. House accepted, in front of the people, that Wilson's message was something he should be given credit for. He told Auchincloss that he was "immensely pleased" with the reply to be given to the pope. Auchincloss Diary, August 24, 1917.

58. House Diary, August 19, 1917; Lansing's Desk Diary, August 21, 1917; *FR-US, 1917, Supp. 2,* 1: 166.

59. Justus, *Macchi di Cellere,* pp. 80, 81-82; Lansing's Desk Diary, August 21, 1917; *FR-US, 1917, Supp. 2,* 1: 167. Sonnino suggested that a "good, firm reply, drawn up by the President and sent in advance of other allied replies would greatly impress public opinion." Sonnino did not think much of the note, saying that it was "un bel niente" as a basis for negotiations. He did not see any reason for quick action. Sonnino, *Diario,* 3: 182-183.

60. Sharp to Lansing, Paris, August 21, 1917; *FR-US, 1917, Supp. 2,* 1: 171-172.

61. Ibid., pp. 167-168; Johnson, *Vatican Diplomacy in the World War,* pp. 30-31.

62. Spring-Rice to Balfour, Washington, August 21, 1917, FO 371, vol. 3083, PRO.

63. House to Wiseman, August 22, 1917, House Papers. A day earlier Phillips informed Polk that "our Mutual friend," obviously meaning House, had told him that England, in all probability, would wait for Wilson to act and then approve of it. Phillips to Polk (personal), August 21, 1917, Polk Papers.

64. House to Balfour, August 24, 1917, Wilson Papers, series II; Baker, *Wilson, Life and Letters,* 7:233. Cecil replied to House that it would be "desirable for the British and other Allied governments to accept the President's reply as their own," but that it had to be discussed in advance by the War Cabinet. Cecil to House, London, August 27, 1917, House Papers.

65. Lansing's Desk Diary, August 26, 27, 1917; Phillips to Polk, August 26, 1917, Polk Papers; Baker, *Wilson, Life and Letters,* 7: 236; *FR-US, 1917, Supp. 2,* 1: 177-179.

66. Lansing's Desk Diary, August 28, 1917; Cronon, *The Cabinet Diaries of Josephus Daniels,* p. 198.

67. Leo Valiani, "Nuovi documenti sui tratativi di pace nel 1917," *Rivista Storica Italiana* 75, no. 3 (1963): 570.

68. Actually, the article (entitled "La genesi del documento") refused any idea that the action was made with the previous agreement or upon German suggestion. Gasparri was very excited when he realized that Michaelis was to make a statement in the Reichstag, and he cabled Pacelli to tell Michaelis "not to give any statement which might indicate previous consultations between Germany and the Vatican." Michaelis agreed to state that the note was not instigated by the German government, but came as a result of the pope's own decision. Gasparri to Pacelli, August 20, 1917; Pacelli to Gasparri, August 22, 1917, Sonnino Papers, 48.

69. *L'Osservatore Romano,* August 20, 1917.

70. Speranza to Thomas N. Page (confidential), Rome, October 12, 1917, Speranza Papers, Correspondence 1916-1918; Speranza, *Diary,* 2: 93. Ambassador Page transmitted the text of the interview to Wilson on October 15, 1917, after he had seen Dr. Foa and talked with him in the embassy. Page to Wilson, Rome, October 15, 1917, Wilson Papers, series II. The text of the interviews was in French.

71. *L'Osservatore Romano,* August 29, 1917, in an editorial confirmed almost all points raised by Gasparri in his interview with Dr. Foa.

72. The text of the reply in *FR-US, 1917, Supp. 2,* 1: 177-179; Johnson, *Vatican Diplomacy and the World War,* pp. 32-33; Snell, "Benedict XV, Wilson, Michaelis", pp. 161-164; Martini, "La nota," pp. 20-21.

73. Koenig, *Principles for Peace,* pp. 236-239, 240, 241.

74. The *Washington Post,* the *Washington Times, Inquirer* (Philadelphia), the *American* and *Sun* (Baltimore); the *Gazette-Times* (Pittsburgh); the *Leader* and the *Plain Dealer* (Cleveland); *Courant* (Hartford, Connecticut); the *New York World, Herald, Post;* the *Republican* (Springfield, Massachusetts); the *Herald* (Lexington, Kentucky); the *Register* (Wheeling, West Virginia); *The Commercial Appeal* (Memphis, Tennessee); the *State* (Columbia, South Carolina); the *Tribune* (Salt Lake City, Utah). G. Speranza, "The Pope, the War and the Roman Question," *Outlook,* August 29, 1917, was one of the clearest explanations of the note that appeared in the United States. Karl von Wiegand in an article published in *Boston American,* August 29, 1917, complained that Wilson's reply was a hard blow to the Kaiser and to the political system in Germany in general.

75. Lansing's Desk Diary, August 28, 1917; Lansing to Wilson and Wilson to Lansing, September 17, 1917, State Department Archives.

76. War Cabinet Papers, 23, III, August 30, 1917, PRO; Barkley to Drummond, Washington, August 31, 1917, FO 800, vol. 383, PRO; Johnson, *Vatican Diplomacy and the World War,* p. 33. On August 30, House asked Spring-Rice to write to the Foreign Office and ask them to endorse Wilson's reply in order that the Allies might represent a united front. House Diary, August 31, 1917. On September 1, Cecil replied curtly that "we greatly admire the Note and it has been received with much satisfaction in our press." Cecil to House, London, House Papers.

77. Lansing's Desk Diary, August 28, 1917; Phillips Diary, August 29, 1917; Spring-Rice to Balfour, Washington, September 4, 1917, FO 371, vol. 3083, PRO. Letter to the Editor of the *American Historical Review* 37, no. 4 (July 1932): 817-819. In Wilson's words, however, "Jusserand the next day went up in the air because it seemed to exclude economic punishment of Germany after the war." Baker, *Wilson, Life and Letters,* 7: 253-254. The French newspapers were full of praise for Wilson's reply. See *Temps, Figaro, Victoria, Humanité,* and *Matin* for August 30 and 31, 1917.

78. Lansing to Sharp. Stovall, and Langhorn, State Department Archives; George D. Bruntz, *Allied Propaganda and the Collapse of the German Empire in 1918* (Stanford, Calif., 1938), p. 131.

79. The best analysis of reactions in Germany is Snell, "Benedict XV, Wilson, Michaelis," pp. 164-174; *FR-US, 1917, Supp. 2,* 1: 183-186, 187-188, 191, 192-193, 196-197, 199-200.

80. Phillips to Polk, August 28, 1917, Polk Papers; Phillips Diary, August 28, 1917; Auchincloss Diary, August 29, 1917; Lansing's Desk Diary, August 29, 1917.

81. House Diary, August 29, 1917. Several days later he wrote to Wilson that the reply to the pope was the "most remarkable document ever written for surely there was never one approved throughout the world so universally and by every shade of political opinion." House to Wilson, September 4, 1917, Wilson Papers, series II.

82. House Diary, August 29, 1917; Wilson to House, September 4, 1917, Wilson Papers, series II.

83. Dunn to Bonzano, New York, August 30, 1917; Malone to House, September 2, 1917, House Papers. House Diary, September 4, 10, 1917, describes House's discussion with Wilson on the subject.

84. Walter Page to Wilson, London, September 3, 1917, Page Papers.

85. Baker, *Wilson, Life and Letters,* 7: 245; Cronon, *Cabinet Diaries of Josephus Daniels,* p. 204.

86. Wilson to John Sharp Williams, August 30, 1917; Wilson to Brisbane, September 4, 1917; Baker, *Wilson ,Life and Letters,* 7: 245, 258.

87. Baker, *Wilson, Life and Letters,* 7: 250, 253-254, 273.

CHAPTER 7

1. Rumbold to Balfour (confidential), Bern, August 20, 1917, FO 371, vol. 3083, PRO. Marchetti insisted that the pope knew that the "present war could not be settled by one note, but he hoped that most of the belligerents would accept the ideals he had put forward."

2. Cambon to Balfour, London, August 26, 1917, FO 371, vol. 3083, PRO. Harold Nicolson commented that the pope's optimism would be "crushed by the

President's reply"; Cecil and Lord Hardinge expressed their hopes that the Vatican would drop the idea of a second note.

3. Nicolson to George R. Clerk, September 5, 1917, FO 371, vol. 3083, PRO.

4. War Cabinet Papers, 23, IV, PRO.

5. Spring-Rice to Balfour, Washington, September 6, 1917, FO 371, vol. 3083, PRO.

6. Page to Lansing, Rome, September 11, 1917, *FR-US, 1917, Supp. 2*, 1: 198.

7. Engel-Janosi, *Österreich und der Vatikan, 2*: 333, rightly singles out Germany as the major opponent of any peace action on the part of the Vatican.

8. Pacelli to Gasparri, September 13, 1917; Gasparri to Pacelli, September 13, 1917, Sonnino Papers, 48.

9. Martini, "La nota," pp. 22-23; Gasparri to Pacelli, September 15, 1917. Gasparri failed to secure support from Emperor Charles and Czernin for his action in Berlin. Gasparri to Bonzo, September 15, 1917; Bonzo to Gasparri, September 18, 1917, Sonnino Papers, 48.

10. Gasparri to Pacelli, Sonnino Papers, 48. On September 18, Pacelli advised Gasparri that he requested that the communication of Germany's reply and its publication be delayed. Gasparri to Pacelli, September 17, 1917; Pacelli to Gasparri, September 18, 1917, Sonnino Papers, 48; Martini, "La nota," p. 23.

11. Erzberger in *Germania* (Berlin) May 3, 1921; Gasparri to Pacelli, September 17, 1917, Sonnino papers, 48. Pacelli was told that the government was surprised to hear that the Holy See was not satisfied, since "Germany has made much as a first step, which, in case the Allies prove their good will, would be followed with new proposals." Pacelli to Gasparri, September 21, 1917, Sonnino Papers, 48.

12. Gasparri to Pacelli, September 20, 1917, Sonnino Papers, 48. Salis to Balfour, Rome, September 22, 1917, FO 371, vol. 3083, PRO.

13. Pacelli to Gasparri, Munich, September 21, 1917, Sonnino Papers, 48.

14. For the texts, *FR-US, 1917, Supp. 2*, 1: 217-220; *L'Osservatore Romano, September 23*, 1917; Rothwell, *British War Aims*, pp. 102-104.

15. Lansing to Wilson, State Department Archives. These, as well as the replies from the minor members of the Central Powers, were received in Washington on October 2 and 3, 1917. Hugh Wilson believed that Germany's reply was more an answer to Wilson than to the pope. *FR-US, 1917, Supp. 2*, 1: 250-254.

16. Phillips Diary, October 1, 1917.

17. Phillips Diary, October 1, 1917.

18. Page to Wilson (confidential), Rome, September 26, 1917, Wilson Papers, series II.

19. *FR-US, 1917, Supp. 2*, 1: 214; Phillips Diary, October 1, 1917.

20. Phillips Diary, October 20, 1917.

21. *FR-US, 1917, Supp. 2*, 1: 214, 223.

22. Rumbold to Balfour (confidential), Bern, September 28, 1917, FO 371, vol. 3084, PRO.

23. In a lengthy editorial discussing the problems of the freedom of the sea, it was pointed out that Gibraltar, Malta, and Cyprus constituted the bastions of the British domination in the Mediterranean. These, as well as others, were flagrant examples of the "subjection of the seas which should disappear or be essentially modified if Wilson's conception which the Pontifical note alludes to, is to prevail." The Catholic *Corriere d'Italia,* September 27, 1917, brought out the same argument.

24. Gasparri to Lloyd George, September 27, 1917, FO 371. vol. 3084, PRO; part of it in Martini, "La nota," pp. 24-25; *FR-US, 1917, Supp. 2*, 1: 229; Johnson, *Vatican Diplomacy and the World War*, p. 35.

25. Page to Lansing, Rome, September 26, 1917, State Department Archives. On October 7, in a letter to Monsignor Chesnilong, Gasparri repeated much the same arguments he had advanced to Lloyd George about the abolition of compulsory military service. "La Saint Siège et la Paix," *Galois* (Sens), October 22, 1917.

26. Erskine to Balfour (confidential), Rome, October 2, 1917, FO 371, vol. 3083, PRO.

27. Macchi di Cellere to Lansing (strictly personal and confidential). Lansing appeared annoyed at the British failure to forward Gasparri's letter to the State Department. Lansing to Wilson, October 10, 1917, Wilson Papers, series II.

28. Pacelli to Gasparri, October 11, 1917, Sonnino Papers, 48.

29. Bonzo to Gasparri, Vienna, October 21, 1917, Sonnino Papers, 48.

30. Renzo di Felice, *Mussolini: Il Rivoluzionario (1883-1925)* (Turin, 1965), pp. 332, 365.

31. Page to Wilson, London, October 9, 1917, Page Papers. Page referred to Cardinal Bourne, who had made decidedly misleading remarks on the pope's peace note.

32. Memorandum "Political information," October 11, 1917, Speranza Papers.

33. For more information, see Victor Mamatey, *The United States and East Central Europe 1914-1918: A Study in Wilsonian Diplomacy and Propaganda* (Princeton, 1957), pp. 153-156; Fowler, *Sir William Wiseman*, pp. 96-97; Dragan R. Živojinović, *America, Italy and the Birth of Yugoslavia, 1917-1919* (New York, 1972), pp. 93-96.

34. Pernot, *Le Saint-Siège*, p. 36; Roberto Vivarelli, "Questoine Adriatica e la Politica Estera Italiana durante la Prima Guerra Mondiale," *Studi Senesi*, series III, XIII (Siena, 1964), 3: 387.

35. Rodd to Balfour (private), Rome, November 11, 1917, FO 800, vol. 202, PRO.

36. *FR-US, 1917, Supp. 2*, 1: 286; Mamatey, *The United States and East Central Europe*, p. 154.

37. Page to Lansing (for House), Rome, November 10, 1917, House Papers.

38. The Austro-Hungarian ambassador to the Holy See believed that the new government, under Giolitti, would be inclined to negotiate for peace. Valiani, *Dissoluzione*, pp. 377, 379, 431; Engel-Janosi, *Österreich und der Vatikan*, 2: 330.

39. Francisco M. Broglio, *Italia e la Santa Sede dalla Grande Guerra alla Conciliazione; Aspetti Politici e Giuridici* (Bari, 1966), pp. 40, 341.

40. Gasparri to Pacelli and Bonzo, November 14, 1917; Bonzo to Gasparri, Vienna, November 21, 1917, Sonnino Papers, 48; Gwynn, *The Vatican and the War in Europe*, pp. 57, 60.

41. Villa Urutia to the Spanish Foreign Ministry, Rome, November 8, 1917, Sonnino Papers, 48.

42. Rodd to Balfour (private), Rome, November 10, 1917, FO 800, vol. 202, PRO.

43. Phillips Diary, November 12, 1917.

44. Spring-Rice to Balfour, Washington, November 14, 1917, FO 371, vol. 3084, PRO; Spring-Rice to Balfour, November 16, 1917, FO 800, vol. 209, PRO; Townley

to Balfour, The Hague, November 19, 1917, FO 371. vol. 3084, PRO, reports that the press in Germany expected the issuance of the new note.

45. Pacelli to Gasparri, November 15, 1917, Sonnino Papers, 48. Emphasis added.

46. Salis to Balfour, Rome, November 26, 1917, FO 371, vol. 3084, PRO.

47. Marchetti to Gasparri, Bern, November 26, 1917; Gasparri to Marchetti, November 28, Sonnino Papers, 48. Marchetti used Gasparri's cable to make energetic denials that the new note was forthcoming. Rumbold to Balfour, December 7, 1917, FO 371, vol. 3084, PRO.

48. Page to House (strictly confidential), November 27, 1917, House Papers; Fowler, *Sir William Wiseman,* pp. 96-98, 100-102.

49. The Austro-Hungarian government, for example, endorsed Germany's decision to resume unrestricted submarine warfare while repeatedly assuring the U.S. government that its own submarines would not attack U.S. ships on the high seas. *FR-US, 1917, Supp. 1,* 1: 104-105, 131-133, 161-168.

50. Ray S. Baker and William E. Dodd, eds., *The Public Papers of Woodrow Wilson: War and Peace,* 2 vols., (New York and London, 1927), 1: 132-133; A. May, "Woodrow Wilson and Austria-Hungary to the end of 1917," p. 233.

51. *L'Osservatore Romano,* December 7, 1917, published information about the U.S. declaration of war on Austria-Hungary.

52. Salis to Balfour, Rome, December 21, 1917, FO 371, vol. 3436, PRO.

53. Lansing to Stimson, December 7, 1917, *FR-US, 1917, Supp. 1,* 1: 382.

54. Rodd to Balfour (secret), Rome, December 11, 1917, FO 371, vol. 3084, PRO.

55. Speranza, *Diary,* 2: 112.

56. Engel-Janosi, *Österreich und der Vatikan,* 2: 331-332.

57. Koenig, *The Principles for Peace,* pp. 241-242; Guglielmo Quadrotta, *La Chiesa Cattolica nella Crisi Universale* (Rome, 1921), pp. 147; Speranza, *Diary,* 2: 118.

58. For an extensive discussion of the origins and implications of Lloyd George's and Wilson's speeches, see Arno Mayer, *Political Origins of the New Diplomacy, 1917-1918* (New Haven, 1959), pp. 313-393; Mamatey, *The United States and East Central Europe,* pp. 172-185.

59. *L'Osservatore Romano,* January 7, 8, 9, 1918. On January 8, Page wrote that the clerical press was very favorable to Lloyd George's speech, pointing out similarities with the pope's note. *Papers Relating to the Foreign Relations of the United States, 1918, Supplement 1, 2 vols. The World War* (Washington, D.C., 1933), 1: 17.

60. Salis to Balfour (confidential), Rome, January 8, 1918, FO 371, vol. 3229, PRO; Rodd to Balfour, Rome, January 19, 1918, FO 371, vol. 3229, PRO.

61. *L'Osservatore Romano,* January 10, 11, 1918. On January 13, the paper brought out an extensive article comparing Lloyd George's and Wilson's speeches and the Vatican's views: "I discorsi di Lloyd George e di Wilson e la Santa Sede."

62. *FR-US, 1918, Supp. 1,* 1: 18, 26.

63. Page to Lansing, Rome, January 11, 1918; Page to Lansing, Rome, January 14, 1918, State Department Archives. Rodd also commented that Wilson's message was enthusiastically received by the clericals. Rodd to Balfour (confidential), Rome, January 14, 1918, FO 371, vol. 3229, PRO.

64. Dragan Živojinović, "The Vatican, Woodrow Wilson and the Dissolution of the Hapsburg Monarchy,"1914-1918, *East European Quarterly* 3, no. 1 (1969): 45.

65. Gasparri to Pacelli, Sonnino Papers, 48. Gasparri did not ask Austria-Hungary to cooperate in making a reply to the Allies and Americans.

66. Gasparri to Pacelli, January 20, 1918; Gasparri to Pacelli, undated cable, Sonnino Papers, 48.

67. Translation of an interview Dr. Rodolfo Foa had with His Eminence, Cardinal Gasparri, the manuscript of which was turned over voluntarily to Ambassador Page by Dr. Foa on January 24, 1918. Speranza Papers, Correspondence 1916-1918.

68. Page to Lansing, Rome, January 23, 1918, State Department Archives.

69. G. Lowes Dickinson, ed., *Documents and Statements Relating to Peace Proposals and War Aims (December 1916-November 1918)* (London and New York, 1919), pp. 122-125, 125-132; Mamatey, *The United States and East Central Europe,* pp. 191-192.

70. Pacelli to Gasparri, Munich, February 2, 1918, Sonnino Papers, 48.

71. Gasparri to Pacelli, February 4, 1918, Sonnino Papers, 48.

72. L.L. Richards to Tumulty, January 31, 1918, Wilson Papers, series IV. Richards, a member of the War Trade Board, suggested that the president notify the pope that the Allies have no further communication whatsoever with the present German government.

73. *FR-US, 1918, Supp. 1*, 1: 68.

74. Lammasch, together with other dignitaries of the Catholic church from Austria-Hungary and Germany, came to Switzerland, ostensibly in order to discuss problems of particular interest to the church. *FR-US, 1918, Supp. 1*, 2: 83; Mamatey, *The United States and East Central Europe,* pp. 219-220.

75. *FR-US, 1918, Supp. 1*, 2: 88, 90, 94, 101-103; Michael B. Briggs, *George Herron and the European Settlement* (Stanford, Calif., 1932), pp. 77-82, 94, 302-304; Arthur Poltzer-Hoditz, *L'Empereur Charles et la Mission Historique de l'Autriche* (Paris, n.d.), p. 274, claims that Czernin favored granting autonomy to the nationalities.

76. Gaisford to Balfour (secret), Rome, FO 371, vol. 3133, PRO.

77. Dickinson, *Documents and Statements,* pp. 134-139; Mamatey, *The United States and East Central Europe,* pp. 223-226.

78. Page to Lansing (secret and confidential), Rome, February 9, 1918, State Department Archives.

79. Wilson, exasperated and annoyed, told Ambassador Jusserand early in March 1918 that the activities of the Vatican constituted "un nouvelle manifestation du desir du Vatican de se meler des affaires d'autrui." Albert Pingaud, *Histoire diplomatique de la France pendant la grande guerre,* 3 vols (Paris, 1937-1938), 3: 351.

80. Gaisford to Balfour (confidential), Rome, February 19, 1918, FO 371, vol. 3133, PRO.

81. Fay to Shane Leslie, Rome, February 27, 1918; Fay to Polk, February 27, 1918, Lloyd George Papers. Fay asked Shane Leslie to see Tumulty and orally transmit to him the contents of the letter. He was also to find out whether Tumulty knew about the policy of separating Austria-Hungary from Germany.

82. House Diary, February 24, 1918; Ellis, *Gibbons,* 2: 269-270; H. Montgomery Hyde, *Lord Reading: The Life of Isaacs Rufus, First Marquiss of Reading* (London, 1967), pp, 280-281.

83. François Charles Roux, *Le Paix des Empires Centraux* (Paris, 1947), p. 211; Alberto Monticone, *Nitti e la Grande Guerra (1914-1918)* (Milan, 1961), pp. 258-264; Broglio, *Italia e la Santa Sede,* pp. 50-51, 349-351, 353-361.

84. *FR-US, 1918, Supp. 1,* 1: 126-127; Baker, *Wilson, Life and Letters,* 7: 551, 558, 565.

85. House Diary, February 24, 1918; Seymour, ed., *The Intimate Papers,* 3: 374-375.

86. Lansing's Desk Diary, February 25, 1918; House Diary, February 26, 1918. House told Lansing, after seeing the note, that there was "no peace in sight." *FR-US, 1918, Supp. 1,* 1: 183-184.

87. Lansing's Desk Diary, April 5, 6, 1918; Engel-Janosi, *Österreich und der Vatikan,* 2: 334-335; Malagodi, *Conversazioni della guerra,* 2: 316-321.

88. Reading to Balfour (secret), Washington, March 19, 1918; Balfour to Gaisford, March 20, 1918, FO 371, vol. 3440, PRO; Villa Sinda to the Spanish Foreign Ministry, Rome, March 23, 1918, Sonnino Papers, 48.

89. Dickinson, ed., *Documents and Statements,* pp. 173-174; Mamatey, *The United States and East Central Europe,* pp. 233-234.

90. On April 16, 1918, Rumbold informed the Foreign Office that Ledochowsky, the bishop of Coire, Revertera, Erzberger, and Marchetti had met in February 1917 in Einsiedeln, Switzerland, and had discussed the Emperor's letter. Rumbold to Balfour, Bern, FO 371, vol. 3134, PRO.

91. Salis to Balfour (confidential), Rome, April 13, 1918, FO 371, vol. 3134, PRO. Several weeks later, Salis reported that "neither Gasparri nor the Pope seemed to think that the Allies had done a good day's work by exposing the Emperor." Berlin was to be the winner. Salis to Drummond, Rome, May 6, 1918, FO 800, vol. 329, PRO; Speranza, *Diary,* 2:153.

CHAPTER 8

1. Justus, *Macchi di Cellere,* p. 85; Pernot, *Le Saint-Siège, L'Eglise Catholique,* p. 102; Antonio Salandra, *Souvenirs de 1914-1915: La Neutralité Italienne et l'Intervention* (Paris, 1932), pp. 201-202; Gwynn, *The Vatican and the War in Europe,* pp. 66-67.

2. Pernot, *Le Saint-Siège, l'Eglise Catholique,* p. 33; Henri Marc-Bonnet, *La Papauté Contemporaine* (Paris, 1951), p. 95.

3. Francisco Rufini, "Il potere temporale negli scopi di guerra degli ex-Imperi Centrali," *Nuova Antologia,* 51, 1178 (April 16, 1921), pp. 289-300; Angelo Martini, *Studi sulla guestione Romana e la Conciliazione* (Rome, 1963), pp. 80-84; Sheinman, *Vatikan i katolitsizm,* p. 446.

4. Martini, *Diario, 1914-1918,* pp. 580-581.

5. On February 10, 1916, the *Catholic Tribune* published a lengthy article under the title "The Roman Clause of the London Treaty" and pointed out that the "Allies agreed to oppose any change in the intolerable position of the Pope." The German press (*Frankfurter Zeitung, Dresdener Zeitung,* and others) published articles about Germany's intention to solve the Roman question after the war.

6. Page to Lansing, Rome, January 17, 1917, State Department Archives.

7. House Diary, April 26, 1917; Balfour to Wilson (confidential), May 17, 1917, Wilson Papers, series II; Robert H. Ferrell, "Woodrow Wilson and Open Diplomacy," in *Issues and Conflicts: Studies in Twentieth Century American Diplomacy,* ed. G.L. Anderson (Lawrence, Kansas, 1959), pp. 202-203; Mayer, *Political Origins of New Diplomacy,* p. 300.

8. *Christian Science Monitor* (Boston), October 31, 1917, published almost the complete text of it.

9. Gwynn, *The Letters and Friendships of Sir Cecil Spring-Rice,* 2: 419-420.

10. Page to Lansing, Rome, December 15, 1917, State Department Archives.

11. Page to Lansing, Rome, January 11, 1918. This was repeated later. "Quarterly Report," no. 1 (January 31-March 31, 1918), State Department Archives.

12. Page to Lansing, Rome, January 23, 1918, State Department Archives; Speranza to Page, Rome, January 25, 1918, Speranza Papers. Speranza enclosed a copy of the text of Dr. Foa's interview with Gasparri.

13. Speranza to Page, Rome, January 27, 1918, Speranza Papers. On February 16, Page talked with Sonnino about the Vatican position. Sonnino again reiterated his opposition on the admission of the Vatican to the peace conference, to which Page agreed. *Papers Relating to the Foreign Relations of the United States, 1918, the World War, Supplement 1,* 2 vols. (Washington, D.C., 1933), 1: 122. Hereafter cited as *FR-US, 1918, Supp. 1.*

14. Page to Wilson (confidential), Rome, January 29, 1918, Wilson Papers, series II. On January 31, Wilson forwarded this cable to House but made no comments; Speranza, *Diary* 2: 126.

15. Fay to Gibbons (strictly confidential), Rome, January 23, 1918, FO 800, vol. 202, PRO; Ellis, *Gibbons,* 2: 267-268. Colville Barclay, the British chargé d'affaires in Washington, sent it back to London on February 22, 1918.

16. Fay to Gibbons (strictly private), Rome, February 12, 1918, FO 800, vol. 202, PRO: Ellis, *Gibbons,* 2: 269-270.

17. Gibbons marshaled the following arguments for this demand: (1) the large number of American Catholics in the armed forces; (2) neutralization of the bad impression caused by the publication of the article; (3) the need for the British to take the initiative in this action; (4) the possibility that the U.S. Catholic hierarchy might protest against Article XV, as it was an insult to the pope; (5) modification of the article would strengthen good feelings toward the Allies on the part of the Americans. Gibbons to Balfour, Baltimore, March 6, 1918, Ellis, *Gibbons,* 2: 270-271; Roberto Mosca, "La mancata revisione dell'art. XV del Patto di Londra," in *Benedetto XV, i Cattolici,* p. 402; House Diary, February 24, 1918.

18. Reading to Balfour (private, secret), Washington, March 1, 1918, FO 371, vol. 3440, PRO.

19. Balfour to Reading, March 4, 1918, FO 371, vol. 3440, PRO; Gwynn, *The Vatican and the War in Europe,* p. 66.

20. Balfour to Reading (private), March 13, 1918, FO 800, vol. 202, PRO; Polk Diary, March 14, 1918.

21. Rodd to Balfour, Rome, February 17, 18, 1918, FO 371, vol. 3438, PRO. On February 19, *L'Osservatore Romano* published a long article, stating that Wilson did not reply to the pope's peace note on behalf of all the Allies and that Article XV was an "affront to the Holy See."

22. Gaisford to Balfour (confidential), Rome, February 23, 1918, FO 371, vol. 3438, PRO.

23. *FR-US, 1918, Supp. 1*, 1: 167-168, 173. A copy of the cable from Rome was sent to the White House.

24. Polk to Hefflin, March 13, 1918, State Department Archives; Daniel M. Smith, *The Great Departure: The United States and World War I, 1914-1920* (New York-London, 1965), p. 86; Polk to Newton D. Baker, Boston, January 38, 1938, Polk Papers.

25. *FR-US, The Lansing Papers*, 2: 113-116, Lansing's Desk Diary, March 22, 23, 1918.

26. Balfour to Rodd, March 28, 1918; Rodd to Balfour, Rome, April 5, 1918, FO 371, vol. 3438, PRO.

27. Rumbold to Balfour, Bern, April 1918, FO 371, vol. 3442, PRO.

28. Gasparri to Ogno, April 20, 1918, Sonnino Papers, 48.

29. Gasparri to Salis, Rome, April 29, 1918, FO 371, vol. 3438, PRO.

30. Ellis, *Gibbons,* 2: 273-274.

31. Gasparri to Locatelli, May 22, 1918, Sonnino Papers, 48.

32. Mercier to Balfour, Malines, June 2, 1918, FO 371, vol. 3438, PRO.

33. Balfour to Mercier, London, June 29, 1918, FO 371, vol. 3438, PRO. On July 8, Balfour's letter to Mercier was sent to Rodd, who was instructed to inform Sonnino about it. Pernot, *Le Saint-Siège, l'Eglise Catholique,* p. 37; *L'Osservatore Romano,* June 17, 1918, published a long editorial, insisting that it was insulting that the decision about the pope's representation at the conference depended upon Italy.

34. Kelly to Balfour, May 30, 1918; Bequin to Balfour, June 4, 1918, Redwood to Balfour, June 13, 1918, FO 371, vol. 3438, PRO. Balfour replied to these letters through the Colonial Office on June 21, 1918, enclosing the copy of his letter to Rodd of March 28, 1918.

35. Ellis, *Gibbons,* 2: 274-275.

36. Gasparri to Bonzano, July 30, 1918, Sonnino Papers, 48; Ellis, *Gibbons,* 2: 275-276.

37. Mosca, "La mancata revisione," in *Benedetto XV, i Cattolici,* pp. 403-404; Brand Whitlock, the U.S. minister to Belgium, knew about the action. Whitlock to Lansing, La Havre, August 10, 1918, State Department Archives.

38. Polk Diary, August 7, 1918. At the same time, Di Cellere wrote that he heard from a reliable source that Wilson was unmistakably opposed to the pope's participation in the peace conference. Justus, *Macchi di Cellere,* p. 87.

39. Mosca, "La mancata revisione," p. 407; Živojinović, "The Vatican, Wilson and the Dissolution of the Hapsburg Monarchy," p. 52.

40. Gasparri to Bonzano, May 26, 1918, Sonnino Papers, 48.

41. Jay to Lansing, Rome, August 16, 1918, Wilson Papers, series II; Gasparri to Bonzano, August 19, 1918, Sonnino Papers, 48; Lansing's Desk Diary, August 19, 20, 1918; Paul Reinsch to Lansing, Peking, November 29, 1918, *FR-US, 1918, Supp. 1*, 1: 128.

42. Memorandum of conversation with the Italian ambassador, August 13, 1918, Breckinridge Long Papers, Manuscript Division, Library of Congress, Washington, D.C.

43. In explaining the nature of Article XV, Di Cellere insisted that the publication of the secret treaty was intended as a piece of political propaganda in Italy designed to favor the clericals and to disrupt national unity.

44. Memorandum on conversation with the Italian ambassador, August 17, 1918, Long Papers.

45. Di Cellere to Sonnino, Washington, August 24, 1918; Mosca, "La mancata revisione," p. 406.

46. Polk Diary, November 8, 1918; Page to Lansing, Rome, November 9, 1918, State Department Archives.

47. Rodd to Balfour (private), Rome, November 9, 1918, FO 800, vol. 203, PRO.

CHAPTER 9

1. Dragan Živojinović, "Il problema di Roma nella politica degli Stati Uniti," in *Atti del XLV Congresso per la Storia del Risorgimento Italiano,* Rome, September 20-25, 1970. (Rome, 1972), pp. 501-568; Loretta Clara Feiertag, *American Public Opinion on the Diplomatic Relations between the United States and the Papal States, 1848-1868* (Washington, D.C., 1933).

2. Page to Wilson, Rome, January 5, 1915, Wilson Papers, series II; Page to Bryan, Rome, January 5, 1915, State Department Archives.

3. Wilson to Bryan, January 5, 1915. The cable was sent to Rome on January 7, State Department Archives. Several days later, Page replied that the telegram was duly received and that he intended to make discreet use of it. Page to Bryan, Rome, January 12, 1915, State Department Archives. In answering Page's letter of January 5, Wilson sounded very grateful for the information it contained: "It is a comfort . . . to have someone upon whose insight and capacity to deal with delicate matters I can have such a complete reliance." Wilson to Page, January 28, 1915, Wilson Papers, series II. For the British Mission and its activities, Angelo Martini, "L'invio della missione inglese presso la Santa Sede all'inizio della Prima Guerra Mondiale," in *La Civilta Cattolica* 4, 2818 (1967): 330-344.

4. Storer endeavored to secure the cardinal's hat for his friend Archbishop John Ireland. He was forced by President Roosevelt to resign in 1906. Anson P. Stokes, *Church and State in the United States,* 3 vols. (New York, 1950), 2: 401-403; Maria L. Storer, *In Memoriam: Bellamy Storer* (Boston, 1923), pp. 1-7.

5. Page to House, Rome, February 5, 1915, House Papers.

6. Storer, *In Memoriam,* pp. 44-45.

7. Page to Bryan, Rome, March 17, 1915, *FR-US, The Lansing Papers,* 1: 721-722.

8. Page to Bryan, Rome, May 18, 1915; Bryan to Wilson, May 21, 1915; Wilson to Bryan, May 23, 1915, Wilson-Bryan Correspondence, State Department Archives. On May 28, Cardinal Gibbons thanked Bryan for his help, informing him that this "courtesy will be deeply appreciated by the Holy Father." Gibbons to Bryan, Baltimore. Bryan passed on this letter to Wilson. Wilson Papers, series II.

9. Drummond to Rodd (personal, secret), July 6, 1916, FO 800, vol. 66, PRO. A similar message was sent to Count Salis. Salis was also informed that Horodyski was in close touch with Count Wladimir Ledochowski, general of the Jesuits. Drummond to Salis (private, confidential), August 23, 1916, FO 800, vol. 67, PRO.

10. Benedict XV to Wilson, January 26, 1917, Wilson Papers, series IV. The same day Tumulty forwarded the pope's letter to Lansing, asking his opinion as to possible replies. Tumulty to Lansing, January 26, 1917, State Department Archives; Ellis, *Gibbons,* 2: 218.

11. Lansing to Tumulty (personal and confidential), State Department Archives; Tumulty to Bonzano, January 27, 1917, and Bonzano to Tumulty, January 29, 1917, Wilson Papers, series IV.

12. Rodd to Balfour (private), Rome, February 8, 1917, FO 800, vol. 202, PRO; memorandum (private and confidential), February 1917, FO 800, vol. 383, PRO. After the pronouncements of Lloyd George and Wilson in January 1918, Cardinal Bourne, archbishop of London, warned Lord Edmond Talbot that the silence on the pope's note weakened British prestige and influence at the Vatican. Bourne to Talbot, London, January 13, 1918, FO 800, vol. 329, PRO.

13. Phillips Diary, June 1, 1917.

14. Phillips Diary, June 22, 1917.

15. Lansing's Desk Diary, July 22, 1917. Horodyski remained in the United States until the end of October 1917, when he paid the last visit to Phillips. Phillips Diary, October 23, 30, 1917.

16. Fowler, *Sir William Wiseman,* pp. 117-118.

17. Spring-Rice to Balfour, Washington, July 1917, Balfour Papers, vol. 49740; Spring-Rice to Drummond, Washington, July 13, 1917, FO 800, vol. 383, PRO; Phillips Diary, August 18, 1917.

18. Spring-Rice to Balfour, September 7, 1917; Gwynn, *The Letters and Friendships of Sir Cecil Spring-Rice,* 2: 410-411. A week later, Spring-Rice explained that Cardinal O'Connell, archbishop of Boston, was the leader of the group "holding very different views." Cardinal O'Connell believed that the "power of the Church over the flock ought to be used for political advancement of the universal Catholic church and for the promotion of such ends as may seem good to the directors of the Vatican policy." Spring-Rice to Balfour, Washington, September 14, 1917, Balfour Papers, vol. 49740.

19. Spring-Rice to Balfour, Washington, September 13, 1917, FO 371, vol. 2947, PRO; Leslie, *Cardinal Gasquet,* pp. 220-223, comments on the Catholic church in the United States.

20. Balfour to Salis, September 15, 1917; Salis to Balfour, Rome, September 17, 1917; Balfour to Spring-Rice, September 19, 1917, FO 371, vol. 2947, PRO.

21. Spring-Rice to Balfour, Washington, September 19, 22, 26, 1917, FO 371, vol. 2947, PRO.

22. Spring-Rice (private) to Balfour, Washington, October 12, 1917, FO 371, vol. 2947, PRO.

23. Polk Diary, November 13, 1917.

24. Spring-Rice to Balfour, Washington, November 14, 1917; Spring-Rice to Balfour, December 2, 1917, FO 371, vol. 3084, PRO. The ambassador had in mind Gasparri's interview with Dr. Foa on August 24, 1917. Ellis, *Gibbons,* 2: 266.

25. For Fay's activities in Rome, see Chapter 8.

26. Hugh Wilson to Lansing (for Polk), Bern, January 27, 1918, State Department Archives.

27. Nelson to Wilson, Washington, February 18, 1918; Wilson to Nelson, February 19, 1918, Wilson Papers, series IV. A day later, Fred Blackmon, Democrat of Alabama, sent to the White House a petition signed by citizens of Chilton County, Alabama, demanding that the president refuse to appoint a representative to the Vatican. Blackmon to Wilson, February 20, 1918, Wilson Papers, series IV.

28. Overmyer to Lansing, March 16, 1918. On March 20, Lansing replied to Overmyer that no pressure was being exerted upon the president to appoint a minister to the Holy See. State Department Archives.

29. Horodyski suggested that some American accompany him in order to explain to Pacelli the "American views and ideals before his return to Munich." Stovall to Lansing, Bern, March 15, 1918, State Department Archives.

30. Rumbold to Balfour, Bern, April 9, 1918, FO 371, vol. 3442, PRO; Horody-ski to Drummond, April 5, 1918, FO 800, vol. 385, PRO.

31. Horodyski to Drummond, Rome, May 13, 1918; Salis to Drummond, May 13, 1918; Drummond to Lord Reading, May 18, 1918, FO 800, vol. 385, 329, 224, PRO. Drummond was not impressed, since he could not see how the pope's proposals could be made practicable in view of Wilson's attitude. House let the British government know that he did not think Wilson would be willing to do anything since the "whole Irish and Catholic intrigue . . . has gone hand in hand in some quarters of the country with the German intrigue." House to Balfour, April 3, 1918, Papers of Sir William Wiseman, House Yale Collection, Sterling Memorial Library, Yale University, New Haven, Connecticut; Fowler, *Sir William Wiseman,* pp. 159-160.

32. Rodd (Horodyski) to Drummond (personal), Rome, May 13, 1918, FO 800, vol 224, PRO. Drummond advised Lord Reading that Wiseman would cable it to House. Wiseman to House, tel. no. 621, House Papers.

33. House Diary, May 20, 1918. House wrote that the British ambassador wanted to see him. During this conference they "went over the letters and cables which he had received from his government."

34. Sharp to Lansing, Paris, May 13, 1918; Frazier to Lansing, Paris, May 18, 1918. State Department Archives.

35. Lansing to Stovall, May 4, 1918, State Department Archives.

36. Page to Lansing, Rome, May 17, 1918, State Department Archives. Sonnino agreed completely with Page. In a letter to House, Page expressed his belief that the appointment of a mission to the Vatican would be an "incalculable error . . . . My earnest belief is that we should not be drawn into Vatican politics directly or indirectly. It can bring only complications and disaster." Page to House, Rome, May 26, 1918, House Papers.

37. Rodd to Drummond (secret), Rome, May 18, 1918; Drummond to Rodd, May 24, 1918, FO 800, vol. 383, PRO. Drummond advised Rodd not to pay any attention to Page's protest.

38. Page to Wilson (private), Rome, May 21, 1918, State Department Archives.

39. Lord Reading to Drummond (personal, secret), Washington, May 23, 1918, FO 800, vol. 224, PRO. On May 27, Drummond replied that it was good that Reading did not press the matter further. Drummond to Reading, FO 800, vol. 224, PRO. House's Diary, May 23, 1918, shows that Lord Reading was received at the White House. Fowler, *Sir William Wiseman,* p. 161, asserts that Lord Reading acted "perhaps at Cardinal Gibbons' request," but this is not correct.

40. Di Cellere appeared to be familiar with the failure of the British initiative in Washington. On August 24, 1918, he informed Sonnino that the "recent secret attempt of the Holy See to establish diplomatic relations with the United States was not even taken into consideration." Mosca, "La mancata revisione," p. 406.

CHAPTER 10

1. It is necessary to establish differences between numerous works in order to move through the jungle of apparent, though not real contradictions, confusion, and lack of continuity of the policy of the Vatican.

2. For example, Migliori, *Benedetto XV*, pp. 115-117; Mario Bendiscioli, "Chiesa e Societa nel Secoli XIX e XX," in *Questioni di Storia Contemporanea*, ed. Ettore Rota, 3 vols. (Milan, 1952-1953), 1: 904-905; Institut Pius I, *La Papauté et les Questiones Internationales* (Paris, n.d.), pp. 81-91; Vistalli, *Benedetto XV*, pp. 203, 206; Poltzer-Hoditz, *L'Empereur Charles et la Mission Historique de l'Autriche;* Vittorio E. Orlando, *Miei rapporti di governo con la Santa Sede* (Milan, 1944), pp. 42, 61; Oscar Jaszi, *The Dissolution of the Hapsburg Monarchy* (Chicago, 1961), p. 160.

3. "La politique de Benoit XV," *La Revue de Paris* 25, nos. 20-21 (October 15, November 1, 1918), 873-896, 183-214; *Luigi degli Occhi, Benedetto XV* (Milan, 1921), pp. 17, 34, 51-53.

4. Candeloro, *Il Movimento Cattolico in Italia*, pp. 370-374, Sceinman, *Il Vaticano tra due guerre*, pp. 51-52, 56-57, 70-71, 80; Alix, *Le Saint-Siège et les Nationalismes en Europe*, pp. 114-121; Salvatorelli, *La Politica della Santa Sede doppo la Guerra*, pp. 8-9; Paris, *Le Vatican contre l'Europe*, pp. 34, 44-46; Engel-Janosi, *Österreich und der Vatikan*, 2: 335, 337, 340; Pernot, *La Saint-Siège, l'Eglise Catholique, et la Politique Mondiale*, p. 147; Ellis, *Gibbons*, 2: 256-258; Eduard Beneš, *La Lutte pour l'independence des peuples*, 2 vols. (Paris, 1929), 2: 418, as well as numerous others.

5. Quadrotta, *La Chiesa Cattolica nella Crisi Universale*, p. 159; Marc-Bonnet, *La Papauté Contemporaine*, p. 47.

6. Charles A. Court Repington, *La Première Guerre Mondiale (1914-1918)* (Paris, 1924), pp. 513-519; Carlo Calise, "Il Cardinale Pietro Gasparri," *Nuova Antologia* 68, no. 1464 (March 16, 1933), pp. 225-236: Quadrotta, *La Chiesa Cattolica nella Crisi Universale*, pp. 56-57, 63; Vercesi, *Il Vaticano, l'Italia e la guerra*, pp. 42-43, 64-65; idem, *Tre Popi: Leone XIII–Pio X–Benedetto XV*, pp. 239-304, Lajos Pasztor, "I cattolici ungharesi e la prima guerra mondiale," in *Benedetto XV, i Cattolici*, p. 816; Tamborra, "Benedetto XV e i problemi nazionali e religiosi dell'Europa Orientale," in ibid., pp. 860-864.

7. Danilo Veneruso, "I rapporti fra stato e chiesa durante la guerra nel guidizi dei maggiori organi della stampa Italiana," in *Benedetto XV, i Cattolici*, p. 736.

8. George Goyau, "L'église libre dans l'Europe libre," *Revue des Deux Mondes* 89, no. 52 (July 1919): 5-36; idem, *Papauté et Chrétienté sous Benoit XV* (Paris, 1922) Ernesto Vercesi, *L'Europa nuova e il Vaticano* (Milan, 1921), pp. 30-31, 100; Giorgio Ori, "La recente politica della Santa Sede nell 'Europa nord-Orientale," *Rassegna di Politica Internazionale* 3, no. 3 (August 1936): 623-636.

9. Monticone, *Nitti e la Prima Guerra Mondiale*, pp. 258-264, 393-397; Broglio, *Italia e la Santa Sede dalla Grande Guerra alla Conciliazione*, pp. 50-51, 349, 352, 353-361.

10. Engel-Janosi, *Österreich und der Vatikan*, 2: 337; Valiani, *La Dissoluzione del Austria-Ungheria*, pp. 379, 432; Pingaud, *Histoire diplomatique de la France*, 3: 352; Broglio, *Italia e la Santa Sede Dalla Grande Guerra alla Conciliazione*, pp. 397-400, 401-403, 415-417, 427-429, 436-437. Speranza, in his *Diary*, 2: 153, writes that the pope complained to the bishop of Vincenza that he had no influence with the Austro-Hungarian government.

11. Jaszi, *The Dissolution of the Hapsburg Monarchy*, p. 160; Gwynn, *The Vatican and the War in Europe*, pp. 63-65; for a more detailed discussion, see Lorenz, *Kaiser Karl und der Untergang der Donau Monarchie*, pp. 10-65, 81-86.

12. Malagodi, *Conversazioni della guerra,* 2: 316-321, 321-322. The Serbian government at Corfu was informed that the Vatican was the "greatest enemy of the Yugoslav unification." Dragoslav Janković and Bogdan Krizman, eds., *Gradja o stvaranju jugoslovenske države (l.I.-20.XII.1918),* 2 vols. (Belgrade, 1964), 2: 184; Dragan Živojinović, "Splitski biskup dr Juraj Carić i borba protiv italijanskih pretenzija u Dalmaciji, 1918-1919," *Istorijski Glasnik,* 2-3 (1966): 145-151.

13. Raymond Poincaré, *Au Service de la France: Neuf années de souvenirs,* 10 vols. (Paris, 1926-1933), 10: 175-176, 192.

14. Whitlock to Lansing, Le Havre, June 17, 1918, State Department Archives.

15. Lansing's Desk Diary, May 10, 1918; *War Memoirs of Robert Lansing* (Indianapolis and New York, 1935), pp. 262-267. For an admirable discussion, see Mamatey, *The United States and East Central Europe,* pp. 252-265.

16. Reading to Drummond (personal and very secret), Washington, FO 800, vol. 224, PRO.

17. Reading to Drummond, Washington, May 17, 1918; Drummond to Reading (personal and secret), London, May 21, 1918; FO 800, vol. 385, PRO.

18. Auchincloss Diary, May 23, 1918, House Collection.

19. *La Civilta Cattolica,* March 8, April 26, June 7, 1918; Paris, *Le Vatican contre l' Europe,* p. 45.

20. *La Civilta Cattolica,* June 15, 1918.

21. The failure of the Austrian offensive on the Italian front in June 1918 was disturbing to the Vatican; a fortnight later it announced its support of Germany's proposal for a negotiated peace. *L'Osservatore Romano,* June 27, 1918; Quadrotta, *La Chiesa Cattolica nella Crisi Universale,* pp. 151-152.

22. Lansing's Desk Diary, June 27, 1918; House to Wilson, Magnolia, Massachusetts, June 23, 1918, House Papers; Mamatey, *The United States and East Central Europe,* pp. 268-269.

23. The press published Wilson's July 4 speech at Mount Vernon, in which he declared the need for the destruction of every arbitrary power that can disturb the peace of the world, or its reduction to virtual impotence. Baker and Dodd, *The Public Papers of Woodrow Wilson,* 5: 233-234; Dragan Živojinović, *Amerika, Italija i Postanak Jugoslavije, 1917-1919* (Belgrade, 1970), pp. 125-126.

24. Kann, *The Multinational Empire,* 2: 279; Vercesi, *L'Europa Nuova e il Vaticano,* pp. 18-19.

25. Harry Rudin, *Armistice 1918* (New Haven, 1944), p. 22.

26. Speranza, *Diary,* 2: 179. Wilson announced his proposal for a league of nations in his speech at Mount Vernon.

27. Herron to Wilson, Bern, July 25, 1918, Wilson Papers, series II; Baker, *Wilson: Life and Letters,* 7: 320; Gasparri to Maglione, August 1, 31, 1918, Sonnino Papers, 48.

28. For instance, A.C. Barbize, "Pope Benedict, the Hun and Peace propaganda," A.J. App, "The Germans," in *The Immigrants' Influence on Wilson's Peace Policies,* ed. Joseph P. O'Grady (Lexington, Kentucky, 1967), pp. 37-38.

29. Karl Novak, *Les dessous de la défaite* (Paris, 1925), pp. 131, 134; Rudin, *Armistice 1918,* p. 38; Bertrand Auerbach, *L'Autriche et la Hongrie pendant la guerre* (Paris, 1925), p. 514; Mermeix [Gabriel Terrail], *Les negociations secrets et les quatre armistices* (Paris, 1919), pp. 184-186.

30. Tumulty and Lansing demanded that the president refuse the note and do

it fast, since "an immediate answer will strengthen your [Wilson's] unquestionable leadership of all nations fighting the Central Powers." Tumulty to Wilson, September 16, 1918, Papers of Joseph Tumulty, Manuscript Division, Library of Congress, Washington, D.C.; Lansing's Desk Diary, September 16, 1918.

31. *FR-US, 1918, Supp. I*, 1: 832-842.

32. Jay to Lansing, Rome, September 19, 1918, State Department Archives.

33. Maglione to Gasparri, Bern, September 25, 1918, Sonnino Papers, 48.

34. Hearley to Creel (for Wilson), Rome, September 24, 1918, Wilson Papers, series II.

35. Poltzer-Hoditz, *L'Empereur Charles et la Mission Historique de l'Autriche*, pp. 289-290; Novak, *Les dessous de la defaite*, pp. 515-516.

36. Auerbach, *L'Autriche et la Hongrie pendant la guerre*, p. 511.

37. Repington, *La Premiere guerre Mondiale*, pp. 513-519.

38. Bonzo to Gasparri, Vienna, October 4, 1918, Sonnino Papers, 48. The Vatican press criticized the first Austrian note, which it considered "an incentive for war, not invitation for peace." *La Civilita Cattolica*, October 4, 1918.

39. Creel to Wilson, October 9, 1918, and Wilson to Creel, October 10, 1918, Papers of George Creel, Manuscript Division, Library of Congress, Washington, D.C.

40. Gasparri to Bonzano, October 7, 1918; Benedict XV to Wilson, October 7, 1918, Sonnino Papers, 48; Wilson Papers, series II. The same day, Bonzo was asked to inform Emperor Charles about the pope's step. Gasparri to Bonzo, Sonnino Papers, 48.

41. Gasparri to Bonzano, October 7, 1918, Sonnino Papers, 48; Gibbons to Wilson, Baltimore, October 12, 1918, Wilson Papers, series II. A day after, Gasparri informed the nuncios in Vienna and Berlin about Gibbon's action with Wilson. Gasparri to Bonzo and Pacelli, October 8, 1918, Sonnino Papers, 48.

42. Ellis, *Gibbons*, 2: 256-257; Mamatey, *The United States and East Central Europe*, p. 327; Dagmar Perman, *The Shaping of the Czechoslovak State: Diplomatic History of the Boundaries of Czechoslovakia, 1914-1920* (Leiden, 1962), p. 49; Engel-Janosi, *Österreich und der Vatikan*, 2: 341.

43. *FR-US, The Lansing Papers*, 2: 160.

44. Rudin, *Armistice 1918*, p. 103.

45. Mamatey, *The United States and East Central Europe*, p. 333. Wilson confirmed his stand in a conversation with Sir William Wiseman on October 16, 1918. Wiseman Papers.

46. Wilson to John Sharp Williams, October 17, 1918, John Sharp Williams Papers; Baker, *Wilson: Life and Letters*, 8: 485.

47. Benedict XV to Emperor Charles, October 10, 1918, Sonnino Papers, 48.

48. Joseph Redlich, *Austrian War Government* (New Haven, 1929), pp. 163, 173; Poltzer-Hoditz, *L'Empereur Charles et la Mission Historique de l' Autriche*, pp. 292-293; Rudin, *Armistice 1918*, p. 129; Edmund Glaise von Horstenau, *Il Crollo di un Impero* (Milan, 1935), pp. 254-255; Alfred Pribram, *Austrian Foreign Policy, 1908-1918* (London, 1923), pp. 125-126.

49. Baker, *Wilson: Life and Letters*, 8: 484-485.

50. Ibid., p. 489.

51. The Vatican was informed that Austria-Hungary was to conclude a separate peace if Germany refused to accept Wilson's demands. Pacelli to Gasparri, Berlin, October 16, 1918, Sonnino Papers, 48. The *Corriere d'Italia*, October 18, 1918,

made its readers believe that the Vatican was not yet absolutely certain of Wilson's attitude toward Austria-Hungary.

52. Rudin, *Armistice 1918,* p. 169; David Strong, *Austria: October 1918-March 1919,*(New York, 1939), p. 99.

53. Bonzo to Gasparri, Vienna, October 20, 1918, Sonnino Papers, 48.

54. Page to Lansing, Rome, October 20, 1918, State Department Archives.

55. Mamatey, *The United States and East Central Europe,* p. 327; Živojinović, "The Vatican, Woodrow Wilson and the Dissolution of the Hapsburg Monarchy," pp. 57-58.

56. Vercesi, *L'Europa nuova e il Vaticano,* p. 110; Poincaré, *Au Service de la France,* 10: 399; Frank Cobb Diary, November 13, 1918, Woodrow Wilson Papers, New Acquisitions, Manuscript Division, Library of Congress, Washington, D.C.; Winston S. Churchill, *The Gathering Storm* (New York, 1961), pp. 9-10.

57. Maglione to Gasparri, Bern, October 26, 1918, Sonnino Papers, 48. Gasparri, however, refused to intervene with the Italian government. Gasparri to Maglione, November 3, 1918, Sonnino Papers, 48; Sheinman, *Vatikan i katolitsizm,* p. 446; David Lloyd George, *War Memoirs,* 6 vols. (Boston, 1933-1937), 6: 3315-3316.

58. Giuseppe Mira, *Autunno 1918: Come finì la guerra mondiale* (Milan, 1932), p. 49; Horstenau, *Il Crollo di un Impero,* p. 287.

59. Gasparri to Bonzano, October 28, 1918, Sonnino Papers, 48; Gibbons to Wilson, Baltimore, November 5, 1918, Wilson Papers, series II; Mamatey, *The United States and East Central Europe,* p. 339; Ellis, *Gibbons,* 2: 257-258.

60. Wilson to Lansing, October 29, 1918, Wilson Papers, series II; Rudin, *Armistice 1918,* pp. 189-190; Engel-Janosi, *Österreich und der Vatikan,* 2: 341.

61. Page to Lansing, Rome, November 1, 1918, State Department Archives.

A NOTE ON THE SOURCES

Sources for the reconstruction of the Vatican's involvement in the international affairs of the First World War exist in numerous archives and libraries both in the United States and in Europe. In the United States, pertinent material, mostly unpublished, is located in several private and official collections and archives (see Bibliography). Perhaps because of the fragmentary nature and character of these sources, they have been, for the most part, neglected by historians. Relevant materials are also to be found, in different forms and quality, in archives in Germany and France and the territories of the former Austro-Hungarian Empire. Richer and better organized are the materials in Great Britain and in Italy. Of these, the most illuminating are the papers of the Italian Foreign Minister, Baron Sidney Sonnino. Greater insight into the Vatican—its policies and the personalities of men who made them—can be gained only when the American and European sources are studied together.

The use of the documentation so different in provenience and quality was perhaps unavoidable. The subject under consideration was so many-sided and important that it drew the attention of many European governments and observers. The belligerents and neutrals, Catholic, Protestant and Orthodox nations alike, observed carefully the Vatican's moves and initiatives. And because of the efforts of so many organizations, intelligence services and individuals, we have the opportunity of analyzing the Vatican's activities. Some of these individuals maintained secret contacts with the Vatican, the Cardinals and others in the Catholic hierarchy. Furthermore, since the Catholic church in general and the Vatican in particular had important stakes in the war and among the belligerents, their representatives frequently voiced their views. It became an established practice for Benedict XV and the cardinal secretary of state to receive and invite correspondents, grant interviews and elaborate on their positions in the press. As a result, there appeared a flood of communications, messages and encyclicals, as well as bewildering rumors, denials and explanations.

Yet, for the purpose of this study the Sonnino papers constitute the single most important collection. Vast and unexplored, the collection

represents one of the most precious acquisitions in the field of the history
of the First World War. Documents from and on the Vatican are dispersed
through it, in accord with an arrangement made by Sonnino personally.
The most secret dispatches and instructions from and to the Vatican
amount to almost a thousand pages, covering without interruption the
period from the end of 1916 to the summer of 1919. The documents are
invaluable for the reconstruction of the policies and comprehension of the
innermost thoughts and desires of the Curia on a variety of questions.
Sonnino used the documents sparingly, mostly for his private needs; on
the basis of them he occasionally let the Allied representatives and governments guess the Vatican's plans and activities. Secretive and reticent by
nature, Sonnino enormously enjoyed reading about his arch-opponents
and neighbors, their comments about himself, the Allied policies, the
Central Powers, the United States etc. Sonnino did not even share his
information with other members of the Italian government. On several
occasions Cardinal Gasparri became suspicious of the leak and acted
swiftly to change the code; when this happened, Sonnino had to wait
weeks or months until the diligent military intelligence was successful in
deciphering the new code. This illegal procedure went on until Sonnino
left the office, in June 1919, and was abandoned by the succeeding
government.

The search through the numerous other collections yielded less valuable
information, yet bits found here and there helped put together a mosaic
and unfold the story. They differ from the material found in the Sonnino
papers both in quality and variety, but they are nevertheless indispensable
to the historian of Vatican diplomacy. They describe the views and
reactions of statesmen and politicians who had to deal with the Vatican,
its ambitions, place and functions during the war. Some of the sources are
exceedingly revealing and instructive, others dry and humorless. They
show, in turn, anxiety and disapproval, fear and distrust, disregard and
reluctance to deal with the Vatican. They uncover strong biases and
prejudices prevalent among the Anglo-Saxon nations, and the vexed and
troubled state of mind of the Catholic Church and the Vatican. Strangely,
even some German documents reflect a disdain for the Pope, his motives
and anxiety to act.

SELECTED BIBLIOGRAPHY

I. Unpublished Manuscript Collections

American

Papers of Gordon Auchincloss, The Diary. Edward M. House Collection, Sterling Memorial Library, Yale University, New Haven, Connecticut.

Papers of Ray Stannard Baker. Wilsoniana, MSS Division, Library of Congress, Washington, D.C.

Papers of William Jennings Bryan. MSS Division, Library of Congress, Washington, D.C.

Correspondence between President Woodrow Wilson and Secretary of State William Jennings Bryan, 1913-1915. State Department files, National Archives, Washington, D.C.

Papers of George Creel. MSS Division, Library of Congress, Washington, D.C.

Papers of Irwin Hood Hoover. MSS Division, Library of Congress, Washington, D.C.

Papers and Diary of Colonel Edward M. House. Sterling Memorial Library, Yale University, New Haven, Connecticut.

Papers and Diaries of Robert Lansing. MSS Division, Library of Congress, Washington, D.C.

Papers of Brickenridge Long. MSS Division, Library of Congress, Washington, D.C.

Papers of Walter Hines Page. Houghton Library, Harvard University, Cambridge, Massachusetts.

Papers of William Phillips, The Diary. Houghton Library, Harvard University, Cambridge, Massachusetts.

Papers and Diaries of Frank L. Polk. Sterling Memorial Library, Yale University, New Haven, Connecticut.

Papers of Gino Speranza. Correspondence 1916-1925, New York Public Library, New York.

Diplomatic, Legal, Fiscal Branch, Archives of the State Department. National Archives, Washington, D.C.

Papers of William Howard Taft. MSS Division, Library of Congress, Washington, D.C.

Papers of Joe Tumulty. MSS Division, Library of Congress, Washington, D.C.

Papers of John Sharp Williams. MSS Division, Library of Congress, Washington, D.C.

Papers of Woodrow Wilson. MSS Division, Library of Congress, Washington, D.C.

Papers of Woodrow Wilson, Frank Cobb Diary, New Acquisitions. MSS Division, Library of Congress, Washington, D.C.

Papers of Lester Woolsey. MSS Division, Library of Congress, Washington, D.C.

British

Papers of Arthur J. Balfour, 1st Earl of Balfour. Division of Manuscripts, British Museum, London.

Papers of Lord Robert Cecil, 1st Marquess of Chelwood. Division of Manuscripts, British Museum, London.
Foreign Office, 371. Public Record Office, London.
Foreign Office, 800. Public Record Office, London.
Papers of David Lloyd George. Beaverbrook Library, London.
War Cabinet Papers. Public Record Office, London.

Italian

Papers of Sidney Sonnino, The Vatican File. Montespertoli, Tuscany, Italy.

II. Published Government Documents

Carnegie Endowment for International Peace. *Official German Documents Relating to the World War.* 2 vols. New York: Carnegie Endowment, 1923.
Oesterreichischer Bundesverlag fuer Unterricht. *Oesterreich-Ungarns Aussenpolitik von der Bosnischen Krise 1908 bis zum Kriegsausbruch 1914.* 9 vols. Wien: Wissenschaft und Kunst, 1930.
U.S. Department of State. *Papers Relating to the Foreign Relations of the United States, 1914. Supplement, The World War.* Washington: GPO, 1928.
————. *Papers Relating to the Foreign Relations of the United States, 1915. Supplement, The World War.* Washington: GPO, 1928.
————. *Papers Relating to the Foreign Relations of the United States, 1915.* Washington: GPO, 1928.
————. *Papers Relating to the Foreign Relations of the United States, 1916. Supplement, The World War.* Washington: GPO, 1929.
————. *Papers Relating to the Foreign Relations of the United States, 1917. Supplement I, The World War.* Washington: GPO, 1931.
————. *Papers Relating to the Foreign Relations of the United States, 1917. Supplement II, The World War.* Washington: GPO, 1932.
————. *Papers Relating to the Foreign Relations of the United States, 1918. Supplement I, The World War.* Washington: GPO, 1932.
————. *Papers Relating to the Foreign Relations of the United States, 1918. Supplement II, The World War.* Washington: GPO, 1932.
————. *Papers Relating to the Foreign Relations of the United States, The Lansing Papers, 1914-1920.* 2 vols. Washington: GPO, 1939-1940.

III. Edited Collections of Documents

André, Scherer and Grünewald Jacques. eds. *L'Allemagne et les Problemes de la Paix Pendant La Première Guerre Mondiale. Documents extraits des archives de l'Office Allemand des Affaires Etrangère.* 2 vols. Paris: Presses Universitaires de France, 1962.
Dickinson, G. Lowes, ed. *Documents and Statements Relating to Peace Proposals and War Aims, December 1916 to November 1918.* New York and London: George Unwin and Macmillan, 1919.

Janković, Dragoslav and Bogdan Krizman eds. *Gradja o stvaranju jugoslovenske država (1.I.-20.XXII.1918).* 2 vols. Belgrade: Kultura, 1964.

Koenig, Harry, ed. *Principles for Peace: Selections from Papal Documents. Leo XIII to Pius XII.* Washington: National Catholic Welfare Conference, 1943.

Scott, James Brown, ed. *Official Statement of War Aims and Peace Proposals, December 1916 to November 1918.* New York: Carnegie Endowment for International Peace, 1925.

Wilson, Woodrow. *The Papers of Woodrow Wilson.* Edited by Arthur S. Link. 27 vols. to date.Princeton: Princeton University Press, 1965- .

Wilson, Woodrow. *The Public Papers of Woodrow Wilson.* Edited by Ray S. Baker and William E. Dodd. 2 vols. New York and London: Harper & Brothers, 1927.

IV. Memoirs, Recollections, Diaries, Letters

American

Addams, Jane, Emily Balch and Alice Hamilton. *Women at the Hague: The International Congress of Women and Its Results.* New York: The Macmillan Co., 1915.

Addams, Jane. *Peace and Bread in Time of War.* New York: King's Crown Press, 1945.

Baker, Ray S. *Woodrow Wilson: Life and Letters.* 8 vols. New York: Doubleday and Doran, 1927-1939.

Daniels, Josephus. *Cabinet Diaries of Josephus Daniels.* Edited by E. David Cronon. Lincoln: University of Nebraska Press, 1963.

House, Edward M. *The Intimate Papers of Colonel House.* Edited by Charles Seymour. New York and Boston: Houghton Mifflin Co., 1926-1928.

Kelley, Francis C. *The Bishop Jots it Down: An Autobiographical Strain on Memories.* New York and London: Harper and Brothers, 1939.

Lansing, Robert. *War Memories of Robert Lansing.* New York: Bobbs Merrill Co., 1935.

Lodge, Henry C. *The Senate and the League of Nations.* New York and London: Charles Scribner's Sons, 1925.

O'Connell, Cardinal William. *Sermons and Addresses.* 9 vols. Boston: Pilot Publishing Co., 1930.

Speranza, Gino. *The Diary of Gino Speranza: Italy 1915-1919.* 2 vols. Edited by Florence C. Speranza. New York: Columbia University Press, 1941.

Storer, Maria L. *In Memoriam, Bellamy Storer.* Boston: Private Edition, 1923.

Tumulty, Joseph P. *Woodrow Wilson as I Know Him.* Garden City: Doubleday, Page, 1921.

British

George, David Lloyd. *War Memoirs.* London: Odhams Press, n.d.

Gregory, John D. *On the Edge of Diplomacy. Rambles and Recollections.* London: Hutchinson and Co., 1929.

Gwynn, Stephen, ed. *The Letters and Friendships of Sir Cecil Spring-Rice.* 2 vols. Boston and New York: Houghton Mifflin Co., 1929.

Repington, Charles A. Court. *La Première Guerre Mondiale 1914-1918.* Paris: Payot, 1924.
Rodd, Sir Rennell. *Social and Diplomatic Memoirs, 1902-1919.* Third Series. London: Edward Arnold and Co., 1925.

Italian

Francesco, Crispolti. *Corone e Porpore, Ricordi Personali.* Milan: Treves, 1936.
Gasparri, Pietro Cardinale. *Il Cardinale Gasparri e la Questione Romana.* Con brani delle memorie inedite. A cura di Giovanni Spadolini. Firenze: Le Monnier, 1972.
Justus, V. *Macchi di Cellere all' Ambasciata di Washington, Memorie e Testimonianze.* Firenze: Bemporad e Figlio, 1921.
Malagodi, Olindo. *Conversazioni della guerra 1914-1919.* 2 vols. A cura di Brunnello Viggezzi. Milano: Ricciardi, 1960.
Marescotti, Aldrovandi. *Guerra Diplomatica, Ricordi e Framenti di Diario 1914-1919.* Milano: Mondadori, 1936.
Martini, Ferdinando. *Diario 1914-1919.* A cura di Gabriele Di Rosa. Milano: Mondadori, 1968.
Orlando, Vittorio E. *Miei rapporti di governo con la Santa Sede.* Milano: Garzanti, 1944.
Salandra, Antonio. *Souvenirs de 1914-1915, La Neutralité Italiénne et l'Intervention.* Paris: Payot, 1932.
Sonnino, Sidney. *Diario, 1866-1922.* 3 vols. A cura di Ben F. Brown and Pietro Pastorelli. Bari: Laterza, 1972.

German

Bernstorff, Johann. *My Three Years in America.* New York: Charles Scribner's Sons, 1920.
Bülow, Chancelier Prince du. *Mémoires du Chancelier Prince du Bülow 1897-1919.* 3 vols. Paris: Librairie Plon, 1931.
Erzberger, Mathias. *Souvenirs de Guerre.* Paris: Payot, 1921.
Fox, Cyril S., ed. *This was Germany: An Observer at the Court of Berlin. Letters of Princess Marie Radziwill to General Mario di Robillant, (1908-1915).* London: John Murray, 1937.
Görlitz, Walter, ed. *The Kaiser and His Court. The Diaries, Notebooks and Letters of Admiral Georg Alexander von Müler, Chief of the Naval Cabinet, 1914-1918.* London: Macdonald, 1961.
Naumann, Viktor. *Dokumente und Argumente.* Berlin: E. Rowohlt, 1928.
Tirpitz, Alfred von. *Erinnerungen.* Leipzig: K.F. Koehler, 1919.

Austro-Hungarian

Czernin, Otakar. *In the World War.* New York: Harper and Brothers, 1920.

V. Biographies

Blum, John M. *Joe Tumulty and the Wilson Era.* Boston: Houghton Mifflin Co., 1951.

Blum, John M. *Woodrow Wilson and the Politics of Morality.* Boston: Little Brown and Co., 1956.

Ellis, John T. *Life and Times of James Cardinal Gibbons, Archbishop of Baltimore, 1834-1921.* 2 vols. Milwaukee: The Bruce Publishing Company, 1952.

Felice, Gaetano de. *Il Cardinale Pietro Gasparri.* Milan: Pro Familia, n.d.

Felice, Renzo de. *Mussolini, Il Revoluzionario (1883-1925).* Turin: Einaudi, 1965.

Hyde, H. Montgomery. *Lord Reading: The Life of Isaacs Rufus, First Marquiss of Reading.* London: Heinemann, 1969.

Leslie, Shane. *Cardinal Gasquet, A Memoir.* London: Burns Oates, 1953.

Link, Arthur S. *Wilson: The Struggle for Neutrality, 1914-1915.* Princeton: Princeton University Press, 1960.

Link, Arthur S. *Wilson: Confusions and Crisis, 1915-1916.* Princeton: Princeton University Press, 1964.

Link, Arthur L. *Wilson: Campaign for Progressivism and Peace, 1916-1917.* Princeton: Princeton University Press, 1965.

Migliori, Giam-Battista. *Benedetto XV.* Milano: La Favila 1932.

Moynihan, John H. *The Life of Archbishop John Ireland.* New York: Harper and Row, 1953.

Negro, Silvio. *Vaticano Minore.* Milan: Ulrico Hoepli, 1936.

Occhi, Luigi degli. *Benedetto XV.* Milano: Dall'Oglio, 1921.

Peters, H. Walter. *The Life of Benedict XV.* Milwaukee: The Bruce Publishing Co., 1957.

Taliani, Francesco de. *Vita del Cardinale Gasparri, Segretario de Stato e Povero Prete.* Milan: Mondadori, 1938.

Vercesi, Ernesto. *Tre Popi: Leone XIII-Pio X-Benedetto XV.* Milan: Ed. Athena, 1925.

Vistalli, Francesco. *Benedetto XV.* Rome: Tipografia Poliglotta Vaticana, 1928.

Walworth, Arthur. *Woodrow Wilson, American Prophet.* 2nd ed., revised. Boston: Houghton Mifflin Co., 1965.

VI. General Works

Albertini, Luigi. *The Origins of the War 1914.* 2 vols. Oxford: Oxford University Press, 1952-1957.

Beneš, Edward. *La lutte pour l'independence des peuples.* 2 vols. Paris: Plon, 1929.

Cline, Howard F. *The United States and Mexico.* Cambridge: Harvard University Press, 1963.

Eppstein, John. *The Catholic Tradition of the Law of Nations.* London: Burns Oates and Washbourne, 1935.

Hales, E.E.Y. *The Catholic Church in the Modern World. A Survey from the French Revolution to the Present.* New York: Hanover House, 1958.

Horstenau, Edmund von Glaise. *Il Crollo di un Impero.* Milan: Frateli Treves, 1935.

Kann, Robert A. *The Multinational Empire, Nationalism and National Reform in the Habsburg Monarchy, 1848-1918.* 2 vols. New York: Columbia University Press, 1950.

Link, Arthur S. *Woodrow Wilson and the Progressive Era, 1910-1917.* New York: Harper and Row Publishers, 1954.

Lord, Robert H., John E. Sexton, and Edward T. Harrington. *History of the Arch-diocese of Boston, 1604-1943.* 3 vols. New York: Sheed and Ward, 1944.

Pingaud, Alfred. *Histoire diplomatique de la France pendant la Grande guerre.* 3 vols. Paris: Alsatia Editeurs, 1937-1938.

Renouvin, Pierre. *La Crise Europenne et la Grande Guerre, 1904-1918.* Paris: Felix Alcan, 1934.

Stokes, Anson P. *Church and State in the United States.* 3 vols. New York: Harper's Publishers, 1950.

Tansill, Charles C. *America Goes to War.* Boston: Little, Brown and Co., 1938.

Wilson, Woodrow. *A History of the American People.* 5 vols. New York and London: Harper and Brothers, 1902.

VII. Special Studies

Abrams, Ray H. *Preachers Present Arms, The Role of the American Churches and Clergy in World Wars I and II, with some Observations on the War in Vietnam.* Scottdale, Pennsylvania: Herald Press, 1969.

Alix, Christine. *Le Saint-Siège et les Nationalismes en Europe (1870-1960).* Paris: Sirey, 1962.

Auerbach, Bertrand. *L'Autriche et la Hongrie pendant la guerre.* Paris: Felix Alcan, 1925.

Baudrillart, Alfred. *La Guerre Allemande et le Catholicism.* Paris: Blond et Gay, 1915.

Briggs, Michel P. *George Herron and the European Settlement.* Stanford: Stanford University Press, 1932.

Broglio, Francisco M. *Italia e la Santa Sede dalle Grande Guerra alla Conciliazione. Aspetti politici e giuridici.* Bari: Laterza, 1966.

Brugerette, Jean. *Le Prêtre Francais et la Societa Contemporaine.* 3 vols. Paris: P. Lethielleux, 1937.

Bruntz, George D. *Allied Campaign and the Collapse of the German Empire in 1918.* Stanford: Stanford University Press, 1938.

Candeloro, Giorgio. *Il movimento Cattolico in Italia.* Rome: Rinascita, 1955.

Child, Clifton J. *The German-Americans in Politics 1914-1917.* Madison: The University of Wisconsin Press, 1939.

Crighton, John C. *Missouri and the World War, 1914-1917, a Study in Public Opinion.* Columbia: University of Missouri Press, 1947.

Cummins, Cedric. *Indiana Public Opinion and the World War, 1914-1917.* Indianapolis: Indiana Historical Bureau, 1945.

D'Agnel, Arnaud. *Benoit XV et Le Conflit Européen.* 2 vols. Paris: P. Lethielleux, 1916.

Dominique, Pierre. *La Politique des Jésuites.* Paris: Grasset, 1955.

Engel-Janosi, Friedrich. *Österreich und der Vatikan, 1846-1918.* 2 vols. Vienne-Graz-Köln: Verlag Styria, 1960.

Feiertag, Clara Loretta. *American Public Opinion on the Diplomatic Relations between the United States and the Papal States, 1848-1868.* Washington, D.C.: Catholic University, 1933.

Fischer, Fritz. *Germany's Aims in the First World War.* New York: W.W. Norton, 1967.

Fowler, Wilton B. *British-American Relations, 1917-1918: The Role of Sir William Wiseman.* Princeton: Princeton University Press, 1969.

Gatzke, Hans W. *Germany's Drive to the West: A Study of Germany's Western War Aims During the First World War.* Baltimore: The Johns Hopkins University Press, 1950.

Gelfand, Lawrence. *The Inquiry, The American Preparation for Peace, 1918-1919.* New Haven: Yale University Press, 1963.

Goyau, George. *Papauté et Chrétienté sous Benoit XV.* Paris: Perrin, 1922.

Grieb, Kenneth L. *The United States and Huerta.* Lincoln: University of Nebraska Press, 1969.

Gwynn, Denis. *The Vatican and the War in Europe.* Dublin: Browne and Nolan Ltd., 1941.

Hershey, Burnet. *The Odyssey of Henry Ford and the Great Peace Ship.* New York: Taplinger Publishing Co., 1967.

Higham, John. *Strangers in the Land: Patterns of American Nativism, 1860-1925.* New York: Atheneum, 1963.

Institut Pius I, ed. *La Papauté et les Questiones Internationales.* Paris: n.d.

Jaszi, Oscar. *The Dissolution of the Hapsburg Monarchy.* Chicago: University of Chicago Press, 1961.

Johnson, Humphrey. *The Papacy and the Kingdom of Italy.* London: Sheed and Ward, 1926.

Johnson, Humphrey. *Vatican Diplomacy in the World War.* Oxford: Basil Blackwell, 1933.

Lama, Friedrich Ritter von. *Die Friedensvermittlung Papst Benedikt XV und ihre Vereitlung durch den deutschen Reichskanzler Michaelis (August-September 1917); eine historische-kritische Untersuchung.* Müchen: Kösel und F. Pustet, 1932.

Levin, H. Gordon, Jr. *Woodrow Wilson and World Politics, America's Response to War and Revolution.* New York: Oxford University Press, 1968.

Lorenz, Reinhold. *Kaiser Karl und der Untergang der Donau Monarchie.* Graz: Verlag Styria, 1959.

Lowry, Philip. "The Mexican Policy of Woodrow Wilson." Unpublished PhD thesis, Yale University, 1949.

Mamatey, Victor. *The United States and East Central Europe, 1914-1918. A Study in Wilsonian Diplomacy and Propaganda.* Princeton: Princeton University Press, 1957.

Marc-Bonnet, Henry. *La Papauté Contemporaine.* Paris: Plon, 1951.

Martini, Angelo. *Studi sulla Questione Romana e la Conciliazione.* Rome: Edizioni Cinque Lune, 1963.

May, Arthur. *The Passing of the Hapsburg Monarchy, 1914-1918.* Philadelphia: University of Pennsylvania Press, 1966.

May, Ernest R. *The World War and American Isolation, 1914-1917.* Cambridge: Harvard University Press, 1959.

Mayer, Arno. *Political Origins of the New Diplomacy, 1917-1918.* New Haven: Yale University Press, 1959.

Mermeix, *Les negociations secrets et les quatre armistices.* Paris: Ollendorff, 1919.

Meyer, Henry Cord. *Mitteleuropa in German Thought and Action, 1815-1945.* The Hague: Martinus Hijhoff, 1955.

Mira, Giuseppe. *Autunno 1918, Come fini la guerra mondiale.* Milan: Mondadori, 1932.

Monticone, Alberto. *Nitti e la Grande Guerra, 1914-1918.* Milan: Giufre Editore, 1961.

Notter, Harley. *The Origins of the Foreign Policy of Woodrow Wilson.* Baltimore: The Johns Hopkins University Press, 1937.

Novak, Karl. *Les dessous de la defaite.* Paris: Payot, 1925.

Page, Thomas H. *Italy and the World War.* New York: Charles Scribner's Sons, 1920.

Paris, Edmund. *Le Vatican contre L'Europe.* Paris: Fischbacher, 1962.

Perman, Dagmar. *The Shaping of the Czechoslovak State, Diplomatic History of the Boundaries of Czechoslovakia, 1914-1920.* Leiden: Bril, 1962.

Pernot, Maurice. *Le Saint Siège, L'Église Catholique et la Politique Mondiale.* Paris: Armand Colin, 1924.

Poltzer-Hoditz, Arthur. *L'Empereur Charles et la Mission Historique de l'Autriche.* Paris: Haschette, n.d.

Premoli, Orazio. *Storia Ecclesiastica Contemporanea (1900-1925).* Turin and Rome: Marietti, 1925.

Pribram, Arthur. *Austrian Foreign Policy, 1908-1918.* London: Allen and Unwin, 1923.

Quadrotta, Guiseppe. *La Chiesa Cattolica nella Crisi Universale.* Rome: Bilychnis, 1921.

Quirk, Robert F. "The Mexican Revolution and the Catholic Church, 1910-1929, An Ideological Study." Unpublished PhD thesis, Harvard University, 1950.

Quirk, Robert F. *The Mexican Revolution, 1914-1915: The Convention of Aquascalientes.* Bloomington, Indiana University Press, 1960.

Rappaport, Armin. *The British Press and Wilsonian Neutrality, 1914-1917.* Stanford and London: Stanford University Press, 1951.

Redlich, Joseph. *Austrian War Government.* New Haven: Yale University Press, 1929.

Roux, Francis Charles. *Le Paix des Empires Centraux.* Paris: Payot, 1947.

Rudin, Harry. *Armistice 1918.* New Haven: Yale University Press, 1944.

Salvatorelli, Luigi. *La Politica della Santa Sede doppo la guerra.* Milan: Istituto per la Storia e politica Internazionale, 1937.

Scheinman, M.M. *Il Vaticano tra due guerre.* Rome: Edizione di Cultura Sociale, 1951.

Scheinman, M.M. *Vatikan i Katolitsizm v Kontse XIX—Nachale XX v.* Moscow: Akademii Nauk SSSR, 1958.

Seldes, George. *The Vatican: Yesterday-Today-Tomorrow.* New York and London: Harper and brothers, 1934.

Siney, Marion C. *The Allied Blockade of Germany, 1914-1916.* Ann Arbor: The University of Michigan Press, 1957.

Smith, Daniel M. *The Great Departure: The United States and World War I.* New York and London: John Wiley and Sons, 1965.

Stelio, Marchese. *Francia e il Problemi dei rapporti con la Santa Sede (1914-1924).* Naples: Edizioni Scientifiche Italiene, 1969.

Strong, David. *Austria, October 1918-March 1919.* New York: Columbia University Press, 1939.

Teitelbaum, Louis M. *Woodrow Wilson and the Mexican Revolution 1913-1916: A History of the United States-Mexican Relations.* New York: Exposition Press, 1967.

Turner, Frederick C. *The Dynamic of Mexican Nationalism*. Chapel Hill: University of North Carolina Press, 1968.
Valiani, Leo. *La Dissoluzione del Austria-Ungheria*. Milan: Mondadori, 1968.
Vercesi, Ernesto. *L'Europe nuova e il Vaticano*. Milan: Mondadori, 1925.
Williams, Michael. *The Catholic Church in Action*. New York: The Macmillan Company, 1934.
Živojinović, Dragan R. *Amerika, Italia i Postanak Jugoslavije, 1917-1919*. Beograd: Naucna Knjiga, 1970.
Živojinović, Dragan R. *The United States, Italy and the Emergence of Yugoslavia, 1917-1919*. New York: Columbia University Press, 1972.

VIII. Articles, Essays, Polemics

Anonimé. "La politique de Benoit XV." *La Revue de Paris* XXV, 20-21 (October 15, November 1, 1918): 873-896, 183-214.
App, Austin. "The Germans." In *The Immigrants' Influence on Wilson's Peace Policies,* edited by J.P. O'Grady, pp. 30-35. Lexington: University of Kentucky Press, 1967.
Bailey, Thomas A. "The Sinking of the Lusitania." *American Historical Review* 41 (October 1935): 54-73.
Bendiscioli, Mario. "Chiesa e Societa nel secoli XIX e XX." In *Questioni di Storia Contemporanea,* 3 vols., edited by Ettore Rota, 1:799-955. Milan: Carlo Garzanti Ed., 1952.
Bendiscioli, Mario. "La Santa Sede e la Guerra." In *Benedetto XV, i Cattolici e la Prime Guerra Mondiale*. Atti del convegno di studio tenuto a Spoleto nei giorni 7-8-9 settembre 1962, edited by Giusseppe Rosini, pp. 25-49. Rome: Cinque Lune, 1963.
Calise, Carlo. "Il Cardinale Pietro Gasparri." *Nuova Antologia* 68 (March 16, 1933): 225-236.
Child, Clifton. "German-American Attempts to Prevent the Exportation of Munitions of War, 1914-1916." *The Mississippi Valley Historical Review* 25 (December 1938): 351-368.
Cuddy, Edward. "Pro-Germanism and American Catholicism, 1914-1917." *The Catholic Historical Review* 59 (October 1968): 427-454.
Engel-Janosi, Friedrich. "The Roman Question in the First Years of Benedict XV." *The Catholic Historical Review* 40 (1954): 269-285.
Engel-Janosi, Friedrich. "Benedetto XV e l'Austria." In *Benedetto XV, i Cattolici e la Prima Guerra Mondiale,* pp. 343-356.
Engel-Janosi, Friedrich. "The Church and the Nationalities in the Hapsburg Monarchy." In *Austrian History Yearbook,* edited by John Rath, III: 67-82. Austin, Texas: Rice University, 1967.
Esslinger, Dean R. "American German and Irish Attitudes Toward Neutrality, 1914-1917: A Study of Catholic Minorities." *The Catholic Historical Review* 53 (1967): 194-217.
Feller, John G., Jr. "Notations of Cardinal Gibbons on the Conclave of 1914." *The Catholic Historical Review* 46 (1960): 184-189.
Ferrell, Robert H. *Woodrow Wilson and Open Diplomacy*. In Issues and Conflicts:

Studies in Twentieth Century American Diplomacy, series edited by G.L. Anderson. Lawrence: Kansas University Press, 1959, pp. 193-209.

Gimarc, Jerry Dell. "Illinois Catholic Editorial Opinions During World War I." *Historical Records and Studies* 143 (1960): 167-184.

Goyau, George. "L'Eglise libre dans L'Europe libre." *Revue des Deux Mondes* 89 (July 1919): 5-36.

Jusserand, Jean J. Letter to the Editor. *American Historical Review* 38 (1932): 817-819.

Leary, William M. "Woodrow Wilson, Irish-Americans and the Election of 1916." *Journal of American History* 54 (1967): 57-72.

Leflon, Jean. "L'Action diplomatico-religieuse de Benoit XV en favour de la paix durant la Première guerre mondiale." In *Benedetto XV, i Cattolici e la Prima Guerra Mondiale,* pp. 53-70.

Link, Arthur S. "Woodrow Wilson and Peace Moves." *The Listener* (London) 75 (June 6, 1966): 868-871.

Loiseau, Charles. "Ma Mission auprès du Vatican. (1914-1918)." *Revue d'Histoire Diplomatique* 64 (1960): 100-115.

Luca, Giuseppe de. "Il Cardinale Pietro Gasparri." *Nuova Antologia* 69 (December 1, 1934): 380-385.

Luca, Giuseppe de. "Discorendo col Cardinale Gasparri (1930)." *Nuova Antologia* 71 (November 16, 1936): 195-205.

Martini, Angelo. "La 'Nota' di Benedetto XV per la pace (agosto 1, 1917)." *La Civilta Cattolica* IV, 2696 (1962): 3-29.

Martini, Angelo. "La Nota di Benedetto XV alle Potenze belligeranti nell' agosto 1917." In *Benedetto XV, i Cattolici e la Prima Guerra Mondiale,* pp. 361-386.

Martini, Angelo. "L'invio della missione inglese presso la Santa Sede all'inizio della Prima guerra mondiale." *La Civilta Cattolica* IV, 2818 (1967): 330-344.

May, Arthur. "Woodrow Wilson and Austria-Hungary to the end of 1917." In *Festschrift fur Heinrich Benedikt,* edited by H. Hantsch and A. Novotny, pp. 198-224. Vienna: Verlag Notring, 1957.

Mosca, Roberto. "La mancata revisione dell'art. 15 del Patto di Londra." In *Benedetto XV, i Cattolici e la Prima Guerra Mondiale,* pp. 399-413.

Ori, Giuseppe. "La recente politica della Santa Sede nell'Europa nord-orientale." *Rassegna di Politica Internazionale* 3 (August 1936): 623-636.

Pacelli, Eugenio. "A propos de l'offre de paix du Saint Siège en 1917." *Revue d'Histoire de la guerre mondiale* 4 (1926): 131-140.

Pasztor, Lajos. "I cattolici ungharesi e la prima guerra mondiale." In *Benedetto XV, i Cattolici e la Prima Guerra Mondiale,* pp. 815-832.

Rufini, Francisco. "Il potere temporale negli scopi di guerra degli ex-Imperi Centrali." *Nuova Antologia* 61 (April 16, 1921): 289-300.

Snell, John M. "Benedict XV, Wilson, Michaelis and German Socialism." *The Catholic Historical Review* 37 (July 1951): 151-178.

Tamborra, Angelo. "L'idea di nazionalita e la guerra, 1914-1918." In *Atti del XLI Congresso per la Storia del Risorgimento Italiano* (Trento: October 9-13, 1963). Rome: Instituto per la Storia del Risorgimento Italiano, 1965, pp. 220-283.

Tamborra, Angelo. "Benedetto XV e i problemi nazionali e religiosi dell'Europa Orientale." In *Benedetto XV, i Cattolici e la Prima Guerra Mondiale,* pp. 855-884.

Valiani, Leo. "Nuovi documenti sui trattativi di pace nel 1917." *Rivista Storica Italiana* 75 (1963): 559-587.

Veneruso, Danilo. "I rapporti fra stato e chiesa durante la guerra nel giudizi dei maggiori organi della stampa Italiana." In *Benedetto XV, i Cattolicice la Prima Guerra Mondiale,* pp. 679-738.

Veneruso, Danilo. "Ricerche e problemi relativi ai rapporti tra cattolici e socialisti durante la Prima guerra mondiale." *Critica Storica* 4 (March 31, 1965): 129-156.

Vivarelli, Roberto. "Questione Adriatica e la politica estera Italiana durante la Prima Guerra Mondiale." *Studi Senesi,* third series, 8 (1964): 343-340.

Živojinović, Dragan R. "Splitski biskup dr. Juraj Caric i borba protiv italijanskih pretenzija u Dalmaciji, 1918-1919." *Istorijski Glasnik* 2-3 (Belgrade 1966): 145-168.

Živojinović, Drajan R. "Stav američkog javnog mnenja i vlade prema dogadjajima na Balkanu, 28 jun-28 jul 1914." In *Jugoslovenski Narodi pred Prvi Svetski,* edited by Rat. Vasa Čubrilović et al., pp. 231-260. Belgrade: Srpska Akademija Nauka i Umetnosti, 1967.

Živojinović, Dragan R. "Robert Lansing's Comments on the Pontifical Peace Note of Ausust 1917." *Journal of American History* 56 (1969): 556-571.

Živojinović, Dragan R. "The Vatican, Woodrow Wilson, and the Dissolution of the Hapsburg Monarchy, 1914-1918." *East European Quarterly* 3 (1969): 31-70.

Živojinović, Dragan R. "Il Problema di Roma nella politica degli Stati Uniti." In *Atti del XLV Congresso per la Storia del Risorgimento Italiano* (Rome: September 1970). Rome: Instituto per la Storia del Risorgimento Italiano, 1972, pp. 501-568.

IX. Newspapers, Magazines, Reviews

American

America.

American. Baltimore.

Ave Maria.

Baltimore Catholic Review.

The Baltimore Sun.

The Boston American.

The Boston Pilot.

Catholic Citizen.

The Catholic Columbia Record. Columbus, Ohio.

Catholic Standard and Time.

Catholic Telegraph.

The Catholic Tribune. Dubuque, Iowa.

Chicago Herald.

Chicago Tribune.

Christian Science Monitor. Boston.

Church Union and Times.

The Commercial Appeal. Memphis, Tenn.

Courant. Hartford, Conn.

Die America. Chicago.

Echo. Chicago.
The Erie Dispatch.
Extension Magazine.
Forthnightly Review.
Freeman's Journal and Catholic Register. St. Louis.
The Gazette-Times. Pittsburgh.
The Herald. Lexington, Ky.
Indiana Catholic.
Josephinum Weekly. Columbus, Ohio.
Kansas City Catholic Register.
The Leader. Cleveland.
The Morning Oregonian. Portland.
Morning Star. New Orleans.
New York American.
New York Evening Post.
The New York Times.
The New York World
"Rome on the Potomac: What the Papal Hierarchy is Doing at the American Capital,"
 The Outlook, February 11, 1913, pp. 10-12.
The Philadelphia Inquirer.
The Plain Dealer. Cleveland.
The Register. Wheeling, W. Virginia.
The Republican. Springfield, Mass.
Sacred Heart Review.
San Francisco Examiner.
The State. Columbia, S. Carolina.
The Sun. New York
The Tribune. Salt Lake City, Utah.
Ubendpost. Chicago.
The Washington Post.
The Washington Times.
Western Watchman.

French

Figaro. Paris.
Galois. Sens.
Humanité. Paris.
La Liberté. Paris.
Matin. Paris.
Temps. Paris.

Italian

Corriere d'Italia. Rome.
La Civilta Cattolica. Rome.
L'Osservatore Romano. Rome.

British

Times. London.

German

Germania. Berlin.

INDEX

J